THE ETHICS OF M

What was the ethical perspective of mode
Yeats, Eliot, Joyce, Woolf, and Beckett rep
develop their moral ideas? Lee Oser argu
human nature restores a perspective on m   ..ature that
has been lost. He offers detailed discussions of the relationship
between ethics and aesthetics to illuminate close readings of major
modernist texts. For Oser, the reception of Aristotle is crucial to the
modernist moral project, which he defines as the effort to transform
human nature through the use of art. Exploring the origins of that
project, its success in modernism, its critical heirs, and its possible
future, *The Ethics of Modernism* brings a fresh perspective on modernist literature and its interaction with ethical strands of philosophy. It
offers many new insights to scholars of twentieth-century literature
as well as intellectual historians.

LEE OSER is Associate Professor of English at the College of the
Holy Cross, Massachusetts. He is the author of *T. S. Eliot and
American Poetry* (1998).

THE ETHICS OF MODERNISM

Moral Ideas in Yeats, Eliot, Joyce, Woolf, and Beckett

LEE OSER

CAMBRIDGE
UNIVERSITY PRESS

CAMBRIDGE UNIVERSITY PRESS
Cambridge, New York, Melbourne, Madrid, Cape Town, Singapore, São Paulo, Delhi

Cambridge University Press
The Edinburgh Building, Cambridge CB2 8RU, UK

Published in the United States of America by Cambridge University Press, New York

www.cambridge.org
Information on this title: www.cambridge.org/9780521116282

First published 2007
This digitally printed version 2009

A catalogue record for this publication is available from the British Library

ISBN 978-0-521-86725-2 hardback
ISBN 978-0-521-11628-2 paperback

To Christopher Ricks

The question, *how to live*, is itself a moral idea; and it is the question which most interests every man, and with which, in some way or other, he is perpetually occupied.

Matthew Arnold

Few artists . . . work quite cleanly, casting off all *débris*, and leaving us only what the heat of their imagination has wholly fused and transformed.

Walter Pater

Contents

Acknowledgments

I have benefited from the criticism of Christopher Ricks, to whom this book is humbly dedicated. My mother, Maureen Waters, and my step-father, David Kleinbard, scrutinized the manuscript in its entirety; this book is part of a conversation we have been having for years. My wife, Kate Lieuallen Oser, reviewed my writing at every stage and helped me to develop my ideas. John Hamilton shared his knowledge of Greek. My errors are invariably my own.

I have debated philosophy and literature for seven years with colleagues in a reading group comprising Jeffrey Bernstein, Jeffrey Bloechl, Robert Cording, Mark Freeman, Robert Garvey, James Kee, Joseph Lawrence, William Morse, and John Wilson. These colleagues have challenged, exasperated, and inspired me. I have profited from conversations with William Blissett, Marie Borroff, William Charron, David Chinitz, Vinnie D'Ambrosio, Iman Javadi, John Karel, Douglas Levin, Ben and Micheline Lockerd, John Mayer, Charles Molesworth, James Najarian, Cyrena Pondrom, Grover Smith, Liam Toomey, and Linda Wyman. I wish to thank Anthony and Melanie Fathman, scholarly hosts, for their warm hospitality. I am grateful to my editor at Cambridge, Ray Ryan, and to two anonymous readers at the Press.

I would also like to thank the College of the Holy Cross, especially two hard-working librarians, Diana Antul and Gail Montysco.

Thanks to Eleanor Marie and Briana Steen.

An earlier version of Chapter 2 appeared as "T. S. Eliot and the Case of the Vanishing *Ethics*," in volume 4, number 2 (Spring 2002) of *Literary Imagination: The Review of the Association of Literary Scholars and Critics*, copyright 2002. Used by permission of the Association of Literary Scholars and Critics.

I have drawn freely on my 2004 essay in *Philosophy and Literature*, "Human Nature and Modernist Ethics."

Introduction: literature and human nature

Human nature restores a perspective on modernism that has been lost. Without this perspective, we can see little of the modernist moral project, which is to transform human nature through the use of art. Why should we remember the block of marble, dragged through the squalid province, before the breath of genius gave it life? Or more accurately, why remember the dray and the windgalled animal that pulled it, when we bask in the favor of Toyota and Boeing, NASA and Maersk? And yet the *old question* has unmistakably returned: what good is there in human nature?

Our answer will depend on our school of thought. I understand the issue as a choice between two alternatives, both ambitious and both imperfect. One is the New Darwinism.[1] Its exponents are mostly scientists and social scientists who want to reinvent the liberal arts in the image of Darwin. Their growing success is connected to the larger role of science in uncovering intellectual fraud in the humanities.[2]

Steven Pinker embodies the strengths and weaknesses of the New Darwinist school. A polymath reaching a wide audience with clear prose, Pinker brings Darwinian naturalism to bear both on modernist literature and on modernity itself. In *The Blank Slate: The Modern Denial of Human Nature*, he shows that Darwinian science contradicts modernism on such immensely important topics as sex, psychology, and the meaning of art. Woolf, in particular, attracts Pinker's scorn with her famous statement, "in or about December, 1910, human character changed."[3] Pinker responds: "She was referring to the new philosophy of modernism that would dominate the elite arts and criticism for much of the twentieth century, and whose denial of human nature was carried over with a vengeance to postmodernism . . . The elite arts, criticism, and scholarship are in trouble because the statement is wrong. Human nature did not change in 1910, or in any year thereafter."[4] As Pinker indicates, the modernist turn from human nature reaches well beyond Woolf. Wilde detested "the great Darwinian principle of the survival of the vulgarest."[5]

I

Yeats spoke for a European tradition: "Art is art because it is not nature."[6] "Its impulses are not of a generically human kind," wrote Ortega in 1925, referring to the modernist movement and its "dehumanization of art."[7] Ortega pinpointed the changes at hand: "For the modern artist, aesthetic pleasure derives from . . . a triumph over human matter."[8] The modernist denial of human nature might be more aptly described as a deliberate and studied refusal of human nature. Otherwise, it is Pinker's dislike – and not his perception – of modernism that sets him apart from the modernists.

Pinker is certainly right to see a Cartesian bias in much modern philosophy, and to find its culmination in modernism and postmodernism. And he is right despite the intense efforts of the modernists themselves to overcome the Cartesian divide between subject and object.[9] The Cartesian dominancy has its beginnings in the sixteenth and seventeenth centuries, when Francis Bacon, Galileo, Hobbes, and Robert Boyle laid siege to the medieval fortress of Aristotle.[10] It is only fair to say that, at their intellectual best, the schoolmen sowed the fields of science and learning. But at their worst they succumbed to a logic-chopping and obscure scholasticism. They buried the living spirit of Aristotle before they were themselves laid to rest, and modern science lurched violently into being. On this subject, Eliot quotes Cowley's eloquent ode *To Mr. Hobbes*:

> Long did the mighty Stagirite retain
> The universal intellectual reign . . .
> But as in time each great imperial race
> Degenerates, and gives some new one place:
> So did this noble empire waste,
> Sunk by degrees from glories past,
> And in the schoolmen's hands it perisht quite at last . . .[11]

Modern science was begotten by Descartes upon the void. Dividing the universe into mind and matter, he thought of animals as nothing more than complicated machines, constructed of passive particles. He lumped them with cabbages, sealing wax, and all the stuff of matter, which he called the *res extensa*, as opposed to the *res cogitans* or mind. Locke, finding that Cartesianism led to psychology, advanced an influential idea of disembodied personhood. Kantian ethics is denatured reasoning, and the categorical imperative is what William James calls a "cold-blooded and dispassionate judicial sentence, confined entirely to the mental realm."[12] Hegel opened the floodgates of historicism, the relativizing of morality, which weakens the claims of universal human nature. To support his metaphysic, he disconnects morality from our life as animals: "morality is Duty . . . a '*second* nature' as it has been justly called; for the *first* nature of man is his primarily merely animal existence."[13] Influenced by Hegel, Marx describes the proletariat as suffering not just "the contradiction between its human nature and its condition of life," but "the outright, decisive, and comprehensive negation of that nature": a state of "dehumanization conscious of its dehumanization."[14] Nietzsche's theory of the mask assumes an ironic distance from human nature, whose dictates the author of *Beyond Good and Evil* refers to as "a certain kind of *niaiserie* [folly] which may be necessary for the preservation of just such beings as we are."[15] Heidegger speaks of the "'scarcely fathomable, abyssal' character of the 'bodily kinship' of humans to animals."[16] In his Harvard dissertation, Eliot adopts the linguistic idea of man while relegating our animal nature to an extraneous background. He holds that subject-object relations for animals are "rather lived out than known" because there are "no objects without language."[17] Nor in the same work will Eliot allow that the body triggers emotion.[18] The neglect by Brentano, Husserl, and other phenomenologists of our animal nature, of the body's physiological (non-intentional) contributions to mental activity, extends through Heidegger into the influential work of Levinas and Derrida. Even the anti-rationalist, anti-Cartesian legacy in France, associated with Derrida and Foucault, repeats the Cartesian bias against human nature.

My criticism of Pinker is that he looks at human nature from the outside. For instance, when he analyzes a scene from Woody Allen's *Annie Hall*, the native humor eludes him. The young Alvy Singer is paying a visit to the family doctor:

MOTHER: He's been depressed. All of a sudden, he can't do anything.
DOCTOR: Why are you depressed, Alvy?
MOTHER: Tell Dr. Flicker. [Answers for him.] It's something he read.
DOCTOR: Something he read, huh?
ALVY: [Head down.] The universe is expanding.
DOCTOR: The universe is expanding?
ALVY: Well, the universe is everything, and if it's expanding, someday it
             will break apart and that would be the end of everything!
MOTHER: What is that your business? [To the doctor.] He stopped doing his
             homework.
ALVY: What's the point?[19]

Pinker is asking us not to confuse "ultimate causation (why something evolved by natural selection) with proximate causation (how the entity works here and now.)" He comments: "The scene is funny because Alvy has confused two levels of analysis: the scale of billions of years with which we measure the universe, and the scale of decades, years, and days with which we measure our lives."[20] But the confusion of two levels of analysis is not terribly funny in itself. You might smile gently at the boy who reports "a big problem" when he sinks a toy boat. What makes Allen's joke work is that Alvy sees more than his mother and the doctor see. Apparently, he sees more than Pinker, too, for Pinker is of the same mind as Dr. Flicker, who dutifully remarks that Brooklyn "won't be expanding for billions of years yet Alvy . . ."

As Baudelaire would suggest, Allen's comedy is "grotesque." In his seminal essay "On the Essence of Laughter," Baudelaire writes: "the laughter caused by the grotesque has about it something profound, primitive and axiomatic, which is much closer to . . . innocent life and to absolute joy than is the laughter caused by the comic in man's behavior."[21] Alvy's grotesque innocence touches a range of profound possibilities: that no theodicy is true, that justice cannot be, that there is no final cause, no divine pattern, no God, nothing to accommodate the world to us. In his cosmic sweep, the grotesque comic is "absolute," but "he can only be absolute in relation to fallen humanity."[22] That is why Alvy's mother argues, "What has the universe got to do with it? You're here in Brooklyn! Brooklyn is not expanding!" Brooklyn is fallen humanity. But of course the grotesque comic leaves no room for analysis: "There is but one criterion of the grotesque, and that is laughter – immediate laughter."[23] We grin immediately at Alvy's axiomatic and naive explanation ("What's the point?") because at bottom it is profound and primitive. Pinker, it must be said, has lost track of his own subject. Feeling anxiety? *Don't confuse two levels of analysis.*

Pinker finds human nature where he looks for it: on maps and charts, sets of data, lists of probabilities, and comic strips. Being a reductive kind of Darwinist, he cannot permit himself to speak of human teleology. He supplies moral precepts, and he supplies a statistical account of human nature, but he omits to consider that precepts will not work unless they motivate people to realize their best potential. Strictly speaking, he has no ethics. He makes do with a kind of analytic good sense: "For efforts at social change to be effective, they must identify the cognitive and moral resources that make some kinds of change possible."[24] On the surface, this looks reasonable enough. But morality demands a great deal more than the resources of genetic science. The moral life as we live it eludes what John Stuart Mill called "the analysing spirit"[25] – which is why Mill suffered a crisis in his mental history. Morality is more particular than "efforts at social change" that are guided by maps and charts, sets of data, lists of probabilities, and comic strips. So it is unsurprising that Pinker's rules, injunctions, and pleadings for good behavior lack depth.

The last generation has seen the revival of Aristotelian virtue ethics, which offers the second of the alternatives before us.[26] The rivalry stems from the scale and gravity of the models. In Pinker and the New Darwinism, science would parlay its mixed blessings into "supreme cognitive authority"[27] over other disciplines. Pinker calls for giving "high priority to economics, evolutionary biology, and probability and statistics."[28] By contrast, Aristotelian science is wrapped in a moth-eaten metaphysic.[29] But Aristotle stays closer to the concrete actuality of moral life. As opposed to Pinker's scientific mono-vision, the legacy of Descartes, Aristotle's diverse fields of knowledge reward the local workers, so that the discoveries of the scientist do not rule out the traditions of the poet. Most important, Aristotle considers the world from a central human vantage point, whether he is weighing rival perspectives in science and philosophy, or commenting on Homer. He is never alienated from himself, into a narrow specialization or an empire of facts. Because he defines true self-love in terms of noble acts, ideals can garner praise and public approval (*Nic. Eth.* 1169a7).[30] Aristotle therefore defies the atomization of moral life, and resists the mechanical worldview of Bentham or Pinker.

Since ethics begins with free will, let us approach Aristotle through *On the Soul.* Against the materialists of his era, and Democritus in particular, Aristotle held that the soul originates movement "through intention or process of thinking" (406b25). It was the first step toward a possible middle way between the idea of the soul as a subtle arrangement of material parts, such as we find in modern reductivist science, and the idea of the soul as a ghostly substance, such as we find in Plato and Descartes.[31] Writing in the *Monist,* Eliot sums up Aristotle's position: "Soul is to body as cutting is to the axe: realizing itself in its actions, and not completely real when abstracted from what it does." Eliot rightly comments that Aristotle's "view is seen as an attempt to get away from the abstractions of materialism or of spiritualism with which we begin."[32] But while his *Monist* account stands up, Eliot as poet joins the modernists in the broad Platonic tradition, where the soul precedes its bodily and social existence. Pinker is a materialist who grants "a wisp of mystery," i.e., who grants a spirit named *wisp* power to cast out the devil *mystery.* Aristotle, as Eliot explains, approaches the soul through the body. "The affections of soul," Aristotle says of the emotions, "are inseparable from the material substratum of animal life" (*On the Soul* 403b18). In consequence, he affords the soul a degree of freedom, not "freedom to do anything it desires," which is the extreme version of ensoulment that Pinker attacks.[33] The very words *soul* and *mind* are custodians of the human world and the human scale of things, the realm of beauty in the *Poetics* (1450b36). To quote the wisdom of R. S. Crane, the "humanities . . . are distinguishable from the natural and the social sciences by their special concern with those aspects of man's achievements in sciences, in institutions, and in arts which are most distinctively human in the sense that their causes are not completely reducible either to natural processes common to men and animals or to superpersonal conditions and forces affecting all members of a given society."[34]

On the Soul remains a highly controversial book, perpetually equipped to create factions. M. F. Burnyeat makes the point that Aristotle saw animal matter as being different in kind from other matter. Descartes took a new turn, and saw all matter as one substance. Analyzing Aristotle's theory of perception, Burnyeat suggests that "the physical material of animal bodies in Aristotle's world" has an ingrained awareness. Computers cannot "do to air" what animals "do to air," which is to "make it smell*able*, hear*able*."[35] Therefore, the current functionalist-materialist account of Aristotle, which frees "our mental life from dependence on any *particular* material set-up,"[36] cannot be true, because there is ultimately something mysterious and indispensable about animal life in Aristotle's view. (Incidentally, computers show no signs of coming to consciousness, despite bold predictions.)[37] So I agree with Burnyeat in his critique of the current functionalist account of Aristotle. But I disagree with Burnyeat that we must line up behind the Cartesian mind-body dualism and "junk" the Aristotelian philosophy of mind. Dualism, "the ghost in the machine," has too little to say about the interaction of mind and body.

To pursue the affinities between *On the Soul* and *The Principles of Psychology* would require an excursion well beyond the present work, but it is helpful here to underscore a fact that has been recently and memorably observed, namely, that Aristotle and James oppose the modern perspective on the mind-body problem established by Descartes.[38] James anchors the self, as a moral agent, in the physical conditions of our animal life. His understanding of emotion takes Aristotelian insights into modern physiology:

A disembodied human emotion is a sheer nonentity . . . The more closely I scrutinize my states, the more persuaded I become that whatever "coarse" affections and passions I have are in very truth constituted by, and made up of, those bodily changes which we ordinarily call their expression or consequence;

and the more it seems to me that, if I were to become corporeally anaesthetic, I should be excluded from the life of the affections, harsh and tender alike, and drag out an existence of merely cognitive or intellectual form.[39]

The passage stands in the profoundest contrast to post-Kantian aesthetic theory, which suspends the physical presence of the body in favor of the world-constructing faculties of mind. Modernist art is aesthetic art. Individual consciousness is the privileged medium of the modernist view of things. In Yeats, Eliot, Joyce, Woolf, and Beckett, ethics is itself a form of aesthetics. James's insight into the role of the body puts a radical question to Yeats's quest for "bodiless emotion,"[40] to the theory of "esthetic stasis" in *A Portrait of the Artist as a Young Man*, to Eliot's moral idealization of "the mind of Europe," to Woolf's "moments of being," and to Beckett's abstract disgust at "the eudemonistic slop."[41] Woolf contrasts the Greeks and the moderns: "Accustomed to look directly and largely rather than minutely and aslant, it was safe for them to step into the thick of emotions which blind and bewilder an age like our own. In the vast catastrophe of the European war our emotions had to be broken up for us, and put at an angle from us, before we could allow ourselves to feel them in poetry or fiction."[42] These examples could be multiplied without end, and I have traced their Cartesian antecedents. Yet on the topic of emotional response, Antonio Damasio considers James to be "well ahead of both his time and ours," for the reason that James had "seized upon the mechanism essential to the understanding of emotion and feeling."[43]

"Let us assume," says Aristotle in the *Politics*, "that the best life, both for individuals and states, is the life of virtue, when virtue has external goods enough for the performance of good actions" (1324a). What is "the life of virtue"? To begin with, a virtue governs a passion: virtues and passions are "bound up" together in our "composite nature" (*Nic. Eth.* 1178a16). Aristotle defines virtue as "a state of character concerned with choice, lying in a mean" relative to each individual, since we are all different (*Nic. Eth.* 1106b36). The choice is determined by reason working with practical wisdom, which is an acquired talent for living well, for directing activity towards the most fruitful ends. Aristotle connects the virtues to their effect: the life of virtue is a state of flourishing called *eudaimonia* or "happiness." To be *eudaimon* is to experience the wholeness of a fortunate human life striving to achieve its full potential. Happiness is "a virtuous activity of soul" (*Nic. Eth.* 1099b27). Dealing with moral matters on their own level, Aristotle is blunt about the limits of his analysis: "We must be content . . . to indicate the truth roughly and in outline, and in speaking about things which are only for the most part true and with premisses of the same kind to reach conclusions that are no better" (*Nic. Eth.* 1094b19). Aristotle's moral judgment is never absolute, though neither is it relativist. I agree, in this instance, with Martha Nussbaum: "the Aristotelian virtues, and the deliberations they guide, unlike some systems of moral rules, remain always open to revision in the light of new circumstances and new evidence. In this way . . . they contain the flexibility to local conditions that the relativist would desire, but . . . without sacrificing objectivity."[44] Aristotle observes a ground pattern of common feeling and behavior, on which a multitude of local patterns can be embroidered. For a global society built on the rapport of diverse nations and corporations and peoples, disregard for the ground pattern is potentially as dangerous as disregard for the local patterns.

In his commentary *Aristotle's Ethics*, J. O. Urmson offers a lucid account of what Aristotle means by character. Urmson numbers four general states of character in the *Nicomachean Ethics*. Each of these states is applicable to any particular emotion, with no emotion being, in itself, good or bad. He illustrates the four states with "a sort of table":

	Want	Aim	Act
Excellence	Good	Good	Good
Strength	Bad	Good	Good
Weakness	Bad	Good	Bad
Badness	Bad	Bad	Bad

The table refers to merit in "emotional want, the aim or choice settled on after deliberation, and in action." Urmson supplies an example that shows, I think, a nice comic touch: "The four states could get a modern illustration from the even-tempered man who has no difficulty in waiting coolly in a traffic jam, the hot-tempered man who successfully restrains himself, the hot-tempered man who tries to remain calm but cannot and the man who curses and hoots at all and sundry with complete self-approval."[45] The even-tempered man possesses the virtue of self-control; he has driven the roads before, knows what to do, and willingly does it. The permanent authors, Homer, Plato, the Greek tragedians, Dante, Chaucer, Cervantes, Shakespeare, and Dickens, abound in characters who fit the analysis. Other characters, tragic figures like Oedipus and Hamlet, and soul doctors like Nietzsche's Zarathustra, test, expand, and defy our moral knowledge.[46] But in any case, moral legibility depends, at least in part, on readers who can readily understand Urmson's example, *mutatis mutandis*.

What I shall call *the Aristotelian body* is central to western literature for four main reasons. First, it is integrated with a soul that has a purchase on reality, keeping art in close contact with actual life. Second, it is both individual and social, for man is a political animal and his good depends upon his life with others (*Pol.* 1253a2).[47] Third, it fosters ethical narrativity, the story of "a life that can be conceived and evaluated as a whole."[48] And fourth, it has moral particularity written all over it. Emotions take place in the body, which physically acts out its moral life. Woolf censures Dickens's "psychological geography" precisely because his eye seizes upon physical characteristics.[49] Pickwick, an "observer of human nature,"[50] shows how Dickens himself observes human nature: he watches the body acting. He is a mimetic writer who lays considerable stress on action.

In contrast to the Aristotelian body, what I shall call *the modernist body* is an aesthetic body. It is an image in the mind, an incorporeal voice, a ghost of style. It is epitomized by the persona or mask.[51] To trace its nineteenth-century sources would require a wide survey, ranging from the continent to England to the US, but the major sources certainly include the post-Kantian legacy of transcendental idealism (the body as *Vorstellung*); the flaneurs, dandies, and dancers of the symbolist movement; pierrots and marionettes; Blake's giant "spiritual forms"; Pater's "imaginary portraits"; the speakers of dramatic monologues; minstrel shows; vaudeville; as well as phonograph,[52] radio, and early cinema. In "The Truth of Masks," Wilde remarks: "A Truth in art is that whose contradictory is also true."[53] It follows that the modernist repertoire of masks and personae strikes Aristotle dumb. Character acts well or badly, but the mask reveals the ambiguities of art.

Influenced by Wilde and Nietzsche, Yeats developed his theory of the mask in opposition to the dull morality of the herd. "Active virtue," he writes, "as distinguished from the passive acceptance of a code, is . . . theatrical, consciously dramatic, the wearing of a mask."[54] In his 1918 review of *Per Amica Silentia Lunae*, Eliot singled out Yeats's next sentence for approval: "Wordsworth . . . is so often flat and heavy because his moral sense, being a discipline he had not created, a mere obedience, has no theatrical element."[55] It is the decadence of modern usage that allows "virtue" to suggest that an artist should always act artistically, as if practical wisdom had no bearing on the passions.[56] This confusion about "virtue" as well as "moral sense" breeds further confusion in the modernist lexicon. Yeats's *personality* is roughly equivalent to Eliot's *impersonality*: both men denigrate the practical self engaged in the business of life.[57]

Personality, writes Yeats, "is greater and finer than character . . . When a man cultivates a style in literature he is shaping his personality."[58] Eliot's transfusion into style is much the same: "The progress of an artist is a continual self-sacrifice, a continual extinction of personality."[59] Or to revise: "great literature is . . . the transformation of a personality into a personal work of art . . ."[60]

Though Eliot and Yeats are poets of masks and disembodied voices, it is a peculiar fact about Eliot that as he aged he came to uphold standards that point in the direction of Aristotle: mimesis, the moral import of action, the agency of character. In his 1953 lecture "The Three Voices of Poetry," Eliot returned to the topic of the mask. He might have been ruminating on J. Alfred Prufrock, Tiresias, or the "brown baked features" of the "familiar compound ghost": "What we normally hear, in fact, in the dramatic monologue, is the voice of the poet, who has put on the costume and make-up either of some historical character, or of one out of fiction . . . [D]ramatic monologue cannot create a character. For character is created and made real only in action."[61] Unmasking the monologist, Eliot was in revolt against his own movement. He was trying to return character to its central place in the literary tradition. *The Waste Land*, a good counter-example, is the reverie of a mask, a bodiless voice incapable of action: "Tiresias, although a mere spectator and not indeed a 'character,' is yet the most important personage in the poem, uniting all the rest."[62] Here, Eliot's use of quotation marks ('character') calls the very concept of character into question, just as *The Waste Land* abandons the mimetic conventions behind the concept.

Joyce, Woolf, and Beckett espouse the doctrine of the mask as well. The Dublin of *Ulysses* is populated by masks, as Joyce forges his characters into the semblance of their Greek archetypes. In Nighttown, that man of many ways, Leopold Bloom, is the man of a thousand faces. Supported by cinematic effects, he races through his psyche's theatrical wardrobe, facing each new situation with a different mask. When Woolf describes "the bright mask-like look of faces seen by candlelight,"[63] she is salvaging art from the depredations of time. Beckett adopts the doctrine only to rail at it. After Molloy, Malone, and his other personae have departed, the Unnamable says, "Bah, any old pronoun will do, provided one sees through it."[64] The mask in Beckett comes full circle from Yeats. It no longer offers any improvement over nature or time or society. It is commonplace ("Bah" as in "baa"), the identity through which one "sees" the world and expresses oneself: in a world bereft of meaningful choices, there is only the meaningless play of masks.[65]

Matthew Arnold makes the last major defense of human nature in literature. He makes this defense in his critical writings; his poetry is a different subject. In his uses of Aristotle, Arnold raises permanent questions. Aristotelians and their critics will always debate the role of the state, the possibilities of human happiness, the existence of the virtues, and the limits of realism. What I need to establish, however, is that Arnold's thinking on human nature is broadly Aristotelian. Such a reasonable premise, which I hope to put beyond dispute, requires proof because of Arnold's damaging reception at the hands of the interested parties whom I discuss in Chapter 3.

The 1853 Preface, the central document of that reception history, is an expressly Aristotelian judgment against romantic excess. Arnold launches his critique of romanticism by way of Aristotle: "We all naturally take pleasure, says Aristotle, in any imitation or representation whatever; this is the basis of our love of poetry; and we take pleasure in them, he adds, because all knowledge is naturally agreeable to us; not to the philosopher only, but to mankind at large."[66] There is a certain looseness in Arnold's method. The persnickety have objected to it, but the Preface to a book of poems is not an essay in a philosophy journal.[67] Arnold takes the liberty of combining Book Four of the *Poetics* with the opening of the *Metaphysics*. In both instances, Aristotle begins with human nature, and Arnold echoes him with the adverb "naturally."

For Arnold as for Aristotle, imitation or mimesis relates primarily to action. It is not a correspondence theory of truth or simply a mirror held up to nature. It is an imitation of our passionate experience. Imitation is therefore largely a matter of feeling, which, as Aristotle remarks, is "not far removed from some feeling about reality" (*Pol.* 1340a24). Working from Aristotelian premises, Alasdair MacIntyre suggests that our feelings originate in our physical life as social animals: "The norms that govern feeling and determine its appropriateness or inappropriateness are inseparable from other norms of giving and receiving. For it is in giving and receiving in general that we exhibit affection and sympathy."[68] Inasmuch as the arts give form to feeling, it is highly germane to literature that our "great primary affections,"[69] to quote Arnold's Preface, should stem from our basic condition as social creatures.

Arnold's ethics is naturalistic and teleological. It is based on a contrast between potentiality and act. In *Culture and Anarchy*, for example, "culture," the actualizing of potential, refers to the grounds of human flourishing. Culture enables mankind to labor towards its end or *telos*, human nature complete on all sides. Arnold's analysis of "representative men" follows an Aristotelian pattern. He says in his genial way, "my head is still full of a lumber of phrases we learnt at Oxford from Aristotle, about virtue being in a mean, and about excess and defect, and so on."[70] He associates Hellenism, sweetness and light, with Aristotle, though he wants to revise the philosopher in a way favorable to "the mass of mankind."[71] Arnold's program for English education derives from the *Politics*, in particular Book Five, Chapter Nine, where Aristotle argues that education must suit the form of government if anarchy is to be avoided. In the same paragraph (1310a12–36), Aristotle corrects the "false idea of freedom . . . that freedom means doing what a man likes" (. . . ἐλεύθερον δὲ [καὶ ἴσον] τὸ ὅ τι ἂν βούληταί τις ποιεῖν). Hence, Arnold's wariness of "doing as one likes." Arnold's "best self" has many sources, not least of which is Book Ten, Chapter Seven of the *Nicomachean Ethics*. The use of "right reason," which characterizes the best self, derives from Book Six, Chapter One (1138b25).

Arnold asks critics "to see the object as in itself it really is."[72] Critics, in turn, have bridled at his request. Some see Arnold's realism as a pedantic lie serving the peculiar obsessions of Arnold himself. Certainly, by ranking the artists above the critics, Arnold has gained few friends and many foes. But Arnold's realism is consistent with his appreciation of literature. His compass points are adequate knowledge and human flourishing. When discussing the signifying power of language, he wisely refrains from aggressive metaphysical claims:

The grand power of poetry is its interpretive power; by which I mean, not a power of drawing out in black and white an explanation of the mystery of the universe, but the power of so dealing with things as to awaken in us a wonderfully full, new, and intimate sense of them, and of our relations with them. When this sense is awakened in us, as to objects without us, we feel ourselves to be in contact with the essential nature of those objects, to be no longer bewildered and oppressed by them, but to have their secret, and to be in harmony with them; and this feeling calms and satisfies as no other can . . . I will not now inquire whether this sense is illusive, whether it can be proved not to be illusive, whether it does absolutely make us possess the real nature of things . . . The interpretations of science do not give us this intimate sense of objects as the interpretations of poetry give it; they appeal to a limited faculty, and not to the whole man.[73]

Just to underscore the connection to Aristotle, one might describe Arnold as adopting the peripatetic idiom of *nous* or intuitive knowledge. But for the most part we can leave technical philosophy out of seeing the object as in itself it really is. Arnold most resembles Aristotle in his concern for the healthy effects of art: he starts with those effects, not with any rule or metaphysic designed to achieve them. Similarly, he values criticism that "tends to establish an order of ideas, if not absolutely true, yet true by comparison with that which it displaces."[74] And it is not just the pragmatic basis of Arnold's realism that should be acknowledged. Arnold was acutely aware of the competition between science and humanism, and quick to put his finger on what is, comparatively speaking, science's moral-emotional aphasia.

The ambition of T. H. Huxley, "Darwin's bulldog," inspired some of Arnold's best remarks on humanism. In "Literature and Science," Arnold holds "a genuine humanism is scientific."[75] His argument is the "need of relating what we have learnt and known to the sense which we have in us for conduct, to the sense which we have in us for beauty."[76] Deriving from Plato a defense of general culture and an innate desire for good, he builds a naturalistic foundation: "it is not on any weak pleadings of my own that I rely for convincing the gainsayers; it is on the constitution of human nature itself, and on the instinct of self-preservation in humanity."[77]

In "Science and Culture," Huxley makes his contending case for a "scientific 'criticism of life.'"[78] He asks his audience to seek the truth "not among words but among things."[79] This is the age-old rallying cry of scientists, of all who want to overthrow a musty, word-sick order, such as postmodernism is today. Science is knowledge, and humanism must pay heed. But Huxley does not establish an ethical position, per se, and in his late essay "Evolution and Ethics" he answers this defect with a prophetic error. For Huxley, "the cosmic process has no sort of relation to moral ends." It follows from this ultimately Cartesian view that "the ethical progress of society depends, not on imitating the cosmic process, . . . but in combatting it."[80] We should not gloss over "Ethics and Evolution" too lightly, for the work represents a considered judgment, by a qualified thinker, that verges on the ethics of modernism. It is richly ironic, in light of the New Darwinism, that Clarissa Dalloway's "favourite reading as a girl" included Huxley.[81] Clarissa's friend Peter Walsh summarizes her take on things: ". . . As we are a doomed race, chained to a sinking ship . . ., as the whole thing is a bad joke, let us, at any rate, do our part; mitigate the sufferings of our fellow-prisoners (Huxley again). . ."[82] More, we should take careful note of a scientific capacity for irrationalism, inasmuch as the Cartesianism of Huxley sounds uncannily like the anti-Cartesianism of Pinker, whose separation of "ultimate causation" from "proximate causation" is another call for separating nature from ethics. Either ethical naturalism is possible or it isn't. Either human nature emerged from our evolutionary past or ethical naturalism is a social construct. If you are proposing a naturalistic ethics, don't be surprised that nature takes time. And if you are absolutely put off by the specter of religion raising its ghastly head, the words of Thomas Nagel may offer comfort: "there is really no reason to assume that the only alternative to an evolutionary explanation of everything is a religious one." But, of course, as Nagel dryly observes, "this thought may not be comforting enough."[83]

Arnold believed that naturalistic ethics gave weight to his judgments on poetry. He could not explain how we come to feel the emotional effect of a line from Homer, "for an enduring heart have the destinies appointed to the children of men."[84] But he grasped the fact that some authors *naturally* speak with more depth and authority than others. His position is typical of his Aristotelianism, and it finds support in the work of contemporary virtue ethicists: our emotions and our ethics have the psychological force of gravity, joining us to the natural order – such as it is.[85] Arnold's response to the Victorian crisis in values is every bit as relevant today as it was during his lifetime, for the armada of science is still breasting the void, only its weapons are louder.

Walter Pater, Arnold's rival and the major Victorian forerunner of the ethics of modernism, discovered his aesthetic outlook in the fissures of Lockean empiricism. Book II of *An Essay Concerning Human Understanding* shows Locke developing his epistemology: "Our observation employed either, about sensible objects, or about the internal operation of our minds perceived and reflected on by ourselves, is that which supplies our understandings with all the *materials* of thinking."[86] Aestheticism begins in the rift between the observation of the sensible object and its impression on the mind.[87] Distinguishing himself from Arnold, Pater writes, "'To see the object as in itself it really is,' has been justly said to be the aim of all true criticism whatever; and in aesthetic criticism the first step towards seeing one's object as it really is, is to know one's impression as it really is, to discriminate it, to realise it distinctly."[88] Impressionism, for Pater, is a "step" into the mind's internal operation, away from the general criteria that guide the mass of men. The change registers in his vocabulary as a preference for *seeming* over *seeing*.

Pater supplies, as moral substitute for what is lost, an exhortation to realize the impression "distinctly." In support of this standard, he deploys the word *virtue*:

the function of the aesthetic critic is to distinguish, to analyse, and separate from its adjuncts, the virtue by which a picture, a landscape, a fair personality in life or in a book, produces [its] special impression of beauty or pleasure, to indicate what the source of that impression is, and under what conditions it is experienced. His end is reached when he has disengaged that virtue, and noted it, as a chemist notes some natural element, for himself and others . . .[89]

Virtue here means "power" or "occult efficacy," as in "speaking of an herb, a wine, a gem."[90] Pater adapts this pleasing archaism to the idiom of modern science, of objectivity and method. The difference between the appreciation of the fine arts from Aristotle to Wordsworth, on the one hand, and the aestheticism of Pater, on the other, is a refinement that prescinds the virtue of art from the other virtues.

Pater disapproved of "critical efforts to limit art *a priori*."[91] The term *a priori* has stuck to Arnold, converting his authority into authoritarianism. If the charge is not entirely misplaced, let us try to deduce its meaning. Arnold learned a dialectic from Goethe, by which classicism guards against the dangers of romantic art: its sickness, self-indulgence, and formlessness. It is fair to turn the tables and say that romanticism guards against the dangers of classicism. Pater sums these up very well in a chapter from *Marius the Epicurean* called "Euphuism," which is a recasting by Pater of his argument with Arnold: "Certain elderly counsellors, filling what may be thought a constant part in the little tragi-comedy which literature and its votaries are playing in all ages, would ask, suspecting some affectation or unreality in that minute culture of *form*: – Cannot those who have a thing to say, say it directly? Why not be simple and broad, like the old writers of Greece?"[92] The character Flavian, granted authorship of the (anonymous) *Pervigilium Veneris*, serves as a mirror for reflection on the burdens of the past: "It was all around one: – that smoothly built world of old classical taste, an accomplished fact, with overwhelming authority on every detail of the conduct of one's work."[93] There is violence lurking in Flavian's complaint against the *a priori*, for Pater's "minute culture of form" cannot be separated from his desire to overthrow established canons. It is a kind of sophisticated primitivism, a neo-Platonic longing for purity of form, but lacking the true lifeblood of myth. It is found in Wilde, as well. The aesthetic movement bequeaths to modernism a cult of intimate pure beauty, which is hostile to the Aristotelian world of common standards. Yeats, living the fate of the last romantics, came to recognize Arnold's foresight and the end of the modern era's "morbid effort," its isolating search for aesthetic perfection.[94] Eliot found it more convenient to address the situation in France: his 1948 lecture "From Poe to Valéry" is a farewell to an *art poétique* where "the subject is little, the treatment everything."[95]

Arnold was not a reactionary, if by that term we mean a man who defines himself with a knee-jerk reaction against change. He decried the "want of correspondence between the forms of modern Europe and its spirit, between the new wine of the eighteenth and nineteenth centuries, and the old bottles of the eleventh and twelfth centuries, or even of the sixteenth and seventeenth . . ."[96] He was modern and cosmopolitan in the best sense: "The critic of poetry should have . . . the most free, flexible, and elastic spirit imaginable; he should be indeed the 'ondoyant et divers,' the *undulating and diverse* being of Montaigne."[97] Arnold's upholding the Greek classification of kinds of poetry, "epic, dramatic, lyric, and so forth,"[98] against Wordsworth's attempt at a new order of classification, represents a classical judgment and a pragmatic defense. What counts is what works best over time: the grounds of human flourishing. Modernism renders experience too personal, too diverse, too self-conscious, for classification according to genre. But the modernists could not replace the old genres, which haunt their creative writings and fortify their criticism – even as points of departure, as in Woolf's "Modern Fiction."

Is modernism the victory of Pater over Arnold? Did Pater's "art for art's sake" win out over Arnold's "moral ideas?" Frank Kermode helped establish the orthodox view, that while Pater and Arnold were equally preoccupied with the moral function of art, it was Pater who "found answers which were at once more congenial to artists who wanted to go on being artists, and more liable to debasement."[99] One can respect Kermode's framing those answers in terms of personal culture and "the moral function" of aesthetic pleasure. But Arnold is suddenly timely: he asks us to remember human nature. And it is not just a matter of Arnold's relevance today, for the modernists did not forget human nature as their critics are wont to do. From the era of Graham Hough's *Last Romantics,* through Kermode, Bloom, and David Bromwich, romanticist readings of modernism have settled the aesthetic issue in Pater's favor.[100] But such readings are themselves aesthetic, unmindful of human nature, and they miss what Arnold meant by "relating" scientific knowledge to our sense of goodness, to our sense of beauty. A wind of forgetfulness blows through all such readings. To pigeonhole or to neglect the Aristotelian basis of Arnold's position is, in effect, to forget the modernist effort to transform human nature through the use of art – the modernist moral project.

Some of Pater's most important "answers" to the moral question come in response to Arnold's distinctive phrasing. The method has the immediate effect of stylizing ethics, of bringing ethics into aesthetic territory. This happens when Pater picks up Arnold's repetition of the word "machinery" in *Culture and Anarchy*. Examples from the book include: ". . . we worshipped our machinery so devoutly";[101] ". . . an inward working, and not machinery, is what we most want";[102] and faith "in machinery . . . is our besetting danger."[103] The word gets into Arnold's Aristotelianism: "applying Aristotle's machinery of the mean to my ideas about aristocracy . . ."[104] Pater takes rhetorical advantage to contrast his own "higher ethics" against Aristotelian "machinery." In his essay on Wordsworth, he says that machinery "covers the meanness of men's daily lives, and much of the dexterity and vigor with which they pursue what may seem to them the good of themselves and others; but not the intangible perfection of those whose ideal is rather in *being* than in *doing* . . ."[105] Pater's distinction between "machinery" and "intangible perfection" restates the Cartesian bias against human nature. His moral-minded aestheticism looks forward to the modernist goal of transforming life in the image of art: "To treat life in the spirit of art, is to make life a thing in which means and ends are identified: to encourage such treatment the true moral significance of art and poetry."[106] But while his identification of means and ends anticipates the modernist obsession with style and the revolt against plot, his practice is not in keeping with the modernist push toward revolutionary change. Pater's chronic flaw, the failure of the higher ethics that the modernists would have to rectify, is the gap between the contemplative world of the aesthete and the active world of society. In *Marius the Epicurean*, the proposed solution is a bridge between one's impressions and one's conscience. It is a bridge buttressed not by reason, but by "instinctive election."[107] Pater restricts his role to a new kind of Wordsworthian solitary, the aesthetic saint. Where modernism evicts the landlord, Pater leaves his dreamy harvest at the gate, "for art comes to you professing frankly to give nothing but the highest quality to your moments as they pass, and simply for those moments' sake."[108]

Pater elaborates his moral outlook in a strange genre that he called "imaginary portraits." The chief example is *Marius*, but "The Child in the House" supplies a good example on a smaller scale. It describes the "brain-building" of Florian Deleal, starting with the gradual inscription of his home on the Lockean "white paper" or *tabula rasa* of his young mind. Pater details the boy Florian's life of perfumes and colors. His family flits through the house like bats. His father's death in India is remembered for its effect on his aunt, "how it seemed to make the aged woman like a child again . . ."[109] His mother is remembered for the curious impressions she leaves. Like Marius, Florian seems to suffer from a mild case of autism. His primary affections are locked in "his house of thought,"[110] secured by "that thick wall of personality through which no real voice has ever pierced on its way to us . . ."[111] Florian welcomes the physical world, the human body and its senses, but he welcomes them as means to the impressions he cultivates. His body is aesthetic, not Aristotelian. His narrative is a story of thoughts and impressions, not acts.

By rejecting the Aristotelian-Arnoldian "machinery" in favor of the higher ethics, Florian becomes a *higher self.* He converts his refined taste into moral superiority: "And thinking of the very poor, it was not the things which most men care most for that he yearned to give them; but fairer roses, perhaps, and power to taste quite as they will, at their ease and not task-burdened, a certain desirable, clear light in the new morning, through which sometimes he noticed them, quite unconscious of it, on their way to their early toil."[112] The working poor are trapped, "unconscious," lacking in taste. Florian watches them from his window like a visitor from fairyland, vainly wishing them entry into his ideal world. The gap between the observer and the observed is virtually ontological, like a difference between species.

The higher ethics is an ultra-refined form of consciousness, which typically expresses itself through feelings of pity. When Florian encounters the ruined Marie Antoinette in a drawing by the French painter David, "meant merely to make her look ridiculous," Pater describes the compassionate effect on him: "The face that had been so high had learned to be mute and resistless; but out of its very resistlessness, seemed now to call on men to have pity, and forbear; and he took note of that, as he closed the book, as a thing to look at again, if he should at any time find himself tempted to be cruel."[113] Pater might have been recalling Edmund Burke: "I thought ten thousand swords must have leaped from their scabbards to avenge even a look that threatened her with insult."[114] But where Burke would leap to his feet, Florian effects a subtle, sadomasochistic identification – a delicate impression of desire. He has pity, and he has his way with it. Saint Florian, his namesake, was horribly scourged and martyred during the Diocletian persecution, and the name serves to weave together the idea of aesthetic sainthood and the feeling of sadomasochistic identification.

As Florian comes to suffer the pangs of his highly morbid sensuality, what saves him from his own fears and compulsions is his memory and dreams. In his inner world, "the sense of security could hardly have been deeper, the quiet of the child's soul being one with the quiet of its home, a place 'inclosed' and 'sealed.'"[115] This hermetic space or form is closed to flesh and blood, like Yeats's "condition of fire," like Eliot's "ideal order," like Lady Lasswade's library, where "the brown books in their long rows seemed to exist silently, with dignity, by themselves, for themselves."[116] For the rest of Florian's days, the uncanny object of his deep desires will be his own mind, housing the pleasure of its impressions, safe until death. This kind of aesthetic solipsism worries Mrs. Ramsay: "How then . . . did one know one thing or another thing about people, sealed as they were?"[117] It is a problem that infects moral judgments: "*Mr. M's Bungalow. A view spoilt for ever. That's murder . . .*"[118] Why should a thing be good or bad, except insofar as it answers to the needs of the aesthetic mind? The higher ethics legislates from a place of exile, affirming its perspective over that of the lower world. The bodiless voice that resents the injury to its impressions has a point, but its angry moral judgment is closed to other considerations.

In their criticism of habit, Pater has an advantage over Arnold. As both were doubtless aware, Aristotle, following Plato, derives the word for virtue (ἠθική) from the word for habit (ἔθος). Aristotle makes this connection the cornerstone of his ethics: "Neither by nature . . . nor contrary to nature do the virtues arise in us; rather we are adapted by nature to receive them, and are made perfect by habit . . . It makes no small difference, then, whether we form habits of one kind or another from our very youth; it makes a very great difference, or rather *all* the difference" (*Nic. Eth.* 1103a14–1103b26). The ethical movement from potential to realization depends on the intervention of habits, which are indispensable to society. The law, for example, is said to have "no power to command obedience except that of habit" (*Pol.* 1269a20). But to a romantic, habit is immediately suspect.

The word *habit* shows up fairly often in *Culture and Anarchy*. Arnold succeeds well enough, on Aristotelian grounds, when he points out the effects of bad habits: "If our habits make it hard for us to come at the idea of a high best self, of a paramount authority, in literature or religion, how much more do they make this hard in the sphere of politics!"[119] But to get at the building up of good habits is not so easy:

In all our directions our habitual courses of action seem to be losing efficaciousness, credit, and control, both with others and even with ourselves. Everywhere we see the beginnings of confusion, and we want a clue to some sound order and authority. This we can only get by going back upon the actual instincts and forces which rule our life, seeing them as they really are, connecting them with other instincts and forces, and enlarging our whole view and rule of life.[120]

Since their romantic habits forbade the Victorian critics from giving habit a warm welcome, Arnold needed all the flexibility at his command to get his point across. His appeal to "order and authority" is, however, precisely the type of language that led Pater to protest in his Conclusion to *The Renaissance*: "The theory or idea or system which requires of us the sacrifice of any part of [our] experience, in consideration of some interest into which we cannot enter, or some abstract theory we have not identified with ourselves, or what is only conventional, has no real claim upon us."[121] Pater effectively closes the door on Arnold, and therefore on Aristotle as well. Roughly speaking, Arnold's "whole view" is the *telos*, his "rule of life" is practical wisdom or *phronesis* (*Nic. Eth.* 1140b4), and the task of connecting "actual instincts and forces" with "other instincts and forces" is the ethical task of creating new "habitual courses of action" in order to realize the culture's potential. For Arnold, the appeal to "sound order and authority" expresses a healthy, Aristotelian dislike of anarchists, sophists, and demagogues. For Pater, the same appeal threatens to intrude on the individual's freedom, and to sever life from art.

Pater's criticism of habit looks back in particular to Carlyle's criticism of custom. In *Sartor Resartus*, Professor Teufelsdröckh observes: "Custom is the greatest of Weavers . . . What is philosophy throughout but a continual battle against Custom; an ever-renewed effort to transcend the sphere of blind Custom, and so become Transcendental?"[122] In his Conclusion to *The Renaissance*, where Pater professes his "love of art for its own sake," he describes our best hope in life as an artistic consciousness, alert to "that continual vanishing away, that strange perpetual weaving and unweaving of ourselves." The weaving echoes Carlyle, but for Pater it is the individual self – more crucially than passing institutions of church or state – that is apparitional. Pater pursues not transcendence but "ecstasy": "How shall we pass most swiftly from point to point, and be present always at the focus where the greatest number of vital forces unite in their purest energy?" The question hovers rhetorically, and then Pater begins his next paragraph with an ontological leap of self-consciousness, marked at the start by an infinitive and then by an adverb of infinity: "To burn always with this hard, gemlike flame is success in life." Habit, like cliché, is a fall, a loss in style, energy, and vision: "In a sense it might even be said that our failure is to form habits: for, after all, habit is relative to a stereotyped world, and meantime it is only the roughness of the eye that makes any two persons, things, situations, seem alike."[123] Habit is the enemy of what Pater calls "virtue" and "*ascêsis*," which manifest the particular alone.

The intervention of Wilde, "the Apostle of Aestheticism," becomes highly relevant at this juncture. In "The Decay of Lying," Wilde envisages the downfall of a gifted young man who "either falls into careless habits of accuracy, or takes to frequenting the society of the aged and well-informed."[124] In "The Artist as Critic," he secures art and the higher self from matter and determinism: "By revealing to us the absolute mechanism of all action, and so freeing us from the self-imposed and trammelling burden of moral responsibility, the scientific principle of Heredity has become, as it were, the warrant for the contemplative life."[125] He affords himself a wide margin of aesthetic distance, from which as a playwright he can mock the charming absurdity of plot, character, and feeling. As Woolf would say, "The plot was only there to beget emotion."[126] Taking up Pater's quarrel with Arnold, Wilde enlivens it with paradox: "the primary aim of the critic is to see the object as in itself it really is not."[127] With Pater's "golden book" in hand, he fleers at "ignoble considerations of probability, that cowardly concession to the tedious repetitions of domestic or public life."[128] The golden book is *Marius the Epicurean*, with its fantastically improbable romance of Cupid and Psyche, which Pater translates beautifully from Apuleius. Wilde condemns habit, nature, and probability in order to set "the record of one's own soul"[129] over the mimetic order. In short, he sets the soul against the machinery of Aristotle.[130]

Wilde's soulfulness is gnostic: "one only realises one's soul by getting rid of all alien passions, all acquired culture, and all external possessions be they good or evil."[131] And though it is not fashionable to read *A Picture of Dorian Gray* as a spiritual allegory, I do not think we can understand Wilde's mediation of Pater unless we restore Wilde to his soul. When Lord Henry Wotton finds "there was no motive power in experience,"[132] he is rejecting practical wisdom and naturalist ethics. When he quotes the Gospel of Matthew to Dorian ("'what does it profit a man if he gain the whole world and lose . . . his own soul?'"), he is deploying Wilde's gnostic theory of denaturalized art as the soul's realm. Dorian, whose picture is denaturalized art, replies to Lord Henry that the "soul is a terrible reality," one he is "[q]uite sure" of.[133] Yeats, Eliot, Woolf, Joyce, and Beckett have this Wildean strain inbred in their aestheticism.

Through the agency of Wilde, Pater's unweaving of habit becomes a means of revealing the soul. For Yeats, the visionary horizons of mind-reading experiences overcome "mere habit."[134] He frees himself from the shackles of matter: "The soul cannot have much knowledge till it has shaken off the habit of time and place . . ."[135] He frowns on character because it "is made up of habits retained, all kinds of things."[136] Holding forth at the National Library, another mystical aesthete strikes a familiar pose: "As we, or mother Dana, weave and unweave our bodies . . . from day to day, their molecules shuttled to and fro, so does the artist weave and unweave his image" (*Ulysses* 9. 376).[137] By contrast, Pater's rival makes a mechanical and graceless appearance: "A deaf gardener, aproned, masked with Matthew Arnold's face, pushes his mower on the sombre lawn watching narrowly the dancing motes of grasshalms" (1. 172). Woolf rebels against habit in order to illuminate "the dark places of psychology." The "great Russian writers . . . have lost their clothes,"[138] she writes in "The Russian Point of View," using clothes as a metaphor to denote habit, since the word in its original sense simply means clothing. In return, the Russians gain the soul: "It is the soul that matters, its passion, its tumult, its astonishing medley of beauty and vileness."[139] The mystic Bernard of *The Waves* sheds the habits of character and narrative, rewriting Pater as "I am made and remade continually."[140]

One solution to the problem of habits is to see them *sub specie aeternitatis*. "Eliot," writes Yeats, "has produced his great effect upon his generation because he has described men and women that get out of bed or into it from mere habit . . ."[141] The reference, I think, is to "Preludes," but Yeats ignores the dramatic contest of spirit and matter that shapes the poem: "His soul stretched tight across the skies / That fade behind a city block, / Or trampled by insistent feet . . ."[142] He ignores, in other words, Eliot's place in the choir of gnostic aestheticism. Joyce sketches the Sunday habits of the Dublin crowd: "Like illumined pearls the lamps shone from the summits of their tall poles upon the living texture below which, changing shape and hue unceasingly, sent up into the warm grey evening air an unchanging unceasing murmur."[143] Joyce's passage is close to Eliot's, only richer (belletristic word): it exemplifies what Harry Levin, following the insights of John Synge, calls "a dialectical synthesis of the naturalistic tradition and the symbolistic reaction."[144]

In his book *Proust*, Beckett describes habit as an "automatic adjustment of the human organism to the conditions of its existence." Like Wilde, he thinks of habit as centered in the body's motor activities, which are thoughtless.[145] Habit, therefore, has no "moral significance."[146] It is "the ballast that chains the dog to his vomit."[147] At the end of the aesthetic movement, Beckett sees life and art itself as disgusting habits.[148] Vladimir comments to himself as Estragon dozes, "habit is a great deadener."[149] The language echoes William Paley's 1802 treatise, *Natural Theology*: "Habit, the instrument of nature, is a great leveller; the familiarity which it induces, taking off the edge both of our pleasures and of our sufferings." Beckett found Paley's sentence in the *OED*, under *habit sense 9b*: "Custom, usage, use, wont." It is a *usage* that speaks across aesthetic and ethical boundaries. As Pater saw, questions of habit can give art a real moral liveliness. But the movement that Pater started concludes in Beckett's reaction against aesthetics, which he condemns for its usages and habits.[150]

Pater's quarrel with Arnold begins with Arnold's dissent from an aestheticizing judgment: "A true allegory of the state of one's own mind in a representative history is perhaps the highest thing that one can attempt in the way of poetry."[151] If we reject habit, and if we reject the "theory or idea or system which requires of us the sacrifice of any part of [our] experience, in consideration of some interest into which we cannot enter, or some abstract theory we have not identified with ourselves, or what is only conventional," we may find that all we have is our minds or souls, because they are all we believe in. If we take Pater's aesthetic as an ideal of authenticity,[152] we generate a vicious circle: we reject habit and other interests to arrive at an authentic self; our union of life and art becomes conventional; the self demands the rejection of habits in order to regain its authenticity. In time the authentic self has exchanged creation for liberation, leaving in its trail, like broken husks, the habits, primary affections, and friendships that happiness desires. And to remain free, one must remain skeptical of whatever would limit present freedom. One is compelled to make an ethic of personal liberation serve the "highest thing," a union of art and life designed for spiritual or psychological ecstasy, even as it expunges the Aristotelian body.

The principle of "fair balance," which stems from the virtue of justice, prompts MacIntyre to criticize Aristotle's *megalopsychos* (*Nic. Eth.* 1123a33), the proto-Nietzschean, self-sufficient Alpha Plus who denies "the possibility of there being any genuine virtues of acknowledged dependence."[153] The *megalopsychos*, it turns out, is a hubristic fraud, who starves the virtue of truthfulness. And now I reach my last point about Pater's influence: since we are mutually dependent (in truth and in justice), it follows that our acknowledgment or denial of our mutual dependence affects our sensibility and taste.

No doubt it is Dickens who strikes us as sentimental. Wilde famously quipped: "One must have a heart of stone to read the death of Little Nell without laughing."[154] For orphans like Little Nell and David Copperfield, the ties of affection, being in constant crisis, can form the focus of lachrymose attention. Modernist sentimentality occurs in reaction against ordinary emotion: "Either we are cold, or we are sentimental," writes Woolf in *Jacob's Room*, on the Paterian premise that life is but "a procession of shadows," an affair of "sudden vision" and sudden vanishing.[155] It would be more accurate to say that modernism oscillates between extremes of restraint and release, between dispassionate coldness and feverish intensity. Both extremes are "sentimental" because they set emotion apart from the moral life.

Death is the foremost occasion for the modernist sentiment of coldness. Cuchulain kills his son and dies in terrible isolation. Stephen Dedalus refuses his mother; he will not console her and is estranged at her deathbed. No one actually mourns Rose Pargiter. Because its subject is an insect (albeit a symbolic one) and not a person, "The Death of the Moth" lays bare the impersonality of feeling that prevails when Yeats declaims to horsemen or Krapp watches the blind go down. Here, to be sure, is a friendless and loveless and independent end: "The body relaxed, and instantly grew stiff. The struggle was over. The insignificant little creature now knew death . . . The moth having righted himself now lay most decently and uncomplainingly composed. O yes, he seemed to say, death is stronger than I am."[156] If emotional perspective returns, it is not in a susceptible shudder, but in a sense of incongruity – even of parody: "The struggle was over." Too much style has been lavished on dispatching an "insignificant little creature." The tragedy is ridiculous – absurd. One must have a heart of stone not to laugh at the death of the "little" moth. Near the other extreme, Beckett greets life's ordinary emotions with a deliberately grotesque embrace, as when Estragon longs for an erection or when Nell waxes nostalgic. And there is his own sentimental "(Exit weeping)," in the second of the "Three Dialogues."[157] Beckett comes late, doubtful of the modernist shtick, but even he defers to the first law of modernist pathos: the harder the prison – nature, body, habit, language, self – the greater, more daedal, more authentic the art.

CHAPTER I

W. B. Yeats: out of nature

The moral ideas behind Yeats's early poems stand for inspection in his 1903 collection of essays, *Ideas of Good and Evil.* In one of the book's major expressions of doctrine, "William Blake and His Illustrations to *The Divine Comedy*," Yeats expounds Blake's "opinions" of Dante, which could not have been pleasing to the Catholic bishops of Ireland. He starts by splitting Dante in two. He admits by way of Blake that "Dante, because a great poet, was 'inspired by the Holy Ghost.'"[1] Quickly, though, he turns his attention to Dante's "worldly" philosophy, "established for the ordering of the body and the fallen will."[2] He calls Dante's ethics "the philosophy of soldiers, of men of the world, of priests busy with government, of all who, because of their absorption in active life, have been persuaded to judge and to punish . . ."[3] Yeats's hostility to "the active life" has English and continental sources, for example, in Pater and Villiers. Yeats compounds this hostility with Blake's gnostic theory of the imagination, which he sums up in "The Moods": "Everything that can be seen, touched, measured, explained, understood, argued over, is to the imaginative artist nothing more than a means, for he belongs to the invisible life . . ."[4] As an active, worldly man, Dante is one of the fallen, the "drudges of time and space."[5] He is a creature of "reason builded upon sensation."[6]

Espousing Blake's morality of "unlimited forgiveness," Yeats holds that "artists and poets . . . are taught by the nature of their craft to sympathise with all living things."[7] Yeats would later discard the ideal of sympathy, but in his early work, imagination and sympathy are closely aligned. "Without a perfect sympathy there is no perfect imagination,"[8] he writes. Likewise, "we enlarge our imagination by imaginative sympathy."[9] The weakness of Yeats's romantic morality, as of all antinomianism, is that it lacks a principle of discernment. Blake is said to have stood for a "Christian command of unlimited forgiveness,"[10] though he believed in the purifying violence of the French Revolution. Blake is said to have held many "animosities,"[11] though in observing Blake's hatreds, Yeats never suggests that they seriously contradict Blake's Christian love. Blake is without sin, and Dante must simply be broken into halves, which, like Dr. Jekyll and Mr. Hyde, have no apparent connection.

Yeats was heir to a living romantic tradition where painters and poets supported each other against the orthodox. For Yeats, Pater's praise for Botticelli's illustrations of Dante would have mingled with Blake's opinions. Pater himself had noticed "an insoluble element of prose in the depths of Dante's poetry."[12] Yeats's Dante is the son of Pater's Aristotle, accused of "reducing all things to machinery."[13] And Pater had already dismissed Aristotle as "the first of the Schoolmen."[14] Yeats may also have remembered the reference to Aristotle in *The Marriage of Heaven and Hell*, where Blake characterizes "Aristotle's Analytics" as a skeleton in the dark Satanic mills.

In his introduction to *The Oxford Book of Modern Verse*, Yeats puts literary history in a personal light: "The revolt against Victorianism meant to the young poet a revolt against irrelevant descriptions of nature, the scientific and moral discursiveness of *In Memoriam* – 'when he should have been broken-hearted,' said Verlaine, 'he had many reminiscences' – the political eloquence of Swinburne, the psychological curiosity of Browning, and the poetical diction of everybody."[15] This proud catalogue of prohibitions, a *via negativa* to the temple of art, memorializes Yeats's 1894 meeting in Paris with the symbolist poet Paul Verlaine. It was Verlaine who raised the cry, *Prends l'éloquence et tords-lui son cou*, rendered by Yeats as "Wring the neck of rhetoric."[16] And what precisely was this prolix and contemptible rhetoric that Verlaine denounced? It was the opposite of "personal utterance."[17] It was "the will trying to do the work of the imagination."[18] It was the "impurities" of politics, science, history, and dogmatic religion. In short, it was the language of the world.

Yeats's symbolist affinities were strengthened through his friendship with Arthur Symons. In his book *The Symbolist Movement in Literature*, which he dedicated to Yeats, Symons declared war on "the old bondage of rhetoric, the old bondage of exteriority."[19] *The Symbolist Movement in Literature* inspired Yeats to write "The Symbolism of Poetry," where he established a close rapport between English romanticism and the continental writers whom Symons championed:

All writers, all artists of any kind, in so far as they have had any philosophical or critical power, perhaps just in so far as they have been deliberate artists at all, have had some philosophy, some criticism of their art; and it has often been this philosophy, or this criticism, that has evoked their most startling inspiration, calling into outer life some portion of the divine life, of the buried reality, which could alone extinguish in the emotions what their philosophy or their criticism would extinguish in the intellect.[20]

It may take the reader a moment to digest the notion that Yeats is propounding here, that poetic inspiration should "extinguish" physical emotion, and that philosophy should "extinguish" the rational mind. What Yeats means by philosophy can be gathered from his essay "The Philosophy of Shelley's Poetry," where "ruling symbols" take the place of system and logic: "The poet of essences and pure ideas must seek in the half-lights that glimmer from symbol to symbol as if to the ends of the earth, all that the epic and dramatic poet finds of mystery and shadow in the accidental circumstance of life."[21] As a guide to aesthetic and ethical perfection, a philosophy of symbols leads beyond the heat of emotion. The symbolist poet escapes "the accidental circumstance" of which phys-ical emotion is a symptom. Symons, in his chapter on Verlaine, describes a movement away from the world and into the unconscious: "It is the very essence of poetry to be unconscious of anything between its own moment of flight and the supreme beauty which it will never attain."[22] Similarly, Yeats's desire for "the buried reality" is a pursuit of perfection at the cost of the world. But while Yeats speaks of copying "the pure inspiration of early times,"[23] the old Platonic violence lurks in a poetic philosophy that rejects not only society but all ideas except its own. In the symbolist movement, primitivism and avant-gardism are indistinguishable.

In "Adam's Curse," we can judge the results of Yeats's "deliberate" artistry:

> We sat grown quiet at the name of love;
> We saw the last embers of daylight die,
> And in the trembling blue-green of the sky
> A moon, worn as if it had been a shell
> Washed by time's waters as they rose and fell
> About the stars and broke in days and years.[24]

The technical skill is astonishing, as the poet achieves an effect of ecstasy, of being lifted out of body. One of the means employed is broken parallelism. The "moon" resists the pattern suggested by its syntactical relation to "the last embers of daylight," where "last embers" carries the suggestion of fading emotion, of emotion's being *extinguished*. Instead of an active verb paralleling "die," the moon, by way of the extended metaphor of the shell, takes the passive participles "worn" and "washed," only to be buoyed and sustained by the flowing syntax. It is a lovely surprise, an effect of defying gravity. Yeats exerts not a moral power, but a power of enchantment, as he brings his reader to identify with his mood, which is itself an abstraction from reality, an advance by way of *eros* ("the name of love") toward perfect beauty. But there can be no moral counterpoint, no dramatic irony, no humor, no other voice, for these would dispel the mood. And there is no longer any plot or action of the body among other human bodies to generate a more vivid and earthy emotion.

The visionary poet "must write or be of no account to any cause, good or evil..."[25] His feelings grow out of imaginative knowledge that is sympathetic and contemplative, not moral in any worldly sense. "The Cloak, the Boat, and the Shoes" is an early example of Yeats's mystical morality. It begins:

> 'What do you make so fair and bright?'
> 'I make the cloak of Sorrow:
> O lovely to see in all men's sight
> Shall be the cloak of Sorrow,
> In all men's sight.'[26]

Coleridge helps gloss the passage, with his definition in *The Statesman's Manual* of a symbol as being "characterized . . . [a]bove all by the translucence of the Eternal through and in the Temporal."[27] In "The Cloak, the Boat, and the Shoes," "the cloak" of appearances is translucent with the reality of Sorrow. Seen differently, Sorrow is swift and ubiquitous, it is pure as white wool. All men share the tragic delight in Sorrow. "All men's ears" take pleasure in the English sapphics. Their haunting subtlety evokes the tender loss that is their subject. And this loss, this momentary blankness, touches a mystical verge. Yeats's use of symbols as dramatic metaphors for sorrow is abstract. It enables him to gain a contemplative distance from emotion, and to establish a sympathetic largeness as he views the human scene. And yet the poet wants no distance between him and us. He is "the supreme Enchanter, or some one of His councils," and his readers are the enchanted.[28] He draws us into his experience through the force of the sapphics, through the use of white space on the page, through the hypnotic repetition of the word "all," through the repeated questioning. He applies his technique to suspend time. "The purpose of rhythm," Yeats writes, ". . . is to prolong the moment of contemplation, the moment when we are both asleep and awake, which is the one moment of creation, by hushing us with an alluring monotony, while it holds us by waking variety, to keep us in that state of perhaps real trance, in which the mind liberated from the pressure of the will is unfolded in symbols."[29] Like a narcotic, poetry is made to serve an unworldly freedom. The poet administers his potion entirely to the mind.

In his essay "The Autumn of the Body," we can trace Yeats's developing interest in the tradition of European symbolism. Yeats approves Mallarmé's concern for "the horror of the forest or the silent thunder in the leaves, not the intense dense wood in the trees."[30] He connects Mallarmé's "poetry of essences" to "an ever more arduous search for an almost disembodied ecstasy."[31] In "The Symbolism of Poetry," he refines his theory: "All sounds, all colours, all forms, either because of their pre-ordained energies or because of long association, evoke indefinable and yet precise emotions, or, as I prefer to think, call down among us certain disembodied powers, whose footsteps over our hearts we call emotions . . ."[32] The notion of "indefinable and yet precise emotions," like that of "disem-bodied . . . footsteps," defies "corporeal reason,"[33] but Yeats makes his point about the immediacy of the effect. In "Rosa Alchemica," an early tale in the manner of Pater, we learn that these "bodiless powers" are "what men called the moods."[34] Pater's *Renaissance* stands closely behind Yeats's theory of otherworldly moods: for Pater, the moods of the visionary artist distinguish him from the dramatic artist.[35] In "The Cloak, the Boat, and the Shoes," we can see that Sorrow is a mood. Moods and powers are in fact all "disembodied."

The symbolist dimension of Yeats's thought is a bodiless dimension. Without the body and its actions among other bodies, emotion becomes reflective, twilit and moody. The mysterious presence of beauty, even in so rarefied a form as a color – white or purple – must suffice as a spring of emotion. But the subtlety of the emotion does not negate its power. An erotic flight of the soul, the lyric drama of emotional ascent is similar to what we find in the *Phaedrus*. Desire for a particular object rises into ecstatic, incorporeal love of immutable beauty, which exists beyond space and time. "The silver apples of the moon / The golden apples of the sun" possess, as objects, much less particularity than Maud Gonne. But the symbolic apples, like Maud or Helen of Troy, bear a ghostly beauty, and it is always the same beauty they bear: "for there is only one perfection and only one search for perfection . . ."[36]

The otherworldly strength of Yeats's symbolist tradition is that it forsakes ethics for a religious ideal. The epigraph to *The Rose* (1893) comes from Saint Augustine: *Sero te amavi, Pulchritudo tam antiqua et tam nova! Sero te amavi!*[37] "So late I loved you, O Beauty ever ancient and ever new! So late I loved you!" These Latin words, quoted again by Yeats in his 1910 essay "Ireland and the Arts," imply that the Good and the Beautiful are one. The artist who unites the Good and the Beautiful delivers them from human hands to the "Unseen Life." "In this matter," writes Yeats of the heroic artist, "he must be without humility."[38] It is a suggestive choice of words, because humility comes from the Latin *humilis,* low or humble, which comes in turn from the Latin *humus,* earth or ground. The disembodied poet is without earth or ground. And given such circumstances, it is unsurprising that he garbs himself in priestly vestments and seeks to inspire cultic loyalty: "We who care deeply about the arts find ourselves the priesthood of an almost forgotten faith, and we must, I think, if we would win the people again, take upon ourselves the method and the fervour of a priesthood."[39] With human content diminishing, the priestly quest for disembodied perfection grows more purely stylistic and occult, so much so that "continuous indefinable symbolism . . . is the substance of all style."[40] The bread of artistic transubstantiation, style is exalted before the public as a divine substance. It transforms reality into essence and symbol.

Challenged by Nietzsche's contempt for hypocritical "despisers of the body,"[41] Yeats gradually returned his imagination to earth. His 1906 essay "Discoveries" is a Nietzschean critique of the symbolist movement. The author questions its diet of "states of mind, lyrical moments, intellectual essences."[42] He wants to reclaim the "whole man – blood, imagination, intellect, running together . . ." He wants to heal the divided consciousness of romanticism. He declares, "I am orthodox and pray for a resurrection of the body . . ."[43] He begins to rehabilitate Dante: "emotion must be related to emotion by a system of ordered images, as in the *Divine Comedy*."[44] In *A Vision* he would go so far as to place Dante in his own company, the brightest men of the illustrious seventeenth phase, those who achieve "Unity of Being."

Nietzsche's presence in *Ideas of Good and Evil* is puzzling until we learn that it came about through secondary sources.[45] In "William Blake and His Illustrations to *The Divine Comedy*," Yeats likens Blake both to Shelley and to Nietzsche on the basis of their revolutionary morals – their transvaluation of values. One thinks, for instance, of *The Marriage of Heaven and Hell* and *The Genealogy of Morals,* works characterized by shrewd psychological insights. "The weak in courage is strong in cunning" is Blake's version of *ressentiment*.[46] Blake also looks forward to Nietzsche in the darting brilliance of his aphorisms, which stake the self to a restless, surging energy. Kindred spirits, Blake and Nietzsche have nothing but contempt for "that tuning down of the affects to a harmless mean according to which they may be satisfied, the Aristotelianism of morals."[47]

But how could the roadway of excess lead to anything like Dantean order? The passionate exuberance of Blake and Nietzsche might be defended along the lines of Shelley's interest – itself an expansion of Coleridge's theory of supernatural literature – in affording "a point of view to the imagination for the delineating of human passions more comprehensive and commanding than any which the ordinary relations of existing events can yield." Reflecting on *Frankenstein*, his wife's extraordinary novel, Shelley saw an effort to "preserve the truth of the elementary principles of human nature" while expanding their application beyond the bounds of reality.[48] But it is hard to deny that *Frankenstein* presents a picture of man as a creature bereft of "elementary principles" and ruled by demonic passions. In Victor Frankenstein's world, nature dwindles as a source of moral value, becoming either dead matter for exploitation, or a pre-social source of pleasure. "Human nature," repeated throughout the work like a mad chorus, is riddled with darkness.

In fact it is Mary Shelley's daemonism in *Frankenstein*, and not her husband's rationalization, that is prophetic of Yeats – though it is unclear how well, if at all, Yeats knew the novel. The daemon understands Victor Frankenstein better than any friend or beloved. It separates Frankenstein from other men. It is his own creation, which destroys him. Yeats is exploring the subconscious in *Per Amica Silentia Lunae* when he writes, "The Daemon, by using his mediatorial shades, brings man again and again to the place of choice, heightening temptation that the choice may be as final as possible, imposing his own lucidity upon events, leading his victim to whatever among works not impossible is the most difficult."[49] As "mediatorial shades," figures like Maud Gonne or Frankenstein's beloved Elizabeth turn – away from nature – into psychological figures and ultimately figures of speech for the daemonic oracle. For Yeats and Mary Shelley, the daemon of excess is the creative medium of fate.

Nietzsche had the prescience to equate "spirits" and "demons" with psychological "drives" in section six of *Beyond Good and Evil*. And what was especially fertile about Nietzsche's demonic thinking, and timely from Yeats's point of view, was its moral fire. Yeats's romantic tradition had never clearly answered the charge of moral inconsequence. Shelley was Arnold's "beautiful and ineffectual angel, beating in the void his luminous wings in vain."[50] It is helpful to recall the original basis of the charge. When, for example, the Shelleyan poet in *Alastor* dreams of an encounter with his ideal lover, she takes a moment to moralize:

> Her voice was like the voice of his own soul
> Heard in the calm of thought . . .
> Knowledge and truth and virtue were her theme,

> And lofty hopes of divine liberty,
> Thoughts the most dear to him, and poesy,
> Herself a poet.[51]

Unless we are rapt beyond speech, we are likely to notice that the dream-maiden's insights into her difficult subject are simply lost to us. We will never know her lesson on the relation of knowledge to virtue. And though virtue is a thought "most dear" to her lover, she soon abandons the "solemn tones" of philosophy for the "wild numbers" of passion, a prelude to the pair's love-making. Virtue and sex go together, somehow. It is not far off to call Shelley's morality a beautiful promise in a wet dream. Only his lovesickness, the pathos of his desire, pulls us up with a shock.

Yeats's "Daimon," "daemon," "antithetical self," or "anti-self" (the multiplication of names reflects obsessive psychologizing) is Nietzsche's self-transcending man in the grip of his obsessions: "Inexpressible and nameless is that which gives my soul agony and sweetness and is even the hunger of my entrails."[52] Wilde had developed much the same theme when, discussing Wagner's music, he referred to "that ΕΡΩΣ ΤΩΝ ΑΔΥΝΑΤΩΝ, that *Amour de l'Impossible*, which falls like madness on many who think they live securely out of the reach of harm, so that they sicken suddenly with the poison of unlimited desire, and, in the infinite pursuit of what they may not obtain, grow faint and swoon or stumble."[53] In "The Celtic Element in Literature," Yeats had praised the "unbounded" passion of "a love poem in *The Songs of Connacht* that is like a death-cry: 'My love, O she is my love, the woman who is most for destroying me . . .'"[54] But it was Nietzsche who converted the passionate theme into the moral drama of psychomachia. "There is much that is difficult for the spirit," says Zarathustra, "the strong *reverent* spirit that would bear much: but the difficult and the most difficult are what its strength demands."[55]

Certainly there were other influences behind Yeats's development, but here I am concerned with the moral psychology that shaped Yeats's modernist poetic. Nietzsche had taken the Faustian dynamic of self-transcendence and self-affirmation, and recast it as a division within the self between master and slave, the "two *opposing* values . . . 'good and evil.'"[56] "Evil," writes Yeats, "is the strain one upon another of opposites."[57] This is positive evil, an assertion of moral choice and "value." When Yeats refers to "the vision of evil" he means more than a privation of good. Evil is an Augustinian consent of the will, but with a Nietzschean twist: Yeats locates creativity itself in the discord of moral conflict. Love can conquer justice, and justice prove the weaker. To quote Zarathustra, "necessary are the envy and mistrust and calumny among your virtues.

Behold how each of your virtues covets what is highest: each wants your whole spirit that it might become *her* herald; each wants your whole strength in wrath, hatred, and love . . . Man is something that must be overcome; and therefore you shall love your virtues, for you will perish of them."[58]

At the supreme height of the daemon's influence, the man of fate "overcomes" human nature, "the bundle of accident and incoherence that sits down to breakfast." He achieves a mask or perfection of style: "he has been re-born as an idea, something intended, complete."[59] One can compare Nietzsche's *Birth of Tragedy*, where "all the celebrated figures of the Greek stage – Prometheus, Oedipus, etc. – are masks of . . . Dionysus."[60] Yeats sees the same phenomenon in the lives of the "supreme masters of tragedy," who, through a final triumph of predestinated will, "become conjoint to their buried selves," and "turn all to Mask and Image."[61] The buried self or daimon is the God, Dionysus living in modern times in the subconscious. The "Mask" is the new self forged by the will. The "Image" is the object of desire, when contemplation and desire unite in "the condition of fire," the spiritual harmony where all is made simple for a time.[62]

Nietzsche observed that "the Greeks . . . could not endure individuals on the tragic stage."[63] Similarly, Yeats's tragic heroes are "phantoms in their own eyes."[64] What counts is the mask. A late example is "Long-legged Fly," where Caesar, Helen, and Michael Angelo are superhuman presences, scarcely human beings. Likewise, the tragic heroes of "Easter, 1916" "went out to die calling upon Cuchulain."[65] They were governed, and ennobled, by fate, which mastered them through the psychological force of the Daimon or anti-self, in their case, the half-divine Cuchulain. Their consummate achievement was to overcome human nature by wearing the divine mask.

Yeats prefers his tragic theory to Aristotle's when he writes, "Tragedy is passion alone, and rejecting character, it gets form from motives, from the wandering of passion . . ."[66] For Aristotle, "passion alone" is not sufficient, and character is not rejected. The fine arts imitate action, says Aristotle, understanding action in the larger sense of *praxis*: "an inward process, a psychical energy working outwards; deeds, incidents, events, situations, being included under it so far as these spring from an inward act of will, or elicit some activity of thought or feeling."[67] But Aristotle never suggests that the tragic hero or the audience is capable of pure passion, for *human* nature cannot entirely separate passion from reason. (It follows that Agave is not a tragic hero, she is a tragic dupe.) This is not to say that reason always prevails, or that morality is harmonious, or that the tragic flaw should be moralized. It is to say that emotion retains some cast of thought for people who are not acting like beasts. A rational, human element survives in the moral impression of tragedy, even if the profoundness of the impression leads beyond language toward the ineffable or God.

Yeats's antipathy to character reflects the goal of his tragic art: the incorporeal ecstasy of vision. In *A Full Moon in March*, the Swineherd cannot consummate his love for the Queen. He is the dung and she the ideal. No living man can besmirch the full moon. But after his beheading, the Swineherd's passionate destiny is realized through an act of ventriloquism that recalls the religious origin of drama, at least as Nietzsche pictured it: "to see oneself transformed before one's own eyes and to begin to act as if one had actually entered into another body, another character."[68] Yeats's Dionysianism, like his long turn to the East, expresses a need for greater passion and stranger vision than Christian Europe was willing to countenance. "The Eastern poet," Yeats writes with Dionysian yearning, "saw the Moon as the Sun's bride; now in solitude; now offered to her Bridegroom in a self-abandonment unknown to our poetry."[69] At the new moon and the full, the soul enters a state of incorporeal purity, of potency and act, respectively, that overcomes the fleshy individuality of the Renaissance. The sense of disembodied perception, which Yeats pursues throughout his work, is an effect of stylistic abstraction from the human substance – from the body's ethical gravity.[70]

Only a generation ago, Yeats was given an enthusiastic reception that generally took him at his word. He was widely reported to have achieved Unity of Being, to have joined soul and body, image and rhetoric, vision and nature.[71] But all that – or nearly all of it – has gone by the board. Poetry has lost its timeless aura, and Yeats and other poets have proven extremely vulnerable to ideological critique. That Yeats's metaphysic has not aged well is an understatement. That it is worth no more than a fly in a snowstorm is a live hypothesis. But while I do not share Yeats's religious faith in the imagination, I do not want to debunk the imagination, which would be like debunking that doubtful organ, the mind. Yeats saw that we can no more escape the metaphysical issues of art than we can escape our own shadows. His younger contemporary Aldous Huxley put the matter this way: "It is impossible to live without a metaphysics. The choice that is given us is not between some kind of metaphysic and no metaphysic; it is always between a good metaphysic and a bad metaphysic, a metaphysic that corresponds reasonably closely with observed and inferred reality and one that doesn't."[72] By pursuing his intuitions to their farthest reach, Yeats confronted the metaphysical questions that rule over art and history.

Yeats refers to Unity of Being as "of all states of mind not impossible, the most difficult to . . . man, race, or nation; because only the greatest obstacle that can be contemplated without despair, rouses the will to full intensity."[73] Since Unity of Being is not the obstacle but the goal, what could the obstacle be, given what we know about Yeats's philosophy? Let us return to his theory of the emotions. Despite the reformation announced in "Discoveries," the theory never departs from the early essay "The Moods," with its Neoplatonic descent of passionate "messengers."[74] In *The Trembling of the Veil,* Yeats says of the Anima Mundi that it "has a memory independent of embodied individual memories."[75] A disembodied mind, it is described as the source of all images – a theme that goes back to "The Philosophy of Shelley's Poetry," if not earlier. As for the transition from the Great Memory to consciousness in historical time, "there is no meeting of spirit and sense but only change upon the instant, and it is by the perception of a change, like the sudden 'blacking out' of the lights of the stage, that passion creates its most violent sensation."[76] "Lapis Lazuli" describes the "Black out" as nature's eclipse: "Heaven blazing into the head . . ."[77] How, then, can spirit and sense interpenetrate and join in Unity of Being? The obstacle facing Yeats presents itself as the obstacle that Descartes answered with the *conarium* or pineal gland. I refer to the classic metaphysical conundrum of putting a ghostly, Platonic type of soul into a human body.

It is true that in "The Wild Swans at Coole," "A Prayer for My Daughter," and *Meditations in Time of Civil War,* an ideal of beauty finds its home in the natural world. It is a lesser ideal by Yeats's intensest daemonic standards. Yeats settles for pastoral and the country house, where he nurses his imagination, in these and other poems of aristocratic nostalgia, going back to "In the Seven Woods." Such poems are undialectical with respect to nature and vision, or action and thought. They are metaphysical, but they do not reveal the actualizing of human potential. In the *Meditations,* for example, the poet must dream and not act, and the soldiers must act and not dream, all being driven by the "Primum Mobile that fashioned us."[78]

In some of Yeats's greatest poems, including "The Second Coming," "Among School Children," and "Leda and the Swan," the body is an image, an aesthetic body expressing a transcendent vision. It follows that the aesthetic body's governing agent or soul is a vision, which has its source outside the body. Even in those poems that are emphatically of the body, like the Crazy Jane poems, the body is sacrificed for ecstatic passion:

> I had wild Jack for a lover;
> Though like a road
> That men pass over
> My body makes no moan
> But sings on:
> *All things remain in God.*[79]

Jane has her own theology, an affront to the Bishop's Catholicism. Her body is "like a road" to her, for her vision is directed, like the saint's, wholly elsewhere. As a poet of sublime refrains, Yeats traffics in oppositions between the common sight and the choric insight. In "Crazy Jane on God," the soul leaps up to heaven. In "Crazy Jane Grown Old Looks at the Dancers," heaven moves the body. In neither case does the refrain support the union of body and soul.[80]

But the obstacles I have just outlined do not necessarily overthrow the quest for Unity of Being. They can be understood as elements in an unfolding drama, with its background in the Byzantium of *A Vision*. It is the core of the myth around which Yeats worked his later revisions and refinements: "The first version of this book, *A Vision*, except the section on the twenty-eight Phases, and that called 'Dove or Swan,' which I repeat without change, fills me with shame."[81] The well-known description from "Dove or Swan" offers an Irish answer to *The Stones of Venice*:

I think that in early Byzantium, maybe never before or since in recorded history, religious, aesthetic, and practical life were one, that architect and artificers – though not, it may be, poets, for language had been the instrument of controversy and must have grown abstract – spoke to the multitude and the few alike. The painter, the mosaic worker, the worker in gold and silver, the illuminator of sacred books, were almost impersonal, almost perhaps without the consciousness of individual design, absorbed in their subject matter and that the vision of a whole people. They could copy out of old Gospel books those pictures that seemed as sacred as the text, and yet weave all into a vast design, the work of many that seemed the work of one, that made building, picture, pattern, metalwork of rail and lamp, seem but a single image; and this vision, this proclamation of their invisible master, had the Greek nobility, Satan always the still half-divine serpent, never the horned scarecrow of the didactic Middle Ages.[82]

In Yeats's visionary Byzantium, the middle class and its gray rationalism are banished. Christianity is purged of its dross, chiefly the "didactic" matter of sin. The people are impersonal, semi-conscious. Realizing the will of "their invisible master," who is Yeats's version of Nietzsche's "amoral artist-god,"[83] they are blessed with the gift of crafting eternity. They are incapable of abstraction. Here, then, is something like Unity of Being: reconciliation of the many and the one, of spirit and matter, of the practical life and the religious life. Only the presence of religious controversy threatens the whole fabric. It disturbs the Neoplatonic descent of images, moods, and emotions from the few to the multitude – what Yeats in *The Trembling of the Veil* calls "nation-wide multiform reverie," "stream of suggestion," and "Unity of Image."[84]

The poet of "Sailing to Byzantium" aspires to Unity of Being through a powerful dialectic of nature and vision. His journey begins with the "birds in the trees – those dying generations" and ends with an undying image, a golden bird, prophetic consciousness of the heaven of art. The arc of the poem is away from the bustle of nature, much as Byzantine art forsakes Hellenistic realism for timeless religious vision. And yet the golden bird requires the dying generations for the dialectic to happen.

Sturge Moore's objection to "Sailing to Byzantium," that the "goldsmith's bird is as much nature as a man's body,"[85] is a crux in the interpretive tradition.[86] It proceeds, in a letter to Yeats dated April 16, 1930, from Moore's agreeing with Wittgenstein that "nothing at all can be said about ultimates, or reality in the ultimate sense."[87] It is from this sphere of concern that he offers his remark. And in his response to Moore, Yeats makes a fine distinction. He writes, "You objected to the last verse of *Sailing to Byzantium* (*sic*) because a bird made by a goldsmith was just as natural as anything else. That showed me that the idea needed exposition."[88] Yeats did not find grounds for objection in the golden bird's having a relation to nature. The point, after all, was to ascend the Great Chain of Being from nature to the heaven of art. Yeats found grounds for objection in the golden bird's being *just as natural as anything else*. It is not a matter of Yeats's establishing "the absolute difference, as of different orders of reality, between the Image, and what is, in the usual sense, alive."[89] It is a matter of relating body to image, and nature to vision, for metaphysic must bow to faith if differences are non-relational and "absolute." The soul goes "out of nature" to achieve its supernatural existence, and there are gaps in the dialectic, but there is not a sudden leap, as we often see in Yeats. Instead, there is a crossing from the natural to the supernatural, including mediatorial shades ("the singing masters"), and a dialectical interplay of nature and vision.

"Byzantium," generally interpreted along the lines of "Kubla Khan" as an allegory of the creative process, is more fragmentary and difficult. But it does reflect Yeats's effort to achieve Unity of Being. It begins with the "drunken soldiery abed" under a "starlit or a moonlit dome," and it concludes with "the dolphin-torn, the gong-tormented sea."[90] The gong is lunar. It refreshes the symbolism of the dome, while illustrating and sounding (like a gong) the metamorphic fecundity or self-begetting power of the imagination. In the final stanza, the sea of nature is manifested as a sea of symbols. But the natural sea remains a force in the poem. It is "torn" and "tormented" in a perpetual state of becoming. It is a source of tension and creativity, a spur, a particular reality. My point here is that nature is mastered and spiritualized as art, but it is not simply evacuated. The Emperor requires his soldiery and his sea. The "disdain" and "scorn" that art expresses for "all complexities of mire or blood" does *not* betoken their complete elimination.

The Byzantium poems were a promise of something higher, which Yeats could not achieve. Through his dialectical interplay of perspectives, he wanted to be true to the earth, the realm of becoming, while rising to the knowledge of being. Inspired more by *The Birth of Tragedy* than by *The Renaissance*, for Nietzsche's sense of the visionary is more active than Pater's, he was laboring to attain an omni-vision, but he could approach it only in stops and starts. In 1928 he wrote achingly of Plato and Plotinus: ". . . it is something in our own eyes that makes us see them as all transcendence." The problem, he confessed, was with himself: the soul should have all nature under its dominion.[91]

Bent on his impossible quest, the later Yeats drew increasing support from Bishop Berkeley. He especially liked the interpretation of Berkeley put forth by Wyndham Lewis in the Conclusion to *Time and Western Man*, published in 1927. Lewis believed in the objective vision of the individual artist. He connected the rise of modern scientific philosophy to the rise of "mass-democracy" and "its *group-mind*."[92] In "our present situation," he argued, "science and art should be kept rigidly apart."[93] Yeats zealously agreed. He told Moore: "I have read *Time and Western Man* with gratitude, the last chapters again and again."[94]

In his Conclusion, Lewis commanded Yeats's attention with the remark that "berkeleyan idealism is by no means incompatible with the kind of vivid realism that is being advocated in these pages."[95] Lewis was attempting an admittedly imperfect synthesis of the idealist Berkeley and the realist G. E. Moore, judged to be "much nearer" to each other philosophically than either was to the "idealo-realism" of Alexander, Whitehead, Cassirer, and Gentile. Yeats would soon describe Berkeley as "idealist and realist alike."[96] But when the poet tried his newfound synthesis out on Sturge Moore, the philosopher's brother wasn't buying:

"He [Lewis] finds my brother's realism very much to his mind but seems to think this can consist with Berkeley's ideas about things existing only in his mind, in which, if he really thinks this, he is certainly wrong."[97] Like his brother, Sturge Moore believed in scientific objectivity. His candid replies to Yeats on this point provide much of the drama in their correspondence. Yeats saw idealism as an alternative to science, and somehow took heart from the writings of G. E. Moore. Sturge Moore protested: "If it were proved that the objective view hitherto held by science were untenable [Moore is thinking of Einstein's supplanting Newton] the alternative would not be 'idealism,' I conceive, but merely a larger admission of ignorance. 'Idealism' has to explain away science."[98] This required yet a blunter follow-up: "You have no inkling of my brother's argument."[99]

Never mind! Berkeley gave Yeats an Irish answer to Locke, to "English empirical genius, English sense of reality."[100] "And God-appointed Berkeley proved all things a dream," Yeats writes in "Blood and the Moon," the statement serving, strangely, to moor Yeats to Ireland, the historical and material Ireland.[101] Lewis describes in Berkeley a movement of thought from the common-sense view, that objects of the external world are "unthinking things," to the ultimate truth of reality. We live in a world of "dead, inanimate matter" until we start to reflect, and common sense discovers its fulfillment in idealism.[102] Likewise, Yeats moves from the common-sense forms of nature to idealized supernaturalism: "An agony of flame that cannot singe a sleeve."[103] He can claim to do epistemological justice to the matter of nature because nature and image are separated only by the dialectical play, or power, of perspective.

Lewis's version of Berkeley remained central to Yeats as he again looked eastward for what he believed the West had lost: "heroic ecstatic passion" that could overcome the body's limits and triumph over materialism.[104] The method of Yeats's writings on Brahminism is syncretic. He is full of surprising correspondences between East and West: "In one of the Patanjali commentaries there is a detailed analysis of the stages of concentration that would be Hegelian did they include the self in their dialectic."[105] The object of these writings – and of Yeats's passion – is to overcome the divided consciousness, the romantic dualism of self and not-self, of vision and nature. And instead of crying *Eureka!*, Yeats cries *Chitta!* "It is *Chitta*, perhaps, which most separates Indian from European thought."[106] *Chitta* is "mental substance" or "mind-stuff." It supplies an eastern revision of Berkeleyan idealism: "If I shut my eyes and try to recall table and chair, I see them as transformations of the *Chitta*. Indeed, the actual table and chair are but the *Chitta* posited by the mind, the personality, in space, where, because

two things cannot occupy the same place, there is discord and suffering."[107]
The great difference between Berkeley and Brahma is that Berkeley's God
remains strictly transcendent, while Hinduism allows Yeats a direct conjunc-
tion with the Divine Self: "By withdrawing into our own mind we discover
the *Chitta* united to Heart and therefore pure."[108] Yeats had found his Holy
Grail: *Chitta* dispels the Newtonian vacuum of space and thereby joins spirit
and matter.

In his Introduction to the second edition of *A Vision*, in 1937, Yeats is
coy in his seeming modesty, questioning his own success as the cosmic
safe-cracker. In the name of "reason," he denies believing "in the actual
existence of my circuits of sun and moon." He seems, if we like, to dismiss
some parts of his book as "plainly symbolical." He then concludes, in the
name of "imagination," that the work's cosmology helped him "to hold in
a single thought reality and justice."[109] Now, where did Yeats do his
banking, with reason or imagination? And what a modest little claim:
holding in a single thought reality and justice. At any rate I do not think
we can say with certainty that Yeats thought *A Vision* just a myth.

In *The Birth of Tragedy*, Nietzsche connects reality and justice in his
famous remark, "it is only as an *aesthetic phenomenon* that existence
and world are eternally *justified* . . ."[110] He calls for a rebirth of myth:
"a concentrated image of the world that, as a condensation of phenomena,
cannot dispense with miracles."[111] But Nietzsche, in the Yeatsian view, did
not know enough. Nietzsche's philosophy, in the astrological verdict of
Phase Twelve of the twenty-eight incarnations, is "subjective."[112] Yeats
wanted to include the subjective in a higher synthesis. He wanted a
unified theory of knowledge, not just the appearances or "phenomena,"
but the whole shebang, inside and out, a mystical reality. He wanted the
mask as flesh. In the end, he would outdo Aristotle and Dante, and crown
himself *il Maestro di color che sanno*.

Yeats admitted doubts only when he was unable to "work out" the
details of his prophecy for Europe's death and rebirth. His method was
obsessively to test the facts before him against his system, "to substitute
particulars for an abstraction like that of algebra."[113] The facts did not fit.
All seemed lost, when Yeats declared victory anyway:

But nothing comes – though this moment was to reward me for all my toil.
Perhaps I am too old . . . Then I understand. I have already said all that can be
said. The particulars are the work of the *thirteenth sphere* or cycle which is in
every man and called by every man his freedom. Doubtless, for it can do all
things and knows all things, it knows what it will do with its own freedom but it
has kept the secret.[114]

This is to beat a hasty retreat from "of all states of mind not impossible, the most difficult" to the transcendence and mystery of God. It is a moment, like the Ulysses episode in Dante, when the self confronts that which is outside its circle and its powers. But it is a moment bereft of any moral attention, tragic or comical, of any real feeling at all.

At this awkward juncture, let us consider the responses of two influential critics. In Yeats's system, Richard Ellmann explains, "Each lifetime is the scene of a tug-of-war between four 'faculties' of the human mind, the daimon, the dead, certain miscellaneous spirits, the Thirteenth Cycle, and other voices. The contest is so intricate, and its outcome so unpredictable, that what starts out . . . as a deterministic system is reframed . . . until it contains a large measure of free will . . ." And if we are still unconvinced, Ellmann says frankly, Yeats "felt . . . free to believe and disbelieve in free will . . ."[115] A generous faith in the creative imagination is essential to the poet. And not only the poet, the critic too is entitled to negative capability, even if Ellmann seems to go whistling past the metaphysical nightmare that feeds Yeats's mesmerizing art. Harold Bloom is less deferential: "The desperate freedom Yeats imported into *A Vision* as the Thirteenth Sphere . . . does not alter the irony that *A Vision* remains only another example of . . . 'the dogma of gradual process,' by which the quasi-historical thought of our time has worked to establish a more tenacious and oppressive belief in fate than has ever before existed."[116] Bloom appears to have warmed to his subject. He is, in any case, dead-on accurate about the irony, which hoists Yeats smack into the company of the dialectical materialists, crushing the individual's subjectivity and strength in the moon's final quarter.

I connect the ethical collapse of *A Vision* to Yeats's denial of science. But there is, I think, much in his position that commands respect. "Fragments" shows the strength of Yeats's argument, which harkens back to Blake's contempt for deism:

I

Locke sank into a swoon;
The Garden died;
God took the spinning-jenny
Out of his side.

II

Where got I that truth?
Out of a medium's mouth,
Out of nothing it came,

Out of the forest loam,
Out of the dark night where lay
The crowns of Nineveh.[117]

Locke as Adam, the spinning-jenny as Eve, and a clipped farewell to Eden:
the poet makes up for in gnomic intensity what he lacks in discursive reason –
the language of Locke. He argues that Locke's machinery has betrayed God
himself, reducing him to a master machine. At the same time, he suggests
that Locke's view is incomplete, one of many "fragments," only "his side"
of things. Although the "Garden" dies in history, its godlike perfection,
alluded to with the alliterative capital "G," exists beyond space and time in
the Anima Mundi. Locke's disintegrated psyche has brought about a
catastrophic fall from Unity of Being, but "truth" is larger than Locke,
and larger than the poet himself, who must also speak in fragments. In Part
II, Yeats answers his self-consciousness with a riddle. In effect, he meditates
on his poem as an utterance from "out of" unknown depths, where the
Lockean mind, closed to innate ideas, cannot penetrate. Whitmanian
anaphora suggest the endless creativity of the divine mystery, while the
slant rhymes (especially in the pronounced flatness of the last line) convey
a strange facticity that challenges science. The poem is a rebuke of scientific
truths that, to quote Nietzsche, "obviously do *not* come from the depths."
Wissenschaft cannot speak to our souls' desire for high passion and Unity
of Being, because it "has absolutely *no* belief in itself, let alone an ideal
above it . . ."[118]

At the turn of the century, Yeats stood among a small vanguard of post-
Nietzschean writers who detested the cosmological vision of seventeenth-
century scientific rationalism. He, Whitehead, and Husserl (soon to be
followed by Weber and Heidegger), were among the first to learn from
Nietzsche's grave doubts about the basis and value of science. "Is the
resolve to be scientific about everything," Nietzsche asked, ". . . [a] subtle
last resort against – *truth?* And, morally speaking, a sort of cowardice and
falseness?"[119] But Nietzsche was not interested in further metaphysics.
A creative skeptic, he abandoned the search for the unity of knowledge,
and left a later generation to resume it.

In the event, a metaphysical gold rush ensued that lasted until the
Second World War, with modernism participating in the frenzy of
speculation. Yeats's letters to Moore show his particular appreciation
for Whitehead's *Science and the Modern World*. In his important book,
Whitehead defends poetry as a form of knowledge, while outlining a
metaphysical synthesis that rivals "the philosophical situation as expressed
by Descartes."[120] To supply an example of science's legitimate concern

with the natural order, Whitehead quotes William James, who paused from his labors over the *Principles of Psychology* to grumble to his brother Henry: "I have to forge every sentence in the teeth of irreducible and stubborn facts."[121] Whitehead remarks: "All the world over and at all times there have been practical men, absorbed in 'irreducible and stubborn facts': all the world over there have been men of philosophical temperament who have been absorbed in the weaving of general principles. It is this union of passionate interest in the detailed facts with equal devotion to abstract generalisation which forms the novelty in our present society."[122] At the furnace of knowledge, James resembles Yeats in his effort to adjust "particulars" to "general principles." But James's respect for matter is foreign to the poet's enterprise. Yeats forged an aesthetic, ethical, and religious unity, a vision of the wholeness of being. But unlike James and Whitehead, he stubbornly dismissed the "irreducible and stubborn facts" of natural science in favor of his independent subjectivity. He knew that facts could be faked and that science lacked a foundation, but he dissolved matter with the idealizing force of his own mind.

It is a theme of this book that you cannot put the mind back into nature unless you respect them both. And that respect, an act, it may be, worthy of discipline and love, protects the moral life. Yeats pursued the great metaphysical goal of relating mind to matter, but his type of imagination was part of the problem and therefore incapable of the solution. He must have noticed Whitehead's warning that Cartesianism "leads directly not merely to private worlds of experience, but also to private worlds of morals."[123] He certainly fitted the description, for his ideas about reality made him a most unusual philosopher: a determinist who denied science the power to "instruct or persuade about its own particular subject-matter" (*Rhet.* 1355b28). He put art before nature, and understood nature only in terms of art. It follows that the private world of his mind became the universe of his work. He inverted the scientific universe, where a colossal vacuum had displaced the spirit. All became spirit, but matter was lost. Yeats never saw his own face on that daemon of the modern age – science.

CHAPTER 2

T. S. Eliot: the modernist Aristotle

A completely ironic poet passes beyond the realm of poetry into an inscrutable solipsism. After discovering the master ironist Jules Laforgue, the young Eliot grew more and more inscrutable himself. From the start of the manuscript poems in *Inventions of the March Hare*, objects and routines pile up, without the possibility of an action to resolve their significance. The ironically titled "Convictions (Curtain Raiser)" opens the collection with scenes of marionettes, including some knightly marionettes who discourse on moral philosophy:

> And over there my Paladins
> Are talking of effect and cause,
> With "learn to live by nature's laws!"
> And "strive for social happiness
> And contact with your fellow-men
> In reason: nothing to excess!"
> As one leaves off, the other begins.[1]

Funny as it is to hear "learn to live by nature's laws!" from the mouth of a puppet, the joke comes at a high cost to the poet. He dwells in a world of suffocating convention, from which he is liberated only in mind. His mindless cast airs its "convictions," overheated platitudes recorded by the poet with an occasional parenthesis, which marks the small difference of his freedom: "My marionettes (or so they say) / Have these keen moments every day."[2] Trapped by the same formalities of meter and manner, the poet and his marionettes bear a family resemblance. They dramatize his dilemma of what to say and do, as he studies the human mechanism and its moral repertoire. Certainly Eliot takes from Laforgue "the elegant posturings of the poet-in-disguise,"[3] but the disguise weighs on him with the dismal force of habit.

Laforgue was tubercular, so was his wife, and the disease claimed his mother when he was very young. No wonder he regarded his body with resignation:

Encore un de mes pierrots est mort;
Mort d'un chronique orphelinisme;
C'était un coeur plein de dandysme
Lunaire, en un drôle de corps.[4]

Another of my pierrots is dead,
Dead from being chronically orphaned;
He had a heart full of dandyism
From the moon, in a bizarre body.

Symons refers to these verses from *Locutions des Pierrots* as "a kind of mockery of prose."[5] He quotes them in *The Symbolist Movement in Literature*, which Eliot discovered in 1908, when he was a Harvard junior composing slender lyrics. The jangling wit (en*core, mort, mort, or* phelinisme, *coeur,* and *corps*), the expectorating gutturals, and the elaborate conceit would have resonated with Eliot's interest in the metaphysical poets, especially Donne. But the metaphysical element is compounded with a later type of romantic psychology, a theatrical self-consciousness that Eliot imitates in "Convictions (Curtain Raiser)." Laforgue ridicules his own feelings through a parody of the human form, which he presents as a white-masked clown, a pierrot adapted from the French pantomime.

In his Clark Lectures of 1926, Eliot views Laforgue through the medium of Schopenhauer and his disciple Hartmann. Taken together, Schopenhauer and Laforgue reveal a good deal about Eliot's formation as a poet. For example, here is the passage with which Eliot, in his 1921 essay "The Metaphysical Poets," introduces his English readership to Laforgue:

O géraniums diaphanes, guerroyeurs sortilèges,
Sacrilèges monomanes!
Emballages, dévergondages, douches! O pressoirs
Des vendanges des grands soirs!
Layettes aux abois,
Thyrses au fond des bois,
Transfusions, représailles,
Relevailles, compresses et l'éternal potion,
Angélus! n'en pouvoir plus
De débâcles nuptiales! de débâcles nuptiales![6]

O diaphanous geraniums, warriors casting spells,
Obsessive sacrileges!
Excitements, debaucheries, refreshing showers! O wine-presses
For the harvests of grand evenings!
Layettes at bay,
Thyrses in the deep wood!

Stiff drinks, reprisals,
Church going, compresses and the eternal potion,
Angelus! Let there be no more power over us
For the marriage debacle, the marriage debacle!

To read this torrential catalogue as a metaphysical conceit, one must grasp
the Schopenhauerian matrix behind it. The geraniums are diaphanous
because we are seeing through appearances to the reality underlying
romance and courtship. The endangered layettes, the Dionysian thyrses
in the deep wood, the Wagnerian potion or love philtre, are allusions to
romance and sexual madness, pregnancies in crisis and unspeakable urges.
Then there are the conventional responses, the bells, prayers, and compresses, ending in a mock "*Angélus!*" and the final exasperated shudder of
"*n'en pouvoir plus / De débâcles nuptiales! de débâcles nuptiales!*" For
Schopenhauer and Laforgue, romantic love and the sacrament of marriage
are a trap: they are the means by which the cosmic will tricks two people
into making a particular baby.

Eliot learned from Laforgue how to distance his emotion. He observes
that in Laforgue's poetry "the system of Schopenhauer collapses, but in a
different wreck from that of *Tristan und Isolde*."[7] For Schopenhauer, art
offers "a solution to the problem of existence" by freeing the intellect from
"the aims of the will."[8] For Laforgue, Schopenhauer offers no balm for the
sufferer, but only a spectacle of self-division, an ironic state of watching
oneself – as a phenomenon of the will – being split into a thinking person
and a feeling person.[9] Laforgue is a tortured romantic whose recurring
symbolism pits the deadly sun of generation against the kindly moon
(or moonshine) of imagination. Wagner, by contrast, celebrates the
emotional tumult of noble figures overwhelmed by magic and wrecked
by their aching sexuality. Eliot is ambivalent about Wagner, by turns
worshipful and cynical.[10] In *The Waste Land*, he pays tribute to *Tristan
und Isolde*. But Laforguean irony intrudes in Eliot's manuscript poem
"Opera," which takes the same work as its subject:

We have the tragic? oh no!
Life departs with a feeble smile
Into the indifferent.
These emotional experiences
Do not hold good at all,
And I feel like the ghost of youth
At the undertakers' ball.[11]

To deny "the tragic" is to deny the physical pleasures of catharsis. It is a
move Eliot would repeat in his drama. The poet passes moral judgment

on his feelings: "These emotional experiences / Do not hold good at all." They do not survive inspection, they have no "good" in them, and their abstraction results in his "indifferent" and divided state. Eliot would continue to refine and vary such expressions of moral solitude, but what we can see with stark clarity in "Opera" is his Laforguean self-consciousness at work. He disengages his mind from the physical world of form and convention, even as he adapts Laforgue to the probity of the strict New Englander, the force of conscience and spiritual independence. What remains is an abstract reflection of the moment at hand, a "ghost" with a voice.

Unlike Eliot, Laforgue can be arrogantly sexual. His poetry simmers with sex-puns. He is much more frank than Eliot, who called him "immature" and "rough."[12] And yet, in moments that Eliot laid stress upon, Laforgue expressed the sincerest longing for true erotic companionship:

> *L'âme et la chair, la chair et l'âme,*
> *C'est l'Esprit édénique et fier*
> *D'être un peu l'Homme avec la Femme.*[13]

> The soul and the flesh, the flesh and the soul,
> It is the proud spirit of Eden
> A little bit to be a Man with a Woman.

For a brief tercet, Laforgue's metaphysic of spirit and flesh veers closer to Dante than to Schopenhauer. "The Metaphysical Poets" has Eliot quoting another *cri de coeur*:

> *Elle est bien loin, elle pleure,*
> *Le grand vent se lamente aussi . . .*[14]

> She is far away, she weeps,
> The high wind laments also . . .

Symons said of Laforgue: "He will not permit himself, at any moment, the luxury of dropping the mask: not at any moment."[15] But Eliot noticed exceptions that gave the French poet a heart-wrenching pathos. In this respect, Eliot's argument is surely right: "in Laforgue there is continuous war between the feelings implied by his ideas, and the ideas implied by his feelings."[16] Laforgue, as Eliot suggests, is a sufferer, whose irony is "an expression of suffering."[17]

With a truly farcical lack of success, Arnold in 1853 warned against poetry "in which the suffering finds no vent in action; in which a continual state of mental distress is prolonged, unrelieved by incident, hope, or resistance; in which there is everything to be endured, nothing to be done."[18] Arnold had left the altar of aesthetic consciousness because he did not want literature to be a "true allegory of the state of one's own mind."[19] His counter-thrust was as follows: "The poet . . . has in the first place to select an excellent action; and what actions are the most excellent? Those, certainly, which most powerfully appeal to the great primary affections: to those elementary feelings which subsist permanently in the race, and which are independent of time. These feelings are permanent and the same; that which interests them is permanent and the same also."[20] The basis of Arnold's argument is threefold: first, human nature exists; second, it is universal and permanent; and third, it connects the poetry of action to "the great primary affections." In short, Arnold's premises betoken a synthesis of Aristotle's thought on ethics and the arts.

No one will raise an eyebrow if I say that Eliot's poetry owes much to Laforgue's poetry and little to Arnold's criticism. As a modernist poet, Eliot is a sufferer, whose irony is relieved, not by incident or hope, but by moments of intense sincerity. Like Laforgue, he sets emotion and intellect at odds. He divorces the thinkers from the doers, the life of the mind from the life of the body, erotic visions from brutal facts. Absurd physiques are typical of the pre-conversion poems, from Prufrock "pinned and wriggling on the wall" to "the hollow men . . . / Headpiece filled with straw." Sweeney is human nature, nasty, brutish, and "broadbottomed." Eliot's great poems, from "The Love Song of J. Alfred Prufrock" to *Four Quartets*, are theaters of self-consciousness, allegories of the state of his mind.

So how could Eliot possibly reconcile his criticism with either Arnold or Aristotle? Judged solely by its opening pages, *The Sacred Wood* appears to be Arnoldian. Here, for instance, is one of Arnold's signature passages as quoted by Eliot in his Introduction:

In the Greece of Pindar and Sophocles, in the England of Shakespeare, the poet lived in a current of ideas in the highest degree animating and nourishing to the creative power; society was, in the fullest measure, permeated by fresh thought, intelligent and alive; and this state of things is the true basis for the creative power's exercise, in this it finds its data, its materials, truly ready for its hand; all the books and reading in the world are only valuable as they are helps to this.[21]

But Eliot – once we get to know him – has really nothing to do with this. The true Eliotic note is quite different:

No poet, no artist of any art, has his complete meaning alone. His significance, his appreciation is the appreciation of his relation to the dead poets and artists. You cannot value him alone; you must set him, for contrast and comparison, among the dead. I mean this as a principle of aesthetic, not merely historical, criticism.[22]

Eliot is more truly at home "among the dead," in a hermetic space of "staring forms / . . . leaning, hushing the room enclosed."[23] His aesthetic proclivities owe more to Pater than to Arnold. In Eliot's poetry of fragments, the elision of connecting matter suggests a corollary elision of social matter. The bridge between self and community collapses: "London bridge is falling down falling down falling down."[24] The individual waits "in his prison,"[25] the Fisher King waits in his desert. With little trust in human nature or in society, Eliot seeks to overcome his distance from Sophocles and from Shakespeare on the solitary wings of genius. He takes to the aesthetic ether, where pure mind meets the "ideal order" of "existing monuments." The "historical sense" serves his purpose insofar as it is a faculty of the aesthetic mind.[26]

History itself, as opposed either to the "historical sense" or to the "mythical method," is a body of facts awaiting comparison and analysis – which "need only the cadavers on the table . . ."[27] In his 1923 essay "The Function of Criticism," Eliot revisits the theme of "Tradition and the Individual Talent," while applauding the "complete development" of "the sense of fact" as "perhaps the very pinnacle of civilisation."[28] By contrast, when Arnold discusses "tradition," he lacks the specialist's zeal for excavating fact from the soil of value. He adopts Aristotle's dictum that "poetry is something more philosophic and [more serious] than history" (Poet. 1451b5). Aristotle bases this observation on general human nature, and Arnold finds its confirmation in "the superiority of diction and movement" that marks the best poetry.[29]

As it happened, Eliot confided to a friend he was using Arnold as a "stalking horse, or as a cloak of invisibility-respectability to protect me from the elderly . . . [Or] as a scarecrow with a real gun under his arm."[30] Within his own circle, "the mantle of Matthew Arnold" was anathema.[31] And yet the Eliot of The Sacred Wood raises the Arnoldian standard of disinterestedness,[32] and endorses seeing "the object as it really is,"[33] after snubbing Arnold as "a propagandist for criticism."[34] It was at best a marriage of convenience, which would darken and intensify as Eliot grew religious.

Aristotle manages to appear more often in The Sacred Wood than any other philosopher, ancient or modern.[35] He is the closest approximation to "the perfect critic." His "scientific mind" is the counterpoint to Hegel's emotional mind.[36] He is said to have "looked solely and steadfastly at the object."[37] His status as "a moral pilot of Europe" is at issue.[38] Eliot quotes On the Soul above the third section of "Tradition and the Individual Talent," implying a connection between Aristotle's nous and the mind of

Europe. More generally, *The Sacred Wood* bristles with a philosophical command not seen in English criticism since the *Biographia Literaria*. Eliot is serious and resourceful in his use of Aristotle, but his project is attended by insurmountable difficulties.

What Eliot tried to do was to accommodate his own kind of scrupulous writing, an Anglo-American obsession with *le mot juste* that assumes the skeptical epistemology of linguistic idealism,[39] to an ethical tradition linking Aristotle and Dante. Allying himself with the analytic intelligence of Aristotle, the author of *The Sacred Wood* battles against critics who "substitute emotion for thoughts."[40] F. H. Bradley, the subject of Eliot's Harvard dissertation, had fought for identical reasons against Arnold and Mill in *Ethical Studies*. And like Bradley in his censure of Mill, Eliot focuses on a loose definition of poetry:

The sentence ["poetry is the most highly organized form of intellectual activity"] . . . may be profitably contrasted with the opening phrases of the *Posterior Analytics*. Not only all knowledge, but all feeling, is in perception. The inventor of poetry as the most highly organized form of intellectual activity was not engaged in perceiving when he composed this definition; he had nothing to be aware of except his own emotion about "poetry." He was, in fact, absorbed in a very different "activity" . . . from that of Aristotle.[41]

The grounds are empirical and individualistic: if "all knowledge . . . is in perception," then we can rule out innate ideas and anamnesis (i.e., recollection of knowledge from a previous existence). Aristotle is often empirical. But as a point of Aristotelian anthropology, *all* feeling is not in perception: feeling, by virtue of its interpersonal character, by its very depth, precedes the self. Hazlitt says of Shakespeare and Milton: "They owe their power over the human mind to their having had a deeper sense than others of what was grand in the objects of nature, or affecting in the events of human life."[42] Eliot, in a lightning stroke, changes Aristotle into a modernist. And this change is accompanied by an almost imperceptible revision of the *Posterior Analytics*. Aristotle had said: "All instruction given or received by way of argument proceeds from pre-existent knowledge" (71a1). There is no reference to "feeling" or "perception," words that bear an association, in Eliot's learned usage, with "aesthetics," a word that derives from a Greek verb (αἰσθάνομαι) meaning "to sense" or "to perceive."

Under the guise of literary criticism, Eliot in *The Sacred Wood* enters the continuing debate in modern philosophy about the relation between aesthetics and ethics, a field of discourse dominated by Kant's third *Critique*. In his theory of aesthetic judgment, Kant had opened the possibility, which he himself did not endorse, of a full-fledged departure of the beautiful from the good.[43] A crucial question in the field is how the feelings and emotions aroused by the art object (i.e. "art emotions") connect to the broader life of feeling and emotion. The meaning of art is at stake in the question.

Bernard Bosanquet offers a precedent for Eliot in his well-known work *A History of Aesthetic: From the Greeks to the Twentieth Century*, especially the section "Aristotle on Tragedy," which speaks eloquently of the religion of art.[44] Bosanquet exalts the aesthetic in the high nineteenth-century manner, which describes the historical triumph of the aesthetic consciousness. It is known that Joyce used the book while writing *Ulysses*. I have not found evidence that Eliot consulted it (other works by Bosanquet feature in his dissertation), but Bosanquet's high aestheticism, which readily adapts Aristotle to the aesthetic cause, making the tragic catharsis an art emotion, is congenial to the mood of *The Sacred Wood*.

William James's approach differs markedly from Bosanquet's. Writes James: "In the aesthetic emotions the bodily reverberation and the feeling may both be faint. A connoisseur is apt to judge a work of art dryly and intellectually, and with no bodily thrill. On the other hand, works of art may arouse intense emotion; and whenever they do so, the experience is completely covered by the terms of our theory."[45] James's theory places unusual emphasis on the body's role in the emotional life.[46] Prior to James, there arose an immoveable barrier between vision and morality for romantic writers on both sides of the Atlantic. Despite the work of James, Eliot restores the barrier and protects the nineteenth-century religion of art. In remarking that "all feeling . . . is in perception," Eliot privileges "the intelligence itself swiftly operating the analysis of sensation to the point of principle and definition."[47] It may be replied that he has in mind "some quality of sensuous thought, or of thinking through the senses, or of the senses thinking, of which the exact formula remains to be defined."[48] But "sensuous thought" for Eliot is not embodied. His praise for the poet Jean de Bosschère is deployed in his own cause: "M. de Bosschère is in fact almost a pure intellectual; leaving, as if disdainfully, our emotions to form as they will around the situation which his brain has selected . . . Instead of refining ordinary human emotion (and I do not mean tepid human emotion, but human however intense – in the crude living state) he aims direct at emotions of art."[49] Likewise: "What constitutes the terrible authority of Villon's testaments is that he saw his feelings, watched them, as coldly as an astronomer watches a comet; and without this cold and scientific observation he could never have given his feelings their permanent intensity."[50] Aristotle and James do not lend their authority to Eliot's isolation of the aesthetic,[51] simply because the nature of feeling does not allow it: feeling begins in the body and then comes to consciousness.

As we absorb the following superb passage from Tourneur's *Revenger's Tragedy*, the author of "Tradition and the Individual Talent" would ask us to distinguish between the "structural emotion . . . provided by the drama" and the "new art emotion" that coheres in the affinity between the "structural emotion" itself and "a number of floating feelings" that are specific to the poetry:[52]

> And now methinks I could e'en chide myself
> For doating on her beauty, though her death
> Shall be revenged after no common action.
> Does the silkworm expend her yellow labours
> For thee? For thee does she undo herself?
> Are lordships sold to maintain ladyships
> For the poor benefit of a bewildering minute?
> Why does yon fellow falsify highways,
> And put his life between the judge's lips,
> To refine such a thing – keeps horse and men
> To beat their valours for her? . . .[53]

Eliot sees the passage in terms of its form: he sees an organic unity comprising numerous emotional parts, all of which he holds at a certain self-conscious distance. To recall James, one may conclude that Eliot falls, along with his impeccable taste, into the category of "a connoisseur . . . apt to judge a work of art drily and intellectually, and with no bodily thrill." Fear for oneself, pity for the tragic victim, lose their immediacy in the analysis, though possibly they are accounted for by the "structural emotion." Then Eliot formulates a new doctrine: "Poetry is not a turning loose of emotion, but an escape from emotion . . ."[54] To make this escape, is it not to escape the relationship between aesthetic interest and real interest, the very relationship on which the tragic effect depends?

It will be remembered that Arnold was concerned with "primary affections" and "elementary feelings," not with "art emotions" that sharply divide the aesthetic from the ethical. The classical hero is a paragon for Arnold, because classical authors appeal to the "permanent elements" of our nature. In Homer, for instance, the Greek mind discerns a difference between heroic excellence (virtue in the earliest sense) and social justice.[55] Achilles's momentous choice, between anonymous old age and glorious early death, awakens his self-consciousness and enriches the moral drama and pathos of his meeting with the aged Priam. Having chosen to enter the world of action, Achilles inhabits the mean between extreme self-consciousness and complete unselfconsciousness. Prufrock and Gerontion at one extreme, and Sweeney at the other, are like the damned, dwelling outside any living tradition of moral life.

For Eliot, the hero had to be transformed. In "What the Thunder Said," the poet undergoes a trial of mystical heroism, a quest for perfection that can be achieved only through selfless dedication to God. The poet-priest, through his apocalyptic struggle, tries to revive a dead world; in his Notes to *The Waste Land,* Eliot documents some examples of this attempt in myth and religion. The focus of his effort is the ego. He sacrifices the ego by estranging the normal life of emotion from aesthetic feelings (art emotions). Eclipsing the ego, he creates a lyric halo or corona around the culture of the West. However, Eliot does not deny the individual. The myriad voices of *The Waste Land* admit of many readings, but the egocentric feeling of lyric control is never absent.

Literature, I am arguing, shows its social nature in a wide variety of ways. It shows its social nature in the nervous system and the blood stream, when it affects the feelings of the author and the reader. The physiological link between art and ethics is the key. Through the presence or absence of this link, the artist declares himself to be either a literary citizen or a literary exile. Either he locates himself in the giving and receiving of a community, or he enters into different exilic modes, be it the barbarism of Sweeney, or the skeptical self-consciousness of Prufrock, or the mystical questing of *The Waste Land.* But in no case can the artist wholly escape the moral life. He has only a choice of approach.

Eliot prepared his Clark Lectures by studying neo-Thomism, which spoke to problems of social order that had "preoccupied him since his first acquaintance with the work of Babbitt and Maurras."[56] At Cambridge he went on to state that what Laforgue "wants . . . is either a *Vita Nuova* to justify, dignify and integrate his sentiments toward the jeune fille in a system of the universe, or else some system of thought which shall keep a place [for and] even enhance these feelings and at the same time enable him to feel as intensely the abstract world."[57] It is a nimble remark, for it sidesteps Eliot's own caveat: "in creation you are responsible for what you can do with material which you must simply accept. And in this material I include the emotions and feelings of the writer himself, which, for that writer, are simply material which he must accept – not virtues to be enlarged or vices to be diminished."[58] What good is "some system of thought," if you are seized by emotional "material which you must simply accept?" The system of thought may have historical, philosophical, or religious interest, but it may simply be foreign to your slice of life – your *tranche de vie*, in Remy de Gourmont's phrase. Laforgue, as we have seen, could sound a Dantean note to effect. But to a man of Laforgue's sensibility, with respect to questions of sex and politics and God, Dante was too remote to be a model.

Prior to the Clark Lectures, Eliot had championed tradition in a way that had avant-garde possibilities. He had defended the authority of genius and avoided the supposed Arnoldian *faux pas* of the *a priori*. In *The Sacred Wood*, he had tactfully grouped Arnold with the dons: "Arnold, it must be admitted, gives us often the impression of seeing the masters, whom he quotes, as canonical literature, rather than as masters."[59] In "The Function of Criticism," he had echoed Arnold's injunction against "doing as one likes," proclaimed a Tory bias, and added some avant-gardist refinements. But now he was closing off the avant-garde possibilities of his earlier position. Having outgrown Laforgue, he was measuring the French poet with the yardstick of Dante. And he was citing Dante for his moral ideas.

In less than two decades, Eliot had gone from being an iconoclastic American disciple of Laforgue to being an English luminary, "classicist in literature, royalist in politics, and anglo-catholic in religion."[60] When he looked for a way of explaining the unity of his *oeuvre*, of explaining himself over and against Arnold, he turned once more to Bradley and to philosophy, which he considered to be Arnold's weakness. Bradley's genius had nourished many of Eliot's ideas and formulations, and Bradley's words glossed line 412 in Eliot's Notes to *The Waste Land*.[61] Moreover, Bradley's resemblance to Arnold both in style and in point of view offered a close parallel to Eliot's own problem.

Eliot concludes his 1927 essay "Francis Herbert Bradley" with a judgment that, if we read it aright, might justify the many paradoxes of his career: ". . . Bradley, like Aristotle, is distinguished by his scrupulous respect for words, that their meaning should be neither vague nor exaggerated; and the tendency of his labours is to bring British philosophy closer to the great Greek tradition."[62] The closing comment makes a connection between philosophy and style. Bradley had welcomed the insights of Kant and Hegel into British thought, and he had done so with unusual clarity, precision, and wit. But Eliot is advancing a larger claim about Bradley's work, and about *Ethical Studies* in particular. He is arguing that Bradley's "common sense," allied with his verbal accuracy, places him in the tradition of Aristotle.[63]

The strongest basis for Eliot's claim is the peculiar likeness between *Ethical Studies* and the *Nicomachean Ethics*. As moral philosophers, both

Aristotle and Bradley describe human beings as political animals faced with individual choices. Both approach society as more than the aggregate of its parts. And both assume the reality of human nature.

But view it from a different angle, and the resemblance between Aristotle and Bradley begins to waver. In the *Nicomachean Ethics*, self-consciousness is important. It is the means to comprehending friendship. For Bradley, self-consciousness is the means to comprehending social life in its entirety. Where "whole" denotes the "social organism," he writes: "'Realize yourself as the self-conscious member of an infinite whole' means 'Realize yourself as the self-conscious member of an infinite whole, by realizing that whole in yourself.'"[64] The self situated in this way is defined with the term *concrete universal*. Its moral nature owes more to Kant and Hegel than to Aristotle. Bradley offers a Hegelian way of overcoming the Kantian divide that separates one's *inclination* to act out of personal advantage or thoughtless habit, from one's moral *duty* to act out of respect for the law. Kant had overcome this divide through the "categorical imperative," the lofty cosmic harmony of a subjective principle (the maxim) and an objective principle (the practical law). Bradley improves on Kant by setting the self in the organic context of "my station and its duties."

In words that recall Kant's *Groundwork of the Metaphysics of Morals*, Bradley maintains that "nothing is good but a good will."[65] But having repeated Kant's move, central to the Enlightenment, of bringing the self-conscious will into the ethical foreground, Bradley struggles to dislodge it. He has a dialectic in his thinking that enables the "mere private self" to blend into the moral life of the community.[66] And though the word *duty* has a denatured and Kantian sound to it, Bradley stresses that our common moral judgments are accomplished by habit and practical wisdom – in an Aristotelian fashion.

One would be tempted to call *Ethical Studies* a synthesis of ancient and modern philosophy, except that its tensions and fault lines are unmistakably modern. Under the broad influence of Hegel, Bradley advances a doctrine of historical relativism. Like Leslie Stephen in this respect, he seeks to reconcile "Mr. Darwin's conjecture as to the development of man from a social animal"[67] with a scheme of teleological progress and moral evolution:

history is the working out of the true human nature through various incomplete stages towards completion, and "my station" is the one satisfactory view of morals. Here . . . all morality is and must be relative . . . Yet . . . the morality of every stage is justified for that stage; and the demand for a code right in itself, apart from any stage, is seen to be asking for an impossibility.[68]

It can be argued that Bradley's relativism weakens the law by calling into question its permanence. The effect was foreseen by Hegel: a widening of the distance between the law and the self-conscious individual. Since the moral code belongs only to a stage of development, the artist and poet, "however obscurely," are virtually called upon to anticipate the next stage. It follows that, by evoking the metaphysical heights, Bradley diminishes his own argument. He reveals the main doctrine of *Ethical Studies* to be earnestly and provincially Victorian: "There is nothing better than my station and its duties, nor anything higher or more truly beautiful."[69]

Aristotle, in a famous passage near the end of the *Nicomachean Ethics* (1177b32), proposes a view of the contemplative life, the life according to reason, as conative or striving. We strive on earth to realize what is divine in our nature, to become our true or best selves. Because the contemplative or philosophical life participates in the activity of God, it surpasses all other activities in happiness. It is not opposed to the life of the city, though it is separated from political and military affairs.[70] Bradley, by contrast, follows Luther in holding that God is "alienated" at a polar extreme from the common life. His solution is "to put your whole self, your entire will, into the will of the divine."[71] The passage is quoted by Eliot in his essay on Bradley,[72] and it accords with the mystical heroism of *The Waste Land* and *Four Quartets*. To be conscious of one's will in this way is, as Bradley affirms, to make one's life a Protestant act of faith. This kind of intense self-consciousness straining to be wholly good is limited to religion: "In mere morality this faith is impossible."[73] Bradley divides the ordinary morality of my station and its duties from the morality of religious consciousness, incidentally refusing Hegel's belief in the nation-state as the organic unity responsible for guiding the spirit. His dual aim is to protect the base of ordinary ethics from the utilitarians, while allowing religion to minister to the sick soul, which exists in a state of alienated self-consciousness that my station and its duties cannot cure.

It is while abusing Arnold that Bradley hurls a stick or two in Aristotle's direction. Eliot quotes Bradley's "Arnold-baiting" in the essay I quoted earlier, "Francis Herbert Bradley." The passage comes from a footnote in the last chapter of *Ethical Studies*:

"Is there a God?" asks the reader. "Oh yes," replies Mr. Arnold, "and I can verify him in experience." "And what is he then?" cries the reader. "Be virtuous, and as a rule you will be happy," is the answer. "Well, and God?" "That is God," says Mr. Arnold; "there is no deception, and what more do you want?" I suppose we do want a good deal more. Most of us, certainly the public which Mr. Arnold addresses, want something they can worship; and they will not find that in an hypostasized copy-book heading, which is not much more adorable than "Honesty is the best policy," or "Handsome is that handsome does," or various other edifying maxims, which have not yet come to an apotheosis.[74]

As a satirist, Bradley is preceded by Voltaire, whose Panglossian "best of all possible worlds" exploits the unreasonableness of Leibniz's principle of sufficient reason. "Be virtuous, and as a rule you will be happy" is less fortuitous. It is true that Arnold, like Aristotle, connects virtue to happiness. But Arnold does not want to reduce virtue or happiness to a "rule." And neither, by a long shot, does Aristotle. Arnold's model is the *Nicomachean Ethics*, a book where Aristotle explicitly refrains from rule-making. Eliot, for his part, extols the passage: "Such criticism is final. It is patently a great triumph of wit and a great delight to watch when a man's methods, almost his tricks of speech, are thus turned against himself."[75] And so the foremost Anglo-American critic of his time, in a eulogy for the last great English metaphysician, stamps on the grave of the last great English critic.

Eliot's 1930 essay "Arnold and Pater" renewed the long attack on Arnold. "'Art for art's sake,'" Eliot comments, "is the offspring of Arnold's Culture; and we can hardly venture to say that it is even a perversion of Arnold's doctrine, considering how very vague and ambiguous that doctrine is."[76] Eliot is right that Arnold and Pater were moralists, and he displays his religious concerns by slighting the differences between them. He is right that Arnold and Pater put culture ahead of religion – Arnold departs from Aristotle in doing so (*Pol.* 1328b13). But Eliot exceeds the bounds of reasonable argument by imputing to Arnold "the Stoicism and Cyrenaicism of the amateur classical scholar."[77] Throughout his career, Eliot's demands for expertise and specialization run counter to Arnold's broad and living humanism. A. E. Housman is more trustworthy: "when it comes to literary criticism, heap up in one scale all the literary criticism that the whole nation of professed scholars ever wrote, and drop into the other the thin green volume of Matthew Arnold's Lectures on Translating Homer . . . and the first scale, as Milton says, will straight fly up and kick the beam."[78]

Eliot berates his rival to gain one central point: "The total effect of Arnold's philosophy is to set up Culture in the place of Religion, and to leave Religion to be laid waste by the anarchy of feeling."[79] Rejecting any ethical basis that is not an act of revelation or faith, Eliot denigrates Arnold's claim that "the religious side in man . . . is not the whole of man," a statement he interprets as meaning that religion "must be kept in its place."[80] Let it be said that Eliot is acutely perceptive in spotting the coercive elements in Arnold's liberal program, which is unfriendly to religion. The romantic effort to set up culture in the place of religion, Eliot's own effort in *The Sacred Wood* (rescinded in the 1928 Preface), was deeply misguided – nightmarish is not too strong a word. But Arnold's cultural standards, his desire to bring classical ethics into the democratic world, do not promote "anarchy of feeling."[81] The truth is that Eliot's religious definition of man clashes with Arnold's humanism.[82] The ethics of *After Strange Gods* (the Page-Barbour Lectures of 1933) is grounded upon revelation, quite unlike the *Nicomachean Ethics*. Twenty years later, Eliot would maintain his position, when he commended Josef Pieper for "affirming the dependence of philosophy upon revelation."[83] This is basically an echo of Bradley's remark, in *Essays on Truth and Reality*: "Philosophy demands, and in the end it rests on, what may fairly be termed faith. It has, we may say, to presuppose its conclusion in order to prove it."[84] Bradley's thinking grows out of a distinctly modern skepticism that is alien to the Greek mind, which is instinctively and not self-consciously religious. My point is that Eliot's skepticism, deeper and fiercer than Bradley's, bars the individual from the affections of human nature and dissolves the practical wisdom necessary for building communities other than theocracies. For Eliot, the only answers were church and faith.

Lecturing at Harvard in the 1930s, not long after the publication of "Arnold and Pater," Eliot dug up Arnold for a last farewell – I picture Cromwell's corpse, swinging for the crows and the King. In his talk, Eliot scuttles the notion of "primary affections" because they are vague. His critique grows more precise, however, as he considers the "boredom and sense of restriction in the simple primary affections . . ."[85] Eliot continues his neglect of Arnold's Aristotelian ethics, of Arnold's Wordsworthian ethics, of any depth in Arnold beyond the Victorian moralism that Eliot finds tedious and repulsive. He condemns "boredom" as the product of routine, habit, and suffocating convention – the environment of his anomic youth. He craves emotion based on a poetic vision, denied to Arnold, of "the boredom, the horror, and the glory."[86] In the latter case, "boredom" is the introspective *ennui* of Baudelaire, the modern discovery of terrible self-knowledge.

Eliot goes on to revise his earlier charge of pedantry, saying that Arnold "was apt to think of the greatness of poetry rather than of its genuineness."[87] His trumping Arnold with "genuineness" shows the clear advantage that accrues to the living critic over his dead counterpart, since Arnold, when he could breath and talk and defend himself with the finest critical intelligence in England, had likewise upheld the standard of "genuine poetry" that "is conceived and composed in the soul."[88] Like authenticity, genuineness is a psychological and an aesthetic criterion. It fills the ethical breach when nothing solider is available. The religious poet appeals to his own kind of genuineness: "That there is an analogy between mystical experience and some of the ways in which poetry is written I do not deny . . ."[89] After the war, such thoughts would further define Eliot against rival critics: "Esthetic sensibility must be extended into spiritual perception, and spiritual perception must be extended into esthetic sensibility and disciplined taste before we are qualified to pass judgment upon decadence or diabolism or nihilism in art."[90] It is a fulfillment that Arnold lacked the religious grounds to pursue.

Be that as it may, Bradley's attack on Arnold has had lasting effects. Extended by Eliot, it combined with a general hostility against Aristotle (for example in Schopenhauer, Marx, Nietzsche, Pater, Tolstoy, Wilde, Dewey, G. E. Moore, and Russell) to ensure that Aristotle faded from the Arnoldian literary culture that we associate in America with Lionel Trilling. In his *Matthew Arnold*, Trilling echoes Bradley's scorn for Arnold's "clap-trap," "that to be virtuous is always to be happy, or that happiness must always come from virtue."[91] It is fairly obvious that Trilling regards the *Nicomachean Ethics* as a Greek fossil. Underscoring what W. J. Bate would call "the more strictly Victorian side of Arnold,"[92] Trilling diagnoses "the overemphasis on sex in Arnold's theory of morality."[93] It is impossible here to do justice to Trilling's highly refined psychology of the arts. But his rough treatment of Aristotle, and his attack on the ethics of Arnold (and of William James) as an *"Aberglaube* [superstition] of morality," invite a moment's consideration.[94]

In his influential book, Trilling divorces Arnold from Aristotle by arguing that Arnold misread him. Housman ranked Arnold among "the great critics of the classical literatures."[95] No less an authority on the *Poetics* than S. H. Butcher echoed Arnold to summarize Aristotle's view of poetry as "a criticism of life."[96] But Trilling refused to credit Arnold's understanding of Aristotle. He comments on the 1853 Preface:

Arnold's basic insight is a sound one – that the most invigorating literature is that which *resolves* itself, and that action is the best means of resolution. Only so is Aristotle's tragic *catharsis* secured and the tragic *catharsis* is still the fullest literary emotion. The tragic *catharsis*, however, even if it be the richest, is not the only literary emotion, nor the only one that gives Joy. Arnold, reiterating the Aristotelean poetic, betrays the Aristotelean method, for where Aristotle is inductive, discovering psychological principles in the study of literature, Arnold argues *a priori*, discovering principles of literature in his conception of psychology.[97]

The tragic effect of *catharsis* is relevant to the 1853 Preface, but Arnold does not actually mention the word. He says, "a cultivated Athenian . . . required that the permanent elements of his nature should be moved."[98] Trilling either misses or simply discounts the gist of this remark. His deployment of the term "tragic *catharsis*" indicates that, like Eliot, he saw "literary emotion" as being different in kind from normal emotion. His conclusion that Arnold "argues *a priori*" takes up the familiar burden of Pater.

Trilling appears to have followed Eliot to Bradley, and to have received some timely instruction along the way. Remembering the sneers of the aesthetic movement, which had converted *Culture and Anarchy* into a judgment against its author, Eliot commented: "In Arnold . . . there is a powerful element of Puritan morality . . ."[99] Trilling, we have seen, drew from the same well of opinion: "For Arnold . . . morality is essentially a check, a bridle, a renunciation."[100] Between Bradley, Eliot, and Trilling, Arnold's belief in virtue as an intrinsic good, in the emotional and moral life as having a natural basis, is entirely obscured. Trilling made so bold as to doubt whether the author of *St. Paul and Protestantism* knew what he was talking about: ". . . at the risk of impugning the Aristotelian definition, which makes morality an act of consciousness, will and habit, Arnold introduces a power from without so that the moral play of man and universe may be reciprocal."[101] Though Trilling finds that Arnold is being superstitious, there is clear metaphysical sanction for Arnold's "power from without" in the teleological framework of Aristotle's thought (*Meta.* 1072b). Secure in his work of partial representation, Trilling assails *Literature and Dogma* as the work of an "absolute moralist," the advocate of "an *a priori* morality intuitively perceived . . ."[102] In support of this damnifying judgment, he cites Arnold's remark: "We did not make ourselves and our nature, or conduct as the object of three-fourths of that nature; we did not provide that happiness should follow conduct, as it undeniably does."[103] "The sentence unleashed all of Bradley's thunder," writes Trilling. But Trilling is mistaken. Bradley did *not* cite that particular sentence, which is basically Aristotelian in character, with a gravity not so easily dismissed. More important, Arnold did not say "that to be virtuous is always to be happy, or that happiness must always come from virtue."[104] Arnold had read the Book of Job. Those are Bradley's words, from his attack on Arnold in *Ethical Studies.* Trilling's uncritical adoption of them perpetuates an abuse: like Bradley, he implies that Arnold did not intend *conduct* in its primary (and Johnsonian) sense of "general practice."[105] One cannot escape the impression that Bradley and Trilling put words in Arnold's mouth.

When Trilling quotes Bradley's thunder, it is thunder directed at Arnold's phalanx of abstractions (e.g. "righteousness," "law," and "Power"). Neither Bradley nor Trilling goes to the philosophical core of the matter in *Literature and Dogma*, where Arnold directs us to his source in Aristotle:

. . . [Aristotle] does not appeal to a speculative theory of the system of things, and deduce conclusions from it. And he shows his greatness in this, because the law of our being is *not* something which is already definitively known and can be exhibited as part of a speculative theory of the system of things; it is something which discovers itself and *becomes*, as we follow (among other things) the rule of renouncement.[106]

This simply does not fit Trilling's description of Arnold's "*a priori* morality." To be sure, Arnold's "rule of renouncement" has a stern puritanical ring. Arnold explains it as the rule of the soul over the body, but his unhappy phrase-making does little to illuminate whatever good might attend a habit of renunciation. I am not cheering for *Literature and Dogma*. But it should be acknowledged that Arnold's understanding of human nature is naturalistic and Aristotelian. Arnold's is not the dead, scholastic idol whom Francis Bacon long ago demolished – it is quite explicitly the empirical Aristotle whom, according to Trilling, Arnold had misappropriated in the 1853 Preface.

It is an historical irony that Eliot, in the late 1920s and 1930s, rejected Arnoldian liberalism for the sake of High Church Anglo-Catholicism, royalism, and a conservative, anti-democratic version of Athens, while Trilling, a decade later, transformed Arnoldian liberalism so as to rid it of suspicious-looking conservative elements. In our current period, Michael Levenson has interpreted Bradley's attack on Arnold as an attack "on the notion that we can construct all that we require of religion, morality, politics and philosophy on the basis of individual psychology."[107] Levenson's *Genealogy of Modernism* fixes the last strap on Arnold's Victorian straitjacket. Following Trilling, Levenson overlooks the Aristotelian side of Arnold's thinking, which is not solely a matter of "individual psychology," and without which Arnold's literary criticism loses much of its "basis." Yet more recently, James Wood dusts off the Bradleyan caricature of Arnold for the haughty title essay of *The Broken Estate*.[108]

Eliot's poetry demanded a rejection of the demotic or vulgar virtues with their purchase on the primary emotions, but his cultural criticism tells a different story.[109] In *The Idea of a Christian Society*, Eliot introduces his "political philosophy" by way of Aristotle, who "wrote studies full of universal wisdom."[110] Like Bradley, Eliot returns to the ethical premises of

Aristotle, but he follows the example of Aquinas in connecting Christianity to classical ethics: "*virtuosa . . . vita est congregationis humanae finis.*"[III] *The Idea of a Christian Society* calls for a "Christian organization of society . . . in which the natural end of man – virtue and well-being in community is acknowledged for all, and the supernatural end – beatitude – for those who have the eyes to see it."[II2] Nonetheless, it would be somewhat superficial to remark that religion healed the division of thought and feeling that characterized Eliot from the first. Of the later Eliot, one might more truly say that his heart was in Salem while his head was in Rome.

The Cocktail Party is Eliot's last major effort to fuse together his creative material and his Christian ethics. First performed in 1949, the play is a superb piece of writing, dramatically unified and richly inventive in its symbolic texture. Eliot breaks from his past as a dramatist by pursuing a connection between the two ends of man: the natural and the supernatural.[II3] Sir Henry Harcourt-Reilly, Julia, and Alex are the Guardians. Like Plato's guardians, they exert a wise influence over their charges; like Calvin's elders, they preside over the passage from earthly life to holiness. Reilly, the witch doctor of the tribe, is a counter-Freudian analyst, debunking the pretensions of the modern psyche. Edward and Lavinia Chamberlayne are adulterous lackloves, the bourgeois party-goers whom the Guardians rescue. Until the final act, theirs is a marriage in hell; the intensely sad scene (Act I, sc. 3) of Edward's and Lavinia's mutual recriminations is prophetic of a rising divorce rate. Poet and socialite Celia Coplestone begins the play as Edward's lover, but ends it a Protestant saint.

After her affair with Edward, Celia, haunted by intimations of God, comes to Reilly seeking advice:

REILLY: I can reconcile you to the human condition,
             The condition to which some who have gone as far as you
             Have succeeded in returning. They may remember
             The vision they have had, but they cease to regret it,
             Maintain themselves by the common routine,
             Learn to avoid excessive expectation,
             Become tolerant of themselves and others,
             Giving and taking, in the usual actions
             What there is to give and take. They do not repine;
             Are contented with the morning that separates
             And with the evening that brings together
             For casual talk before the fire
             Two people who know they do not understand each other,
             Breeding children whom they do not understand
             And who will never understand them.

CELIA: Is that the best life?
REILLY: It is a good life. Though you will not know how good
         Till you come to the end. But you will want nothing else,
         And the other life will be only like a book
         You have read once, and lost. In a world of lunacy,
         Violence, stupidity, and greed . . . it is a good life.[114]

The style shows those qualities that Eliot prized in Hooker and Andrewes: "determination to stick to essentials, . . . the desire for clarity and precision on matters of importance."[115] Yet the deliberate and orderly manner is shot through with symbolist effects. The alliteration of "reconcile," "returning," "remember," "regret," "routine," and "repine" creates a canine undertone that suggests Reilly's knowledge of human savageness. With the reiteration of "understand," a *conduplicatio* that hollows out the word like a chime, Eliot teases us into sensing the limits of our usual round of thoughts and phrases. Then there is the metaphorical reference to a visionary "book." Like the Bible, the book binds together the natural and the supernatural. It enhances Reilly's mystical authority, much as the Bible bestows authority on a preacher. And it enables Eliot to strengthen a central motif: the largeness of Reilly's perceptions and the smallness of our own.

Reilly's speech recalls Bradley's *Ethical Studies* by combining an active idea of ethics with a visionary disdain for morality. The shared life can be a "good life," but it is still alienated, in Bradley's sense of the word, from the divine. Eliot upholds the ethical integrity of persons in the community of "giving and taking" that is the source, in Aristotelian terms, of our shared life of feeling. People become "tolerant," the increase of tolerance being for Eliot a benefit of humanism in a religious society.[116] In a 1986 production of *The Cocktail Party* in London, the actor playing Reilly thumped his desk to accentuate the phrase "It is a good life."[117] But the community huddles before a fire that evokes Plato's cave. Owing to sin, giving and taking lose much of their affective weight. Sinners fool themselves about their desires and passions. The life of virtue falters under the combined pressure of Eliot's insatiable skepticism and his implacable faith. In the speech, "casual" harbors an etymological play on a Latin word for "fall," and "breeding" recalls the opening lines of *The Waste Land*. Celia has already come to the conclusion that "one is always alone"[118]: the more self-conscious the person, the greater the sense of spiritual struggle and estrangement from one's community.

What happens in *The Cocktail Party* – what happens in much of Eliot's Christian art – is that Eliot transforms an aesthetics of exile into a theology of exile. His exilic mode enacts what he lamented as a

Cartesian distance between the self and its emotions. The fall of western culture into modernity is the theme of Eliot's Clark Lectures, where Eliot writes, "I insist on a general line of descent from the seventeenth century to the nineteenth," a line of "intellectual psychologism" that connects Descartes to Bradley.[119] It is a point both of ethics and of science that Cartesianism warps the physiology of our emotional responses by imposing too great a distance between the mind and the body. In the play's final act, Lavinia and Edward save their marriage *and* Celia is reported to "have been crucified / Very near an ant-hill."[120] Our response to these outcomes, as spectators of the drama, is flattened and confused by their absurd discord. From start to finish, Eliot applies an art of interruption, of fragmented action, not only for certain comic effects, but to disrupt our emotional investment in the characters, so that we cannot escape our spiritual burden. When Alex uncorks the news about Celia's death, the spectator can register his response only through a filter of self-consciousness, because the broken plot has alienated the audience members from the nominal community on the stage.

I come back to Bradley in order to affirm the moral coherence of *The Cocktail Party*, such as it is. As in *Ethical Studies*, self-consciousness ultimately transcends the mutual consciousness of friendship, and directs the self on its lonely journey to God. As in *Ethical Studies*, the community has a moral basis, though a higher, religious morality exists for a select few. But the play's divisions may have less to do with Bradley than with the *dual perspective* that attends us as individuals who are political animals. It is arduously difficult, with little reward for the effort, to fathom both these viewpoints within a single consciousness. More, we express our dual nature, which is sometimes in our deepest experience contradictory, in a host of ways. We glimpse our inherent duality behind Bradley's two levels of moral life, common and religious, physical and spiritual, with their escalating demands on the self. The same rival emphases distinguish Plato from Aristotle: Plato's vision is for the elect, the Guardians, the philosophers capable of leaving the Cave; Aristotle, as Arnold recognized, speaks to practical questions of democratic life. Likewise, we may observe the duality of human perspective in yet another Eliotic tension, between the private covenant of grace (a compact between God and the individual saint) and the public covenant of the people to build a city of God. The comedy of *The Cocktail Party* is metaphysical: it is the theoretical resolution of ethical and spiritual problems that, on the stage of life, challenge our sanity and our civilization.

CHAPTER 3

James Joyce: love among the skeptics

"Ibsen," writes Joyce in the *Fortnightly Review* essay that astonished his fellow undergraduates, ". . . treats all things . . . with large insight, artistic restraint, and sympathy." The young author begins his next sentence by echoing Arnold's sonnet "To a Friend," which pays homage to Homer, Epictetus, and Sophocles. At issue is Ibsen's handling of an episode in *When We Dead Awaken*: "He sees it steadily and whole, as from a great height, with perfect vision and an angelic dispassionateness, with the sight of one who may look on the sun with open eyes."[1] Joyce lauded the classical temperament of Ibsen's work, especially his sense of character. But Joyce's classicism, unlike Arnold's, is aesthetic. For Joyce, a classical style is "the syllogism of art." Classicism is "a constant state of the artistic mind."[2] It is not a requirement that the permanent elements of human nature be moved.

Ibsen's artistic vision was confirmed for the young Joyce not by Arnold, but by Pater and Flaubert.[3] "If all high things have their martyrs," writes Pater, "Gustave Flaubert might perhaps rank as the martyr of literary style."[4] By a suggestive coincidence, Stephen Dedalus shares his name with the first Christian martyr, the eloquent Saint Stephen – much as Florian Deleal takes his name from a martyred saint. Certainly Joyce was remembering Flaubert's letters when he had Stephen remark: "The artist, like the God of the creation, remains within or behind or beyond or above his handiwork, invisible, refined out of existence, indifferent, paring his fingernails."[5] Wilde did not pretend to play God, when he said in his Preface to *Dorian Gray*, "No artist has ethical sympathies."[6] It was Flaubert's perspective, an effect of autonomous stylistic perfection, that dazzled and enticed the young modernists. Eliot wrote a friend in 1917: "I like to feel that a writer is perfectly cool and detached, regarding other people's feelings or his own, like a God who has got beyond them."[7] But amidst his later reversals, he came to doubt the creed of sublime neutrality: "the author, in that Olympian elevation and superior indifference attributed to great artists, and which I can only imperfectly understand, has detached himself from any moral attitude toward his characters . . ."[8]

It is not hard to link Joyce's classicism to romantic irony.[9] Hegel had mapped out the heights of ironic subjectivity to which Ibsen, Flaubert, and Joyce would ascend. The "form" of this subjectivity, writes Hegel, "is a subjective void, i.e. it knows itself as this contentless void and in this knowledge knows itself as absolute."[10] Babbitt, in his learned analysis of romantic irony, describes the false classicism of the romantic genius. Socrates, he says, used skepticism and irony in a dialectic that pointed beyond Socrates: "What Socrates opposes to convention is his universal self." Joyce, on the other hand, fits the romantic mold by offering not his universal self, but only "his 'genius,' . . . his unique and private self."[11] A genius is free to dispose of the world according to his will. "Why indeed," asks Babbitt, "should the poet allow any restriction to be placed upon his caprice in a universe that is after all only a projection of himself?"[12] For Babbitt, Flaubert's classicism is in fact a "disillusioned" romanticism, a bitter realism about sex.

It is, however, reasonable to defend romantic irony as healthy skepticism toward moral authority. On this interpretation, Joyce's skepticism is a form of freedom. It resists the passionate dictates that lead men to violence and war. It lends itself to good government, and enriches what the nineteenth-century French historian François Guizot called the "diversity" of European culture.[13] I note that the Platonic Socrates refers to Daedalus as "founder of my line."[14] It can be suggested that, through the name of the semi-autobiographical Stephen Dedalus, Joyce extends the line of Socrates. He is skeptical and impious and a myth-maker who, like Socrates, gives a saving form to fate.

What most exempts Joyce from Babbitt's criticism is that, although Joyce practices a great deal of romantic irony, his moral purpose is constructive. In 1903, he praised Ibsen for assisting "the breaking-up of tradition, which is the work of the modern era."[15] The next year, having conceived *Dubliners* and written its first story, "The Sisters," he told his brother Stanislaus: "I am trying . . . to give people some kind of intellectual pleasure or spiritual enjoyment by converting the bread of everyday life into something that has a permanent artistic life of its own . . . for their mental, moral, and spiritual uplift."[16] Buck Mulligan understands Stephen: "you have the cursed jesuit strain in you, only it's injected the wrong way" (1.209). The comment speaks to Joyce's knowledge of himself: "You allude to me as a Catholic," Joyce once remarked; "you ought to allude to me as a Jesuit."[17] His Jesuit mind is moral, theological, and missionary. If his aims do not strike us as contradictory (if "the breaking-up of tradition" and the moral assertions of Joyce's art cohere easily in our minds), it is probably because we think that his values are the right ones.

I want to approach Joyce's work as a form of moral education. In *A Portrait of the Artist as a Young Man*, we enter a world of teachers, who possess knowledge that is wide and varied, but cut off, like church Latin, from the fresh turnings of experience. As we read the book, the Jesuit hierarchy gives way to a new arrangement, where Stephen is to the Jesuits as the Jesuits are to the Christian Brothers. By mastering his experience through the English language, Stephen claims artistic and spiritual superiority. The stages of his growth, from early consciousness to refined self-consciousness and creative power, establish for author and reader alike an authentic mode of selfhood – a convincing union of life and art.

It was Pater who gave the idea of authenticity its most perfect expression: "The theory or idea or system which requires of us the sacrifice of any part of . . . experience, in consideration of some interest into which we cannot enter, or some abstract theory we have not identified with ourselves, or what is only conventional, has no real claim upon us." Authenticity is what Gabriel Conroy, another teacher, maintains against the "interest" of Miss Ivors in "The Dead." In Stephen's case, Pater's enemies, the forces that would deny the true self, are overcome by the artist as he pursues his calling. Stephen tells Cranly, in their last conversation before the diary: "I will not serve that in which I no longer believe whether it call itself my home, my fatherland or my church . . ."[18] The intimate ties that bind Stephen to these enemies must be dissolved for the *Portrait* to be complete.

This dissolution did not happen in *Stephen Hero*, to judge from the manuscript that survives. Joyce had to rethink Stephen and his relations to others. In the *Portrait*, family recedes into the background. Stephen's brother Maurice loses his supporting role. Emma Clery, the love interest of *Stephen Hero*, fades into "E – C – ," an etherial muse and a projection of Stephen's psyche. Likewise, Joyce in his revised work attenuates Stephen's friendships at University College. Theodore Spencer makes a good point: "in the *Portrait* we are introduced to Stephen's friends – Cranly, Lynch and the rest – as items, so to speak, in Stephen's mind."[19] With respect to the independent reality of, say, the indelible Cranly, there is room for disagreement, while allowing that Stephen in the *Portrait* is considerably more solipsistic than his predecessor in *Stephen Hero*.

By the same token, *Stephen Hero* is more dramatic than the *Portrait*, in Joyce's sense of drama as "the art wherein [the artist] presents his image in immediate relation to others."[20] One of the central events of *Stephen Hero* is the paper that Stephen delivers at the Royal University. The essay's mixed reception serves to highlight Irish provinciality and the hypocrisy of Irish politics. But Joyce depicts at least one of Stephen's critics with sympathy. It is hard to feel any goodwill toward Hughes when he declares "that the moral welfare of the Irish people was menaced by such theories."[21] Hughes is a time-server. But one of the priests defends Stephen while offering criticism that is intelligent and wise:

Father Butt confessed that it was a new sensation for him to hear Thomas Aquinas quoted as an authority on esthetic philosophy. Esthetic philosophy was a modern branch and if it was anything at all, it was practical. Aquinas had treated slightly of the beautiful, but always from a theoretic standpoint. To interpret his statements practically one needed a fuller knowledge than Mr Daedalus could have of his entire theology. At the same time he would not go so far as to say that Mr Daedalus had really, intentionally or unintentionally, misinterpreted Aquinas. But just as an act which may be good in itself may become bad by reason of circumstances so an object intrinsically beautiful may be vitiated by other considerations. Mr Daedalus had chosen to consider beauty intrinsically and to neglect other considerations. But beauty also has its practical side. Mr Daedalus was a passionate admirer of the artistic and such people are not always the most practical people in the world. Father Butt then reminded his audience of the story of King Alfred and the old woman who was cooking cakes – of the theorist, that is, and the practical person and concluded by expressing the hope that the essayist would emulate King Alfred and not be too severe on the practical persons who had criticized him.[22]

The modest Father Butt is persuasive about Stephen's interpretation of Aquinas.[23] It is not simply a matter of Joyce letting us know that he understands his critics and has foreseen their objections. The social nature of feeling in *Stephen Hero* demands this kind of interaction between Stephen and others. Against the stylistic developments that will lead to the *Portrait* and *Ulysses*, Father Butt holds his personable own. He has a thoughtful argument about the relation of acts to their circumstances and about the relation of beauty to "other considerations." In the *Portrait*, he dwindles into the "leanness and greyness" of a typical Jesuit,[24] the dean of studies whose lost surname confirms his soul's anonymity (his name is only briefly recovered amidst a flotsam of information in "Ithaca" [17.145]). My point is that in the *Portrait* Joyce must diminish such well-rounded figures as Father Butt, whose balanced and intelligent views, which reflect well on the authority of church and state, threaten to blunt the diamond edge of Stephen's authentic life.

Joyce adjusted Stephen's reality to meet the demands of lyrical form. For the child Stephen, guilt and conscience register, not through a pit in the stomach, but through the mind-work of a proto-poem:

> Pull out his eyes,
> Apologize,
> Apologize,
> Pull out his eyes.[25]

In the dreamwork of art, the body sleeps. The mind transfigures the physical emotion, shaping and controlling the dread provoked by Dante's grim warning, that if Stephen does not apologize, "the eagles will come and pull out his eyes." This introspective technique is at issue when Stephen defines the lyrical form to his disciple Lynch. In effect he is explaining his own portrait: "the form wherein the artist presents his image in immediate relation to himself."[26] It is through this Trinitarian mode of self-differentiation that the artist creates his lyrical world.[27] In the patristic version, God the Father presents his image, Christ, in immediate relation to himself, the Holy Ghost. In the Joycean version, Joyce presents his image, the martyr Stephen, in immediate relation to Himself, the Holy Joyce. Stephen's aesthetic baptism at Sandymount Strand (the scene of the bird-girl) is completed when he feels his "soul . . . swooning into some new world, fantastic, dim, uncertain as under sea, traversed by cloudy shapes and beings."[28] Joyce transforms the Aristotelian body of Stephen Daedalus in *Stephen Hero* into the modernist body of Stephen Dedalus in the *Portrait*. As Joyce's "image," the latter-day Stephen is the Word disincarnate, the agent of an original style, not of embodied virtue or desire. And since Joyce's lyrical form promotes this disembodiment, it logically precludes the common paths of life and feeling, like romance with a featherless biped.

Joyce's moral education features a latent element of moral suasion, an appeal to moral sensibilities that Joyce himself must shape and tease into receptive condition. He needs our consent – though he will not bend his knee and ask for it – in order to exalt his union of life and art above other ways of life. He needs our consent because art is solipsism and chaos unless others recognize the form it takes. It isn't enough to filch the Trinitarian mystery. The artist cannot "forge . . . the uncreated conscience" of his race without first gaining their consent. In this respect, Joyce's missionary complex differs from Wordsworth's Napoleon complex: "every author, as far as he is great and at the same time *original*, has had the task of *creating* the taste by which he is to be enjoyed . . . What is all this but an advance, or a conquest, made by the soul of the poet?"[29] If Joyce relies more on "silence, exile, and cunning,"[30] than on imperial power, it is because he sends a Jesuit into a predominantly English world.

After Father Arnall has finished half his sublime sermonizing on hell, Stephen repairs to the classroom at Belvedere, where he collapses at his desk. The verbal patter of his schoolmates interrupts his panicked meditation on death and judgment, on being sentenced to an infernal afterlife:

> He could not grip the floor with his feet and sat heavily at his desk, opening one of his books at random and poring over it . . . He had died. Yes. He was judged. A wave of fire swept through his body: the first. Again a wave. His brain began to glow. Another. His brain was simmering and bubbling within the crackling tenement of the skull. Flames burst forth from his skull like a corolla, shrieking like voices:
> – Hell! Hell! Hell! Hell! Hell!
> Voices spoke near him:
> – On hell.
> – I suppose he rubbed it into you well.
> – You bet he did. He put us all into a blue funk.
> – That's what you fellows want: and plenty of it to make you work.
> He leaned back weakly in his desk. He had not died. God had spared him still. He was still in the familiar world of the school. Mr Tate and Vincent Heron stood at the window, talking, jesting, gazing out at the bleak rain, moving their heads.
> – I wish it would clear up. I had arranged to go for a spin on the bike with some fellows out by Malahide. But the roads must be kneedeep.
> – It might clear up, sir.
> The voices he knew so well, the common words, the quiet of the classroom when the voices paused and the silence was filled by the sound of softly browsing cattle as the other boys munched their lunches tranquilly, lulled his aching soul.[31]

Joyce leads us to identify with Stephen and not with his classmates, whose casual reality arouses paranoid suspicion. If Stephen is anxious for the wrong reasons, at least he knows fear and trembling. He is self-conscious, a highly intelligent and sensitive young artist. He has the authority of Hamlet behind him, of Byron and Shelley, of the heroes of the *Künstlerroman* tradition, from Goethe's *Wilhelm Meister's Apprenticeship and Travels*, to Stendhal's *Life of Henri Brulard*, to Dickens's *David Copperfield*, to Butler's *Way of All Flesh*.[32] This tradition of literature, insofar as it informs our reading, tends to reinforce our sympathy with

Stephen's point of view. But for sheer psychic torture, it is safe to say that the *Künstlerroman* tradition has nothing like Arnall's sermon. The young Stendhal never yielded to the despotism of his Jesuit tutor, the Abbé Raillane, "a sworn enemy to logic and to sound argument."[33] David Copperfield survives his instruction at the monstrous hands of Mr. Creakle. The intellectual and emotional savagery of Arnall far outstrips even Butler's deplorable Dr. Skinner, whom Butler shows to be human at last. Arnall's sermon might possibly drive a highly sensitive young person mad, but Goethe, Stendhal, Dickens, and Butler would survive it.

So these mainstays of the *Künstlerroman* tradition do not wholly explain our sympathy for Stephen. The *Portrait* is an epochal book that persuades us to like a new kind of hero – alienated, an exile. Father Arnall's sermons, aimed at pews of teenage boys, draw on the rhetorical armory with such limitless punishing extravagance that we turn against him as against one who has violated innocence. His terms of address, "O, my dear little brethren in Christ Jesus,"[34] his "quiet friendly tone,"[35] are exposed by Joyce in a scene verging on satire. But there is no counterpoint to the satire, which as a mode or genre depends on the intrusion of common sense. Heron, the rival bird-man, scornful, vain defender of the bourgeois Tennyson over the romantic Byron, does not supply a moral standard. Heron is a dandyish bully and not a true artist. The rest of the boys, speaking "common words" and eating lunch, bear the markings of Nietzsche's "herd." The closest we come to a moral standard is the mild sadism of Mr. Tate: "That's what you fellows want: and plenty of it to make you work." But Tate will not do. Not only do we sympathize with Stephen's terror, we take Joyce's suggestion and look outside the book for an enlightened perspective. Unmenaced by the fires of an adolescent hell, we award the moral palm to the author of the book: to the mature Stephen.

A famous crux of the *Portrait* is the question of Joyce's distance from his protagonist. Joyce's genius for dramatic irony complicates the question, is the *Portrait* autobiography?[36] Some will tend, with Levin and Ellmann, to highlight the autobiographical character of Joyce's writing. Others, with Kenner, will warn against making too much of it.[37] Joyce in middle age told Frank Budgen: "Some people who read my book *A Portrait of the Artist* forget that it is called *A Portrait of the Artist as a Young Man*."[38] This remark, though perfectly just, does not revoke the work's design of joining together life and art: the young artist transcends – from his own perspective and through many mistakes – all that threatens his freedom and his power. Whether Joyce Himself was "well pleased" is a matter that stumps our theology.

As Stephen approaches manhood, Joyce bestows on him an intensely privileged viewpoint that is analogous to spiritual vision. In the following passage, for example, the perceptions of author and hero blend into a single heightened consciousness:

> What birds were they? He stood on the steps of the library to look at them, leaning wearily on his ashplant. They flew round and round the jutting shoulder of a house on Molesworth Street. The air of the late March evening made clear their flight, their dark darting quivering bodies flying clearly against the sky as against a limphung cloth of smoky tenuous blue.[39]

The scene has no clear connection to the previous section, which has the villanelle "Are you not weary of ardent ways?" set in italics and marked off from the succeeding text by asterisks. Since the novel's opening pages, Joyce has used elision, the lack of connecting matter, to foster an extraordinary effect of isolation. Here Joyce intensifies the effect by placing Stephen by himself, with the unknown and nameless birds that symbolize his destiny, in the vivid "air" of earliest spring. The drama is in Stephen's perception, which counterpoints his physical languor, and which will continue to unfold and develop with the realization that the birds are swallows, and that swallows carry associations of springtime and desire reaching from Swinburne and Tennyson back into antiquity. Such writing is a culmination of style, impressionistic and lyrical, with a musical intimacy of form and content, of period and perception, that transcends Stephen's personal situation to assert his growing authenticity of viewpoint.[40]

As he disembodies himself through art, which is the realm of his "spirit," the artist forsakes human nature and its ethical norms of giving and receiving. Cranly gives the right answer to Stephen's catechism, when asked to remember what the artist wants: "To discover the mode *of life or of art* whereby your spirit could express itself in unfettered freedom."[41] Artistic refinement is achieved only through an artistic life. Stephen and Cranly are about to separate, forever. To read Stephen's mission ironically is to cheapen the authentic demands of art and freedom, and the sacrificial necessity of exile. Flight comes at the cost of flight. In a final metamorphosis, Joyce sheds his third-person narration to let Stephen ascend in the triumph of the diary, where art is life and life is art: "Welcome, O life! I go to encounter for the millionth time the reality of experience and to forge in the smithy of my soul the uncreated conscience of my race."[42] Irony approaches asymptotically to zero, the more we are moved by Stephen's soaring high note, in which the artist addresses "life" itself, while grandly alluding to Blake and staking the matter of "conscience" to the heights of art and myth and fate. Put another way, Stephen overcomes his ironic distance from others through an act of persuasion, where the Irish race, and possibly the human race, consent to his, and to Joyce's, transforming artifice. And the more we identify with Stephen, the less it will bother us that he has no idea what life is.

In the halls of rote learning, Clongowes Wood College and University College in the *Portrait*, and Mr. Deasy's school for Protestant boys in *Ulysses*, Joyce professes the singularity of the artist. Stephen's teachers act as foils to the authentic experience of the artist-hero. Their falsehood sets off his truth, their nightmare counterpoints his vision. Accordingly, the Nestor of the *Ulysses* schema is an anti-Nestor. Mr. Deasy animates the dead hand of the past. Succeeding a long line of rectors, instructors, and prefects, he is a little Nobodaddy: anti-Semitic, imperialist, and blind to the light. Dispensing British coin, he speaks with fulsome Edwardian complacency on behalf of Christian-Victorian progress. He is still living in the world of Samuel Butler's parents. As commentators have observed, Deasy surviving into old age would face a bitter irony: the European crack-up. The reader knows it is coming, as does Stephen, who apparently intuits it, as does the author, who is writing in its midst. Against Deasy, Stephen enjoys a rare good inning in *Ulysses*. It is Deasy who inspires Stephen's gnomic utterance: "History . . . is a nightmare from which I am trying to awake" (2. 377). And it is Deasy's civilization that the artist wants to remake in the Blakean smithy of his soul.

Stephen's counter-instruction of Deasy resembles Socratic dialectic. In the service of justice and truth, Stephen's irony is directed at the Deasy type. But in rising to a loftier, more lyrical style of writing at the chapter's end, Joyce reserves his mysteries for his disciples – those with the ability to read him. The priest of art wields "the secret knowledge and secret power" that Stephen once attributed to the Jesuits.[43] His final ironies are esoteric:

– Mr Dedalus!
  Running after me. No more letters, I hope.
– Just one moment.
– Yes, sir, Stephen said, turning back at the gate.
  Mr Deasy halted, breathing hard and swallowing his breath.
– I just wanted to say, he said. Ireland, they say, has the honour of being the only
  country which never persecuted the jews. Do you know that? No. And do you
  know why?
  He frowned sternly on the bright air.

– Why, sir? Stephen asked, beginning to smile.

– Because she never let them in, Mr Deasy said solemnly.

A coughball of laughter leaped from his throat dragging after it a rattling chain of phlegm. He turned back quickly, coughing, laughing, his lifted arms waving to the air.

– She never let them in, he cried again through his laughter as he stamped on gaitered feet over the gravel of the path. That's why.

On his wise shoulders through the checkerwork of leaves the sun flung spangles, dancing coins. (2.432)

At the level of sarcasm, Deasy's shoulders are not "wise." At the level of dramatic irony, the sun will shine on them anyway, much as the air will cooperate with Deasy's lungs, though he is apparently not worthy of life. At the symbolist level of epiphany, the sun signifies divine illumination. It is emblematic not of The Good, not of God, but of the artist, within or behind or beyond or above his black and white "checkerwork of leaves," *Ulysses*. Joyce's symbolist irony, of supplanting mimetic language with writing that has its own autonomy (writing that subordinates nature to art and to the unifying aesthetic consciousness), is an irony deployed against the world and its corrupt moral order. In a monumental act of usurpation, Joyce displaces the Logos, the God of Deasy, with the morally purified word of his own making. The Bloomsday sun betokens the independence of Joyce's language, alluded to by the "coins" that spangle and dance, there for readers who can redeem them. A Blake-quoting Judas, Deasy has his reward of silver and shadows. Joyce himself is Judas and Jesus and Blake, slaying the old gods and proclaiming the new. His "coins" issue from the forge and mint of his own civilization, not that of Deasy or Caesar.

It is truer of *Ulysses* than of any previous novel that the reader is an acolyte. Discipleship is virtually built into reading Joyce's masterwork. It is a book of many classrooms: school and library, public house and bawdy house, home and hospital – not to mention the Dublin streets. And though Stephen and others participate in several symposia, it is Joyce who assumes Stephen's lost mantle. "Toothless Kinch, the superman" (3. 496) fails where Joyce succeeds. Where Stephen succumbs to the paralysis of Dublin, Joyce is Nietzschean in his courage, shattering the sick world and flinging his words, dancing signs, onto the void.

Who could have foreseen the fate of the young hero of Joyce's *Künstlerroman*? It is more than strange that Dedalus should fall like Icarus. Stephen's failure indicates Joyce's self-revision as an artist and his reformed understanding of his art, just where it overlaps with ethics. To judge from a cosmic expansion of style that pushed the traditional novel beyond the breaking point, the author of *Ulysses* found the lyric mode of the *Portrait* a narrow means of unifying life and art. Stephen, from Joyce's mature perspective, was an artistic dead-end – "blind" like the street in "Araby." He did not know or feel enough. His "dread" of "the mystery of his own body," and his desire for "a new soaring impalpable imperishable being," ensured his ephebic, Shelleyan status.[44] The schemata for *Ulysses* underscore Stephen's problems by assigning each chapter a bodily organ, with the exception of the first three chapters, which form Stephen's Telemachia. Joyce had taken to mocking Stephen's disembodied condition.

That being said, Stephen's lonely exilic authenticity remains the starting point of Joycean morality. Without life or love in official Dublin, the agent of goodness is isolated. It is lackeys and dupes, agents of false consciousness and the status quo, who speak collectively in *Ulysses*: the priests, the pressmen, the Citizen, Gerty MacDowell, and Edward VII all use collective forms of address – as do the stylistic imitations of "Oxen in the Sun." Leopold and Molly Bloom use *we* in an authentic manner to refer to men and to women sexually, that is, in a pre-political sense. Generally, though, Joyce deploys *we* as a part of rhetoric, which is to go slumming by high modernist standards. For those of finer taste, rhetoric invites skepticism and humor. It can convey a moral suggestion, but only at an impersonal distance. Within the cerebral realm of exquisite pleasures, a rhetorical consciousness, like Gerty MacDowell's, can engage the reader's sympathy. "Nausicaa" has a pathos unique to literature, though no one has been known to weep at it.

The first occurrence of *we* in the novel comes from Buck Mulligan, talking to Stephen: "My name is absurd too: Malachi Mulligan, two dactyls. But it has a Hellenic ring, hasn't it? Tripping and sunny like the buck himself. We must go to Athens. Will you come if I can get the aunt to fork out twenty quid?" (1.41) Mulligan is astute enough to recognize Stephen's exilic loneliness, and Stephen sees straight through his rival. The "usurper" uses *we* to hide calculating self-interest behind a mask of artistic friendship.[45] More esoterically, Mulligan is inviting the reader – *we* are invited – to observe Joyce's Homeric subtext, and then to embark on a voyage: "We must go to Athens." But we recognize that Mulligan, like all men, including the author of *Ulysses*, is motivated by self-interest. In the Larbaud scheme, he bears the signs of Antinous, the suitor who plots against Telemachus's life, and who is the first to be slain by Odysseus. Joyce's invitation to the reader, tendered through Mulligan, is therefore ambiguous. It splits into an irrational dream language of "let us go" and "let us not go." Aristotle's principle of non-contradiction will not be making the visit to Athens. The philosopher calls this premise of logic "the most indisputable of all principles," even though it cannot be demonstrated: "it is impossible for anything at the same time to be and not to be . . ." (*Meta.* 1006a1). Joyce, one must assume, intends us to grasp the movement he is making, from reason, friendship, and community to the oracular intuitions of the artistic mind, as a movement from surface to depth. To quote his young disciple Beckett: "For the artist, who does not deal in surfaces, the rejection of friendship is not only reasonable, but a necessity. Because the only possible spiritual development is in the sense of depth."[46] Our entry into the novel is an instructive prod at our self-awareness and at our own authenticity. The poor in spirit need not apply. From Joyce's apocalyptic standpoint, it is a question of our being dead or alive.

Stephen lacks one crucial element for Joyce's moral purposes. As we have seen, Stephen has a conscience. His brief scene with Dilly at the bookstall shows he can connect his heart to his head. But he subjects his conscience, like all else, to the play of art. As Kenner suggests, the mental refrain "agenbite of inwit" allows Stephen to turn "pity and guilt into heady rhetoric."[47] This is a moral and an aesthetic problem. Stephen's skepticism, while fueling his authenticity, cannot inspire a movement of love beyond the thick wall of himself. He becomes a narcissistic spectacle, the latest case of Dublin paralysis. Joyce's solution is to take Stephen's authenticity and his skepticism – the hard lessons the young man has learned – and to create a character where they can co-exist with love, which provides a bridge out of the straitened aesthetic self.

The innate power of sympathy is the psychological basis of the love that is needed. And it is of course Leopold Bloom who embodies this power: the moral imagination.[48] Through Bloom's power to love, Joyce may be said to answer Chesterton's critique of Ibsen, that, in the "negative spirit" of Ibsen's work, he had failed to provide a definite model of "the good man."[49] Bloom is an ethical model for the reader, as well as the prophet of Joyce's apocalyptic mission to transform human kind. As role model, he educates the bourgeois readership whom modernization and politics were prying away from the church. As Joyce's prophet, he is a messianic figure, a messenger from on high.

Joyce considered Blake "the most enlightened of western poets."[50] In a 1912 essay, he describes Blake as a writer with "pity for everything that lives and suffers and rejoices in the illusions of the vegetable world, for the

fly, the hare, the little chimney sweep, the robin, even the flea . . ."⁵¹
Bloom's opening vignette with his cat is in this sense Blakean: "Mr Bloom
watched curiously, kindly, the lithe black form . . . They call them stupid.
They understand what we say better than we understand them." The key
is the transition from "curiously" to "kindly," where the moral imagination kicks in. Joyce found a similar belief in Shelley: a sense of the
imagination as a force for good in the world, and a sensibility that is
nearly Manichaean in sundering the visionary from the blind. The cat's
understanding shines all the more brightly against the leaden stupidity of
those who underestimate cats.

Independent of the corrupt religious and legal institutions that crowd
the Dublin streets, Bloom's moral imagination enables Joyce to fill the
moral vacuum of the city. Bloom is equipped with a power unbeholden to
priest, king, judge, or magistrate. He wonders, Hamlet-like, at the blind
stripling: "What dreams would he have, not seeing? Life a dream for him.
Where is the justice being born that way?" (8. 1144). Joyce makes his point
through juxtaposition: the blind stripling passes from Bloom's sympathetic view, to be immediately succeeded by Sir Frederick Falkiner, chief
judicial officer of Dublin, and emblem of the Protestant Anglo-Irish
establishment (8. 1151). In "Cyclops," Sir Frederick is blown to bits in the
serio-comical catastrophe visited upon Dublin by the Irish Polyphemus,
just before the translation into heaven of "ben Bloom Elijah." The idea is
that Bloom's gospel of sympathy will put an end to the nightmare that
Falkiner administers: what Bloom calls "Force, hatred, history, all that"
(12.1481).

Bloom's compassionate mind and passing thoughts, from Handel's
Messiah (8. 1163) to the promised land of Agendath Netaim (8. 1184),
prepare us for his messianic aspect. His new religion of compassion not
only supplants the church, it condemns the murderous cosmos that could
rob a man of his sight or allow a "holocaust" to happen in New York
harbor (8.1146). For thematic parallax, Joyce supplies a counterpoint: he
gives play to an unsympathetic perspective on the stripling near the end of
"Sirens" (11.1281–83). Joyce does not sentimentalize the power of sympathy.
He knows that pity can be milked for dark pleasures, that it can be
consumed by the aesthete. But he suggests that Bloom's morality can
survive the risk.

Joyce's development of the sympathetic imagination marks the passing
of the social morality that we find in *Stephen Hero* and *Dubliners*. To
be sure, the moral life rarely flourishes in these early works. Joyce
commented to his publisher that his intention in *Dubliners* "was to write

a chapter of the moral history of my country and I chose Dublin for the scene because that city seemed to me the centre of paralysis."[52] Usually, the paralysis is terminal. Father Flynn is crushed under the weight of sin. Eveline Hill dies spiritually because her father gives too little in return for her constant care. Bob Doran is trapped into marrying Polly Mooney. But *Dubliners* as "moral history" is not entirely unrelieved by generosity or insight, even if Joyce's intention of "mental, moral, and spiritual uplift" is hard to recognize. "After the Race" portrays capitalism in the spirit of *Rerum Novarum*, Pope Leo XIII's encyclical of 1891, which dealt with the Industrial Revolution and the importance of a just wage. In "A Painful Case," James Duffy instructs the reader with a negative example of Wordsworthian-Nietzschean solitude. And after adopting the Englishness of "Smith," the young boy in "An Encounter" returns posthaste to the mores of his upbringing.[53] When he is accosted by a perverted litterateur in a vacant field, his sudden dependency upon his poor Irish companion shows him that he has been guilty of pride. The "queer old josser" pleads for sympathy, and it is carefully withheld: ". . .and his voice . . . grew almost affectionate and seemed to plead with me that I should understand him."[54] Throughout *Dubliners* one finds, for better or worse, a strong sense of tribal community and moral rules. It is unsurprising that "An Encounter" closely follows an event that took place in the lives of Joyce and his brother.[55]

The paralysis is partly lifted in "The Dead." The Misses Morkan are generous and good-hearted hostesses, despite their being spinsters with a small view of the world. Gabriel upholds "the tradition of genuine warm-hearted courteous Irish hospitality,"[56] despite his mixed motives for doing so. And though he sees its weaknesses, his speech in praise of the Morkans is loving and sentimental without being maudlin. Most people hearing a similarly warm, thoughtful, and entertaining speech in such a setting would relish it.[57] In the Dublin of *Ulysses*, where Joyce subjects the use of *we* to imposing if not impossible levels of skepticism (e.g. 7.37 and 10.878), Gabriel's "we have gathered together under this hospitable roof"[58] would be more vulnerable.

Eliot cites "The Dead" as a work of Catholic sensibility.[59] Certainly the language of the tale is a texture of Catholic allusions from start to finish, and the rhythms of gathering, feasting, and remembrance are liturgical. The closing epiphany is fully modernizing, however. Struck by pity for Gretta, Gabriel experiences a charitable broadening of his sympathies. But though he weeps "[g]enerous tears," his final vision is beautiful and cold: a catharsis of snow. It is faithful to Joyce's discussion of tragedy in his

"Paris Notebook," as well as to Stephen's definition: "the tragic emotion is static . . . The mind is arrested and raised above desire and loathing."[60] Though I would hesitate to call it a "secular illumination," Gabriel's epiphany differs in kind from the warm catharsis of a high mass or a full-blooded tragic drama.[61] So I agree to a point with Eliot, but what I hear is the fading music of Catholic tradition.

There are signs in *Ulysses* that the imagination is inadequate for the moral work that Joyce asks it to do. One of these signs is that the moral imagination places a greater burden on the individual than it places on society as a whole. Shakespeare, for example, is the artist par excellence, who "found in the world without as actual what was in his world within as possible" (9.1041). Stephen goes on to explain: "We walk through ourselves, meeting robbers, ghosts, giants, old men, young men, wives, widows, brothers-in-love, but always meeting ourselves" (9.1044). This general situation, which Stephen dramatizes and exaggerates, will tend to favor expressive types – e.g. artists, critics, and journalists – and leave others at a disadvantage. Joyce had praised Ibsen for his "large insight, artistic restraint, and sympathy." A society of Ibsens would be a society of equals. It would turn its law courts, schools, and churches into theaters, galleries, and opera houses. In Ibsen Land, art and ethics are halves of a sympathetic whole. In Ireland, however, sympathy is not necessarily in keeping with large insight and artistic restraint – often it has quite the opposite effect, as in Gerty's imaginings of Bloom. And though Bloom's sympathetic powers exceed Gerty's in dignity and scope, his capacity for insight is of a lower order than Joyce's.

The odd fact is that Leopold Bloom would not understand Joyce's novel.[62] Artistic genius, which is Joyce's leading virtue in the Nietzschean sense of virtue, has little correlative in Bloom; and Bloom's essential "poldyness" is a far cry from Joyce's greatness. We cannot understand *Ulysses* on the basis of Gerty's sentimental reverie of Bloom, though we can understand the *Lady's Pictorial* (13.151). We cannot understand *Ulysses* on the basis of Bloom's sympathy for Stephen, though we can understand First Corinthians: "Love is patient; love is kind; love is not envious or boastful or arrogant or rude. It does not insist on its own way; it is not irritable or resentful . . ." (13:4–5 NSRV). Saints do not have to be artists; they do not even have to be critics.

More philosophically, Joyce's difficulties with pity or sympathy can be explained in terms of a divergence of views between the ancient and the modern world. In the *Electra*, Euripides has Orestes say that pity is found only among the wise, never among the ignorant. For Aristotle, pity "may be defined as a feeling of pain caused by the sight of some evil . . . which befalls one who does not deserve it, and which might be expected to befall ourselves or some friend of ours. . ." (*Rhet.* 1385b13). Justice, friendship, and other virtues help govern the magnitude of pity. Without the virtues, pity is diminished.

Pity in the modern tradition operates through the individual will, which has no rational tie to knowledge and wisdom.[63] And even if we tether the individual will to reason, other problems arise. Here, for example, is a standard critique of Kant: "The doctrine of the categorical imperative provides me with a test for rejecting proposed maxims: it does not tell me whence I am to derive the maxims which first prove the need for a test. Thus the Kantian doctrine is parasitic upon some already existing morality . . ."[64] So it stands to reason, that inasmuch as pity is learned, inasmuch as it depends for its survival on the virtues, which depend in turn on the moral work of generations, pity will mutate with the mores of society. There is a mediating role for habits and usages to play with respect to sympathy – a role Joyce does not allow for. He and Bloom are both too isolated for their own good.

A second sign of the moral imagination's inadequacy is the Cartesian divide it opens between mind and body. Certainly Joyce affirms the goodness of bodies. But he does not affirm the specific goodness of the *human* body. Ellmann, it might be rejoined, argues persuasively that Joyce overcame the mind-body division. In the Introduction to his biography, he writes that Joyce's "brutes show a marvellous capacity for brooding, his pure minds show bodies remorselessly stuck to them." But it is jarring for an Aristotelian to think of bodies as "remorselessly stuck" to pure minds. Ellmann goes on to say that Joyce "never" holds mind and body apart.[65]

What does this amount to in practice? In the *Portrait*, the dreamlike movement of Stephen's consciousness is at times directed unconsciously by the experience of his body, as when Stephen feels the onset of sickness at Clongowes while remembering "the white look of the lavatory": "He felt cold and then a little hot: and he could see the names printed on the cocks. That was a very queer thing."[66] In *Ulysses*, the stream of consciousness likewise floats atop a somatic report of pleasure, pain, and movement. The body and mind interact like partners in dialogue, which is by turns dreamy or comical. The partners are a bit like Siamese twins. They are not integrated. When Bloom is repulsed by the "dirty eaters" (8. 696) of the Burton restaurant, Joyce registers a vivid account of the proceedings in Bloom's mind:

His gorge rose.

Couldn't eat a morsel here. Fellow sharpening knife and fork to eat all before him, old chap picking his tootles. Slight spasm, full, chewing the cud. Before and after. Grace after meals. Look on this picture then on that. Scoffing up stewgravy with sopping sippets of bread. Lick it off the plate, man! Get out of this. (8. 672)

No one can doubt that, as Bloom observes the action in the restaurant, his body is present. His gorge rises, and the narrator goes on to describe him "tightening the wings of his nose." But the unreality of the stream of consciousness method – by which I refer to the bare fact that Bloom's interior monologue does not provide an accurate model of the mind – emerges precisely from Joyce's treatment of the interaction between mind and body. In reality, the more that physical habit weighs on a decision, the fewer conscious thoughts the decision tends to require. We conserve mental energy through our habits and routines. Joyce's hyperliteracy in effect denies this natural conservation. To judge from the intense wordiness of his cogitations, one would think that Bloom had never experienced a bad restaurant, a place that discloses itself with countless pre-verbal clues that compete with the greedy eye. In the abstract fashion imagined by Hume, Bloom appears to be encountering the billiard balls of life for the first time.

Bloom's mastery over Bella shows the mind's mastery over the body. It is an exercise of "willpower" (15. 3216) that results from a train of thought about female sexuality. The problem is not that Bloom engages the will: virtue, being an activity, also engages the will. But virtue does not engage the will in a vacuum. It is as if Bloom must each and every day recognize the tremendous fact of woman's carnal nature in order to resist Circe. There will always be Circes, and there will always be pathetic fops who worship Venus in furs. But the mature political animal settles into productive habits and a way of life – and hypocrisy is the bow that vice makes to virtue.

The most serious sign of the moral imagination's native frailty is its susceptibility to advertising rhetoric. Dublin in 1904 was experiencing "the age of the great shops and great advertisers," which started in London in the 1880s, and saw the growth of a mass culture and a mass mind.[67] Looking at the social impact of modern capitalism, MacIntyre suggests that if we detach "our affections and our market relationships from their traditional moral background," then "each becomes a source of vice: on the one hand a romantic and sentimental overvaluation of feeling as such, on the other a reduction of human activity to economic activity."[68] The

Blooms lend support to this thesis. For much of his day, Leopold alternates between market activity and his sentimental alias "Henry Flower, Esquire." Molly turns from the consumer paradise to a sentimental image of herself as "a flower of the mountain" (18.1576).

Does Joyce, while trying to show the riches of the authentic self and its power to love, neglect the ways in which capital and technology deplete that self? Applying Marxist analysis to "Penelope," Joseph Heininger concludes: "when Molly appropriates the floral image from the reified products of the cultural marketplace, she validates her personal history and its continuity with the present."[69] Heininger refers to Molly's act of "resistance to the spectacle of consumption" as an act that "decolonizes her mind and body."[70] By contrast, the Beckett of *Endgame* and *Happy Days* makes the point, as pessimistically as possible, that people have no freedom left to "appropriate" the "reified products of the cultural market-place." In Molly's case, the case of a fairly average person without an abundance of moral and intellectual virtues, such products will tend to validate her, not vice versa. "Flower of the Mountain" might be a perfume in Winnie's black bag. Though I do not agree with Beckett or his critic Adorno in their very grim assessments of middle-class life, I think that they see truths that Joyce overlooks.

Jennifer Wicke has less faith than Heininger in utopian resistance. By giving Adorno a kind of happy face, she builds a case for *Ulysses* as Bible of the self-aware status quo: "It is . . . the universe of consumption *Ulysses* takes up aesthetically, and the . . . divide we are ready to make between consumable goods and rarefied literature is a distinction *Ulysses* does not want to make . . ." Is this quite true? Doesn't Joyce intend us to subordinate the *Lady's Pictorial* to *Ulysses*?[71] Wicke continues: "In so saliently replicating the intricate mechanisms of consumption. . ., *Ulysses* prompts us to see . . . our attitudes toward consumption . . . Joyce can teach us how we have been performing the work of consumption all our lives."[72] Of course it is just the way in which Joyce goes about "replicating the intricate mechanisms of consumption" that separates him from lesser talents. And as for "how we have been performing the work of consumption all of our lives," we may feel that *consumption* is a dehumanizing idol of jargon. But give Wicke her due. She can derive her materialist lesson from Joyce's romantic irony, which, by ushering the individual into the subjective void, exempts the individual from standards of taste. So Joyce, the prince of prose, prepares the way for Howard Stern, the "King of All Media," who is "shifting his salacious act to satellite radio and freeing himself from the increasingly harsh glare of federal regulators."[73] To escape the "harsh glare" of the state, King Howard launches his disembodied voice into the void of space, enthroning himself in "the universe of consumption," where Newtonian physics and the media and the cash nexus are one.

When it operates on individual desires at the expense of all else, the free market lends itself to the pleasure calculus of utilitarianism. Joyce, though he is not especially capitalistic, is quasi-utilitarian. To conceive with Freud, "Before born babe bliss had" (14. 60), is to equalize bliss and pleasure. Much the same kind of leveling effect happens in commercial advertising:

> *What is home without*
> *Plumtree's Potted Meat?*
> *Incomplete.*
> *With it an abode of bliss.*
> (5.144)

This is very witty in its Irish dark and doggerel way. "Plumtree's Potted Meat" might bud and flower in *The Waste Land*, and heaven is fed by corpses. But to a reader of Leopold Bloom's virtues and talents, the ad bankrupts the good that supports the nobler meaning of "bliss." And without the nobler meaning, there is no practical difference between "home" and exile, for if it does not harbor some good that the exile desires, "home" is itself exilic and "incomplete." Why would Ulysses return? Why pity the homeless?

Joyce asserts his modernity by making the good life for man an artistic question, which cannot be answered from a public standpoint.[74] More, he provides an example of how the good life works. To borrow David Bromwich's fine phrase about Whitman, he gives "a social definition of self-trust."[75] But having invested too much in the fundamentally mistaken anthropology that extends from Hobbes, Locke, and Rousseau to Nietzsche and to Freud, he is prodigal of freedom, which is naturally much rarer than uranium. He writes *Ulysses* on a *tabula rasa* where human nature is scraped clean. And that is why the self on the model of the Blooms has an autonomy, I should almost say a grace, that is largely imagined. It is untouched by the market's worst seductions. It is safe from the speed and power with which technology and profiteering combine to plunder the Muses.

In his 1903 review of *Aristotle on Education*, a compilation by John Burnet, Joyce dismisses the *Nicomachean Ethics* as "the weak part of the peripatetic philosophy" and readily dispatches the *Politics*: "Individualism, it would seem, is not easily recommended to the Greek mind, and in giving his theory of education Aristotle has endeavoured to recruit for a Greek state rather than to give a final and absolute solution to questions of the greatest interest."[76] Joyce prized Aristotle for his metaphysics and aesthetics; Burnet's exposition of "the practical requirements of the community" had no appeal to the young Dubliner.[77] It happens that Burnet did not excerpt the passages from the *Politics* where Aristotle warns against the infection of corrupting greed: "The origin of this disposition in men is that they are intent upon living only, and not upon living well; and, as their desires are unlimited, they also desire that the means of gratifying them should be without limit" (1257b41). The Athenians were a famously acquisitive people. Aristotle, who philosophized against communism (e.g. 1263b15), was forceful as well in his critique of rabid consumerism: "Some men turn every quality or art into a means of getting wealth; this they conceive to be the end, and to the promotion of the end they think all things must contribute" (1258a10–15). Bloom has no "disposition" to be greedy. Human nature is transformed in him to serve Joyce's vision of a better world. And yet he goes to bed "habitually" thinking about advertising (17.1769). His lack of greed is nothing short of miraculous.

CHAPTER 4

Virginia Woolf: Antigone triumphant

Woolf is the only English person under consideration in this book, so it is fitting here to take a moment to consider the English historical background of the ethics of modernism – a background that affected everyone else. In "Mr. Bennett and Mrs. Brown," Woolf cites Samuel Butler's *Way of All Flesh* (written 1872–84, published 1903) as a herald of the "change in religion, conduct, politics, and literature" that she marks with the date December, 1910.[1] The novel's hero, Ernest Pontifex, is born in 1835, the same year as Butler, and his unhappy experiences open up a brutally satirical perspective on Victorian morality. Ernest's very name is a jab at Thomas Arnold's ideal of earnestness. The narrator Overton, who is Ernest's godfather, describes the young man's puzzlement after the ruin of his ill-advised marriage:

What was morality worth if it was not that which on the whole brought a man peace at the last . . .? It seemed to [Ernest] that in his attempt to be moral he had been following a devil which had disguised itself as an angel of light. But if so, what ground was there on which a man might rest the sole of his foot and tread in reasonable safety?[2]

Butler supplies his own version of the transvaluation of values: the "angel of light" is a "devil" in disguise. Blasting the hypocritical arrangements of marriage and family, he lays bare the meanness of respectability. His iconoclasm foreshadows Woolf's later attacks upon the Victorians. Most important, *The Way of All Flesh* broadcasts the signs of a cultural debacle: England's faltering belief in its institutions, and the waning of its immemorial customs.

    G. M. Young, the eminent historian of the Victorian age, observes that after 1830 England began to lose its Evangelical religion, "a creed which was at once the basis of its morality and the justification of its wealth and power."[3] The Evangelical faith in the Bible, in the divinity of Christ, buckled under the pressure of science and the Higher Criticism. At the same time, the traditions of agricultural life succumbed to the industrial economy of booming cities, where Christianity had little direct impact on the masses.[4] (It was, incidentally, the incipient welfare state and its bureaucracy that would increasingly minister to the myriad problems facing this new public; Woolf's female characters often partake of the new social consciousness.) Butler directs his most ferocious satire at the fraying Evangelical crust of his family. The hero's siblings are prigs. His parents, dull-witted sadists. But he condemns almost everyone he comes in contact with. Teachers, churchmen, parents, Londoners, the lot: lying rogues. If we locate it in the history of ethics, *The Way of All Flesh* testifies to the truth of "Hume's law." It had become impossible for Ernest – and difficult for his nonfictional contemporaries – to derive an "ought" from an "is."[5]

The Way of All Flesh appeared in 1903, which is also the date of *Principia Ethica*, the major work by G. E. Moore and another monument in Woolf's intellectual landscape. In effect, *Principia Ethica* offered a way to overcome the fact-value dichotomy in Hume's law. The way was private, a refuge from the mummery of Victorian life. But its aesthetic possibilities were impressive, and by no means limited to satire.

In *Principia Ethica*, Moore grants wide authority to independent-minded aesthetes, discriminating individuals who can recognize the presence of good by themselves, without the cues of convention. The central idea is Moore's view of goodness as a non-natural, non-analyzable property, like yellow.[6] "Good," he writes, "has no definition because it is simple and has no parts,"[7] the words "simple" and "simply" receiving considerable emphasis throughout. Moore thinks of goodness as attaching itself through consciousness to the beings and things of the common world. For disciples of Moore, it can be said that either you see goodness, or you don't. Because goodness cannot be defined in terms of any other property, no one individual has rational authority over another's intuition of goodness. How were disputes settled? "In practice," writes John Maynard Keynes, "victory was with those who could speak with the greatest appearance of clear, undoubting conviction and could best use the accents of infallibility."[8]

Lytton Strachey believed that Moore had "shattered" Aristotle.[9] It is a judgment worth judging, for its influence both on Woolf and on the school of analytic philosophy that Moore helped establish. When Moore accuses Aristotle of the "naturalistic fallacy," one can reply that naturalistic ethics is alive and well. When Moore accuses Aristotle of reliance on unthinking habit, one can reply that a virtue "must actually engage the will."[10] But it is harder to dismiss Moore's perception of a fatal divide in

Aristotle between the practical happiness of virtuous activity and the divine happiness of the life of the mind. Why live ethically if the ethical life has nothing to do with our true goal, the joys of *theoria*?

If there is an answer to this potentially devastating argument, it lies in the lived nature of Aristotle's ethics. I imagine that Aristotle experienced the hard weight of practical affairs, and that he met few if any pure, joyous contemplatives. He was an administrator and a teacher who knew that students need the virtues to prepare them for the activities of *theoria*, and that good families and good governments are therefore indispensable. I imagine, further, that Aristotle had enjoyed unforgettable hours in a state of philosophical rapture, and that these divine moments co-existed in memory with his everyday perspective, broadening his view and inspiring his effort. I think this god-haunted condition is at least recognizably human. "But the suspicion remains," argues J. L. Ackrill, "that a man who believed in the supreme importance of some absolute could not continue to live in much the same way as others."[11] The remark applies to martyrs of art who locate the absolute in their work. It applies to saints. But Ackrill misses something that Aristotle would immediately have grasped, namely, the tragic possibilities of Ackrill's own argument. If we admit tragic conflict, we can see that Aristotle speaks to the tragic souls of civilized people.

Rarely, in any case, has intellectual violence worn such impeccable airs as it does in *Principia Ethica*. The author's tone of pipe-smoking superiority and crushing logical precision is reminiscent of Sherlock Holmes. Moore writes, "The inference that, if virtue includes in its meaning 'good in itself,' then Aristotle's definition of virtue is not adequate and expresses a false ethical judgment, is perfectly correct: only the premiss that virtue does include this in its meaning is mistaken."[12] In other words, Aristotle's false argument was itself erected on a false foundation. Elementary, my dear Lytton!

Moore's allure was not only violent, it was utopian. He was apocalyptic, dust-binning the Greeks, while ordaining "a new heaven and a new earth."[13] At the heart of his ethical project was his aesthetic creed: "No one, probably, who has asked himself the question, has ever doubted that personal affection and the appreciation of what is beautiful in Art or Nature, are good in themselves . . ."[14] If you want goodness, according to Moore, you must devote yourself to certain states of mind, for the beauties of art and nature and society are "good in themselves" only in a limited way. Their true goodness blossoms in the "complex wholes" of consciousness:

[The] mere existence of what is beautiful has value, so small as to be negligible, in comparison with what attaches to the *consciousness* of beauty. This simple truth . . . is the ultimate and fundamental truth of Moral Philosophy. That it is only for the sake of these things [i.e. what is beautiful in Art and Nature] – in order that as much as possible of them may at some time exist – that anyone can be justified in performing any public or private duty; that they are the *raison d'être* of virtue; that it is they, these complex wholes themselves, . . . that form the rational ultimate end of human action and the sole criterion of social progress: these appear to be truths which have been generally overlooked.

That they are truths – that personal affections and aesthetic enjoyments include *all* the greatest, and *by far* the greatest, goods we can imagine, will, I hope, appear more plainly . . . All the things, which I have meant to include under the above descriptions, are highly complex *organic unities*.[15]

For all intents and purposes, Moore puts Pater's aestheticism on the footing of a utilitarian ethics.[16] Like Pater, he directs consciousness toward maximum beauty. Unlike Pater, he believes it our duty to work for the greater good, but he views this good along the lines of Pater's higher ethics. It will be recalled that Pater contrasted the machinery of Aristotle with "the intangible perfection of those whose ideal is rather in *being* than in *doing*." Pater's "intangible perfection" is the forerunner of Moore's conscious good. Moore bridges the gap between doing and being by making the former ("human action") a mechanical means to the latter.

Woolf undertook an extensive study of *Principia Ethica* in 1908, and came to know its author personally through her brother Thoby's circle at Trinity College, Cambridge.[17] Decades later, she asked her niece if she had read "the book that made us all so wise and good: *Principia Ethica*."[18] There is humor in the question, but no one should doubt that Moore's ethics has an important relation to Woolf's art.[19] She was the daughter of a moral philosopher of note, Leslie Stephen. Her novels abound with philosophical references. She could read Greek. When she faulted Dickens for having no philosophy, she was clearly implying her own philosophical superiority.[20]

The Aristotle that emerges from Moore's pages is a moralizing sham. In the same spirit of ridicule, Woolf exposes the virtue-mongering Sir William Bradshaw, the moralist who spiritually executes Septimus Smith in *Mrs. Dalloway*. Smith repeatedly refers to both his doctors, Bradshaw and Holmes, as "human nature." Moore unmasks Aristotle, as Woolf unmasks Bradshaw and Holmes: they are physicians who invoke "human nature" to bolster an oppressive social order. In *Jacob's Room*, Jacob discovers that the Greek solution to "the problems of civilization . . . is no help to us."[21] "Aristotle" is demoted to a grubby inn-keeper, "a dirty man, carnivorously interested in the body . . ."[22] Like Moore, his fellow Cantabrigian, Jacob has no use for the *Nicomachean Ethics*: "Indeed there has never been any explanation of the ebb and flow in our veins – of happiness and unhappiness."[23]

In *A Room of One's Own*, Woolf adopts Moore's precept of aesthetic duty: "There runs through these comments and discursions the conviction – or is it the instinct? – that good writers, even if they show every variety of human depravity, are still good human beings. Thus when I ask you to write more books I am urging you to do what will be for your good and for the good of the world at large."[24] By Aristotelian standards, her position is sophistical. "We believe good men more fully and more readily than others . . .," says Aristotle (*Rhet.* 1356a), and we know good men by their character. But if good is a non-natural property attaching itself to consciousness, then its existence is not tied to the Aristotelian body.

We can see the fruition of being, as opposed to doing, in Woolf's description of Orlando:

There was something strange in the shadow that the flicker of her eyes cast, something . . . one trembles to pin through the body with a name and call beauty, for it has no body, is a shadow and without substance or quality of its own, yet has the power to change whatever it adds itself to . . . This shadow . . . stole out, and attaching itself to the innumerable sights she had been receiving, composed them into something tolerable, comprehensible.[25]

Woolf in this passage beautifies Moore's non-natural theory of goodness. In fact her only philosophical revision is to have "beauty" become the key term. Moore's idea of the "complex wholes" of heightened consciousness is present in the experience of composition that the narrator relates. Along the same lines, *The Voyage Out* concludes with a description of a unifying pattern in the mind of the gifted St. John Hirst (whose beautiful friend Helen Ambrose reads the *Principia Ethica*): "The movements and the voices seemed to draw together from different parts of the room, and to combine themselves into a pattern before his eyes; he was content to sit silently watching the pattern build itself up, looking at what he hardly saw."[26] Like Orlando, St. John is a vessel, an impersonal bearer of the world-as-art, which fills his mind as a complex "pattern."

It was Moore who inspired Woolf to write, "we are the words; we are the music; we are the thing itself."[27] Rebelling against idealism, Moore argued that words and music are concepts (like goodness and beauty) that attach to the entity of consciousness, which is the thing itself, the real world.[28] Without Moore's influence, "the aesthetic ethics of cultural dissent," as one critic describes *Three Guineas*, would not have emerged as we know it.[29] Moore immeasurably heightened Woolf's moral reach, bringing the authority of ethical discourse into the private realm of aesthetic consciousness, including the lyrical dementia, the apocalyptic derangement of the senses, that recurs throughout her *oeuvre*. "Is it really obvious," asks Moore, "that health, for instance, is a good? Was the excellence of Socrates or of Shakespeare normal?"[30] Pater's triumph over Arnold was already complete.

Like Moore, Woolf wants to break through the Cartesian partition between self and world, and so attain an immediate perception of the goodness and beauty in things.[31] Like Moore, she defies the limits of her own Cartesianism. How can emotion fit into an non-naturalist theory of goodness and beauty?[32] To follow Moore, it does so mentally. He thinks that, *a priori*, a finely-tuned set of emotional responses waits like a harp in the mind to be plucked by the fingers of beauty:

It is perhaps the case that all aesthetic emotions have some common quality; but it is certain that differences in the emotion seem to be appropriate to differences in the kind of beauty perceived: and by saying that different emotions are *appropriate* to different kinds of beauty, we mean that the whole which is formed by the consciousness of that kind of beauty *together with* the emotion appropriate to it, is better than if any other emotion had been felt in contemplating that particular beautiful object.[33]

Moore does not clarify how the aesthetic emotion is known to be appropriate, except that it contributes to the maximum of beauty and goodness under the circumstances of perception. He is not anti-social, but he omits the role of culture in shaping aesthetic appreciation. At the end of *The Voyage Out*, St. John experiences a "feeling of profound happiness" in the manner that Moore prescribes: an emotion of pleasure attaches itself as part of the organic whole of his rich consciousness.[34] The emotion is confined to the mental realm. Like Orlando, St. John experiences Moore's aesthetic version of *eudaimonia*, a disembodied maximum of goodness and beauty.

Though Woolf applied Moore's theory of appropriate emotions to her fiction, she could not anchor it to reality. "The novel as a whole," she says in *A Room of One's Own*, ". . . is a structure leaving a shape on the mind's eye, built now in squares, now pagoda shaped, now throwing out wings and arcades, now solidly compact and domed like the Cathedral of Saint Sofia at Constantinople. This shape . . . starts in one the kind of emotion that is appropriate to it."[35] (Compare Moore: "beauty *together with* the emotion appropriate to it . . .") But why should we respond with appropriate emotions to abstract shapes? For Woolf, we only respond to that rare thing, a successful novel. Such books weather the fiercest scrutiny, she says, "for Nature seems, very oddly, to have provided us with an inner light by which to judge of the novelist's integrity or disintegrity."[36] A novelist of integrity, a Tolstoy, will compass the emotional effect. But as for the provision of Nature – by way of an inner light – for a judgment of formal integrity and the appropriate emotion, Woolf is at a loss. She juggles with "seems" and "very oddly." The whole process, from the "squares" onward, is an enchanting fog. The problem is that, at bottom, "Nature" (as in "the appreciation of what is beautiful in Art or Nature") cannot be made to serve a non-naturalist appreciation of form. It is a problem inherent in Moore.[37] Realism in the novel, in Tolstoy for example, demands its emotional due from the body, regardless of formal structures and complex wholes.

Moore's influence on Woolf, though profound, is not the last word on her ethics. It fits into a larger ethics of authenticity, outlined in "Modern Fiction" with the terms "spirit," "utmost sincerity," "free will," and "saintliness." This ethics of authenticity connects Woolf's literature to her feminist politics and the church of Judith Shakespeare. No doubt Woolf can be apolitical. She expresses her distaste for novels that push the reader "to join a society, or, more desperately, to write a cheque."[38] In *Three Guineas*, she says, "if we use art to propagate political opinions, we must force the artist to clip and cabin his gift to do us a cheap and passing service. Literature will suffer the same mutilation that the mule has suffered; and there will be no more horses."[39] But few will argue the point if I refer to Woolf as a feminist author. There is something deeply "contradictory," to quote Lily Briscoe's musings, in what Woolf does. The progressive impulse pulls toward a post-Christian spiritualizing feminism, while, conversely, the stated refusal to "preach doctrines"[40] pulls toward a more purely artistic interest. Lily as feminist transforms Mrs. Ramsay according to her "vision." Lily as artist pursues "the razor edge of balance between two opposite forces,"[41] the eternal balance of male and female, youth and age, birth and death, for art enjoins a changeless – by degree Johnsonian, stoical, and Indic – doctrine of human nature and fate. By giving imagination a purchase on the essence of things, Moore's philosophy helps Woolf accommodate her contradictions, giving her means to reconcile her feminist politics and her artistic conscience.

In "Modern Fiction," Woolf's signature move is to approach her subject aesthetically: "Life is not a series of gig-lamps symmetrically arranged; life is a luminous halo, a semi-transparent envelope surrounding us from the beginning of consciousness to the end."[42] Woolf sees "life" in terms of light, form, and consciousness, and in her eagerness to see it that way, she presumes what she intends to prove. It is painterly to describe "life" as "a series of gig-lamps symmetrically arranged." Life is not an aesthetic phenomenon – unless you are an aesthete. To define it as a "luminous halo" is to open up a realm of disembodied freedom, where the spirit navigates an opalescent atmosphere, unstained by earthly creatures. Though she deploys a fine syntax and appeals to the common reader, Woolf's fight against "materialism," against the plot of the body and the conventions that attend it, is not a negotiation among powers, but a radical change in direction. In her aesthetic soaring, she redefines, or undefines, both art and man: "the infinite possibilities of the art" insure that "there is no limit to the horizon, and that nothing – no 'method,' no experiment, even of the wildest – is forbidden, only falsity and pretence."[43] Her aesthetic consciousness is a revolutionary will, remaking human reality as it purifies the mind.

This transformative labor is metaphysical: Woolf wants to reinvent what art is and to alter the terms of its reception. She makes use of Pater's "*Anders-streben*,"[44] overlapping effects from different arts, in order to open world and mind to a multiform apprehension that human beings cannot experience in nature.[45] She is a painterly writer, who brings the spatial dimension of the canvas to the temporal procedures of the novel. She is devoted to the musical qualities of language, to the nonsensical harmonies of pure sound. But I have not issued onto the familiar territory of Woolf's formalism just for review. I want to reinstate what has been lost to view: the way in which formalism overcomes human nature.

Woolf's characters shuttle between nature and non-nature, mimesis and abstract form, as Woolf confronts the divide between realism and formalism that occupies her in *A Room of One's Own*. They imitate reality through action, and, as modernist bodies, they populate the organic whole of the aesthetic consciousness. Forgetting the purpose of his trip to London (he is "in love" with a woman named Daisy), Peter Walsh encounters his old flame Clarissa at the end of *Mrs. Dalloway* with the "terror" and ecstacy" of decades earlier. He loses track of his own plot, as "life" brings him full circle. But Peter is not entirely plotless. Adrift on a June day in London, he would be indecipherable without his sketches from memory, involving Richard, Sally Seton, Hugh Whitbread, and others. And Peter gives us more than sketches. He is deft at locating, in the midst of his stream of memories and associations, the characteristic actions of people, like Sally Seton running naked through a hall or Richard's silent rowing. So the novel is like a highly complex state of consciousness, but the likeness breaks down when mimesis intrudes with its weather of physical emotions. Peter is abstracted from his own plot in favor of his formal contribution to the novel's organic unity. But his particularity depends on mimesis, on character sketches in linear time.

Woolf heeds the revelations of the unconscious emanating from Freud, Proust, and Bergson, all of whom denied the bourgeois rationality of character that she found typified in the novels of Wells, Bennett, and Galsworthy. Lily pursues a "common feeling" through time, a singular "wholeness" where the scattered "elements of things" are gathered into one of "those globed compacted things over which thought lingers, and love plays."[46] But Woolf goes only so far in her spatialization of time, with *The Waves* marking the high tide of experiment. Countless episodes of action, luminous vignettes, enhance the pages of *To the Lighthouse*, including the sustained realism of the great seventeenth section of Part One, the wonderfully moving dinner scene. Characters are too ghostly, too unreal, if they remain unacted potentialities. Human beings take definition from time. Augustus Carmichael's bowing to Mrs. Ramsay is indispensable. Likewise, even as Woolf explores the depths of the mind, practical wisdom is not alien to her characters' lives. It remains a background, like Richard Dalloway and his Austenesque paternalism.

As a higher self, Lily is released from the narrative demands of a typical life into a life of art. When she returns to the Ramsay house after Mrs. Ramsay's death, she feels "Nothing, nothing – nothing that she could express at all."[47] Why on earth is she there? Her character, her wants and her purposes, would be absurdly inscrutable, except for her art. Lily's immediate self-withdrawal intensifies the conflict between nature and formalism in the novel:

Sitting alone . . . among the clean cups at the long table, she felt cut off from other people, and able only to go on watching, asking, wondering. The house, the place, the morning, all seemed strangers to her. She had no attachment here, she felt, no relations with it, anything might happen, and whatever did happen, a step outside, a voice calling ("It's in the cupboard; it's on the landing," some one cried), was a question, as if the link that usually bound things together had been cut, and they floated up here, down there, off, anyhow. How aimless it was, how chaotic, how unreal it was, she thought, looking at her empty coffee cup.[48]

Unreality, a whispering undercurrent in *Mrs. Dalloway*, emerges as a full-blown metaphysical mantra in *To the Lighthouse*. Lily is able to resolve the tension between realism and formalism by rendering reality *unreal*. Endlessly ambiguous, unreality is the frontier of absolute freedom. It is an affront to the positivism of Mr. Ramsay (and of Leslie Stephen). But while unreality throws doubts on appearances, it admits the possibility of an ultimate pattern beyond them. Unreality imbues Lily's perceptions with the ghostly tincture of a hidden absolute or metaphysical reality, while dissolving the world of habit with a revelation or "shock," to quote *Moments of Being*.[49] Unreality is a dimension where the self, for the sake of its own authenticity, breaks from "falsity and pretence." Like fairyland, unreality is a realm of artistic power. It is a domain where no law in any language, social or scientific, can check the artist's will.

Lily is authentic in Pater's sense of refusing to allow "the sacrifice of any part of . . . experience, in consideration of some interest into which we cannot enter." She is authentic in side-stepping the demands of plot – in life as in art. But though she allows no one to clip and cabin her, she parlays her personal authenticity into authority over the lives of others, in particular, Mrs. Ramsay. Lily's painting of Mrs. Ramsay harbors a moral judgment:

She remembered how William Bankes had been shocked by her neglect of the significance of mother and son. Did she not admire their beauty? he said. But William, she remembered, had listened to her with his wise child's eyes when she explained how it was not irreverence: how a light there needed a shadow there and so on. She did not intend to disparage a subject which, they agreed, Raphael had treated divinely. She was not cynical. Quite the contrary. Thanks to his scientific mind he understood – a proof of disinterested intelligence which had pleased her and comforted her enormously. One could talk of painting then seriously to a man. Indeed, his friendship had been one of the pleasure of her life. She loved William Bankes.[50]

When Lily removed all mimetic reference to Mrs. Ramsay's son James from the painting, William was a bit "shocked." But Lily does not identify with the Madonna and Child, the subject of Raphael. The artist gives birth to art, not to children. Her iconoclasm is an assertion of ethical self-consciousness that Woolf sees fit to repeat, to engrain in the memory of the reader by describing the scene in "The Window" and remembering it in "The Lighthouse." It is an ethical self-consciousness that refuses Mrs. Ramsay's individuality, and that of her son, for it refuses to be limited by the existence of others, and chooses its own freedom. In translating Mrs. Ramsay onto canvas, Lily elides what is generally the most crucial of all human relationships, the foundation of all relationships to follow. Her painting holds not only religious but also the deepest political and historical significance. Even the freedom-worshipping Locke, in his advocacy of natural rights, observed that a woman's instinctive bond with her children transcends her self-interest. Through Lily, Woolf dissolves the strongest natural bond in society, and she does so in the name of an aesthetic morality of personal liberation. Since motherhood cannot be unmasked, it must be unmade.

Lily's recollection of her original scene with William Bankes takes place in a highly suggestive context. It comes directly after her reflections on Paul Rayley and the "fire" of love: "And the roar and the crackle repelled her with fear and disgust, as if while she saw its splendour and power she saw too how it fed on the treasure of the house, greedily, disgustingly, and she loathed it. But for a sight, for a glory it surpassed everything in her experience."[51] It is certainly not a "glory" that Lily cares to experience more personally or to exalt in her art. In the book's final transformations and unfoldings, her friendship with William the scientist eclipses Paul Rayley's passion for Minta the charmer. And as critic Gabriel Franks has rightly observed, friendships in Woolf "are the half-aetherial sort envisaged by Moore as such important building blocks in the construction of the Ideal," i.e. the best possible world.[52] "Half-aetherial" not only because Lily and William share an aesthetic approach to life, but because Lily, the blessed virgin of the new dispensation, has a sexless rapport with William, who "always left her . . . plenty of time to wash her hands."[53] The successive paragraphs form a triptych: Paul's ideal of physical love; Lily's revising the Madonna and Child; William and Lily's courteous hygiene. The three scenes depict a progressive denaturalizing, from sexual love and maternity to the purities of art and aesthetic friendship.

To understand Lily's transformation of Mrs. Ramsay, one must try to understand the original. She is a most extraordinary melange of signifiers: Victorian sweetheart, loving wife, social worker, saint, Demeter, Aphrodite, Hera, and Madonna. She is Pater's Mona Lisa. She is the Angel in the House. And though she is the devoted wife and mother of many children, she intuits the truth of the post-Victorian dispensation:

She could be herself, by herself. And that was what now she often felt the need of – to think; well, not even to think. To be silent; to be alone. All the being and the doing, expansive, glittering, vocal, evaporated; and one shrunk, with a sense of solemnity, to being oneself, a wedge-shaped core of darkness, something invisible to others. Although she continued to knit, and sat upright, it was thus that she felt herself; and this self having shed its attachments was free for the strangest adventures. When life sank down for a moment, the range of experience seemed limitless. And to everybody there was always this sense of unlimited resources, she supposed; one after another, she, Lily, Augustus Carmichael, must feel, our apparitions, the things you know us by, are simply childish. Beneath it is all dark, it is all spreading, it is unfathomably deep . . . This core of darkness could go anywhere, for no one saw it. They could not stop it, she thought, exulting. There was freedom, there was peace, there was, most welcome of all, a summoning together, a resting on a platform of stability. Not as oneself did one find rest ever, in her experience . . . but as a wedge of darkness. Losing personality, one lost the fret, the hurry, the stir . . .[54]

By all appearances, Mrs. Ramsay affirms the mother, the distaff, the family. But Woolf is transforming the traditional picture, replacing it, much as Lily replaces painterly conventions, with the freedom to be oneself – to be released from one's "personality" into the "stability" of a unified consciousness, "a summoning together." The moment is fateful, and commentators have noted that Mrs. Ramsay's knitting connects her to the Fates. Decisively, then, it is the artists with whom Mrs. Ramsay identifies at this moment, which weaves together past and future. It is morally necessary to the novel that Mrs. Ramsay personally identify with the artists. Otherwise, Lily's transformation of her would be an act of "irreverence" – the concern raised by William Bankes. And it is the artists, Lily and the more mysterious Mr. Carmichael, who realize Woolf's ideal, sacrificing familial ties and affections, in order to salvage the world's goodness and beauty in the transforming vessel of consciousness. Mrs. Ramsay shares the artists' knowledge of the impersonal self as "a wedge-shaped core of darkness." Her phrasing suggests the uterus, the womb or birthspace of a new kind of beauty that is the dialectical negative of her own maternal and fleshy beauty. It also suggests a triangle, one of those forms, like the "dome" Lily associates with Mrs. Ramsay, that leave "a shape on the mind's eye" and contribute to the novel's structure.[55] These forms, triangle and dome, together with their emotional correlatives, are feminine. They contribute to the artist's rendering of a complex, unified aesthetic consciousness, which is itself open to countless perspectives, while the older picture of Mrs. Ramsay knitting is transfigured in Lily's vision.

It can hardly be doubted that Lily alters Mrs. Ramsay to suit her own "vision." She transforms the fleshy maternal woman into a "triangular purple shape."[56] She locates her essence in the "wedge of darkness." For her art's sake, she effaces a child, and converts an individual woman into a stylistic arrangement: an image of her own self-consciousness. Just here, then, is the delicate negotiation between Woolf's spiritualizing feminism and her quasi-classical "balance." And just here Woolf relies on the *Principia Ethica*. Lily's perception of the Second Coming of Mrs. Ramsay is vintage Moore: "Mrs. Ramsay – it was part of her perfect goodness – sat there quite simply, in the chair, flicked her needles to and fro, knitted her reddish-brown stocking, cast her shadow on the step. There she sat."[57]

Such "perfect goodness" exists "quite simply," admitting of no analysis in its ontological purity, while attached to an organic whole of thought and feeling in an act of consciousness. It is art as liturgy and revelation. For disciples of Moore, I have remarked, either you see it, or you don't.

The freedom of unreality ends in violence against the establishment, from God on down the ladder of male hierarchy, through mother and family, and into the prison of human nature. As in Moore, the aesthetic consciousness masks the passions of the will, which aims to transform human reality. But where philosophical generations clash in the name of truth, Woolf represents such violence artistically, under the theme of Oedipal conflict. *To the Lighthouse* opens with a six-year-old boy, scissors in hand, longing to stab his Victorian father. After the deaths of Mrs. Ramsay, Andrew, and Prue, it closes with Lily's re-creating Mrs. Ramsay in Lily's image ("I have had my vision") while James and Cam wage psychological war against Mr. Ramsay. As James realizes in his thoughts of a crushing wheel (Oedipus = "Swellfoot"), the Oedipal victim can be male or female: "So now, when his father came striding down the passage knocking them up early in the morning to go to the Lighthouse down it came over his foot, over Cam's foot, over anybody's foot."[58] Reading the final third of *To the Lighthouse* with Woolf's stomach for unmasking loves and hates, I see scattered traces of an elegy for a vanished world. Mostly I see a revolution of art that exiles the past.[59] Readers of Woolf will remember that "life" is her great subject. "I'm happy like this," Lily reflects. "Life has changed completely."[60] Lily's deference to "life" cannot disguise her active will. Time and the war have changed English life. But for life to change *completely?* That is an event on the order of apocalypse.

The period of Freud's Oedipus Complex was the most Oedipal in modern history. Revolution and war dominated politics. Style overthrew style, philosophy philosophy. The Oedipus Complex is the modernist version par excellence of generational conflict because it minimalizes, denies, or voids the love of parent and child. Giving and receiving, all the primary affections between parent and child, are transformed by the Oedipus Complex into a mask behind which lurk hostility and violence. Accordingly, the "wise child" liberates herself from her parents' moral authority, much as the higher self liberates herself from the plot. The more successful the Oedipal revolt against parent and authority, the more abstract and pure the aesthetic becomes. *The Waves* is the result of this tendency, a highly abstract and lyrically mesmerizing novel whose main characters are effectively parentless.

In *The Years*, through Edward Pargiter's quotation of Sophocles' Greek, Woolf passes the most sweeping judgment against the Victorians by their children in modernist literature. At issue is a compact phrase well known to classicists, line 523 of the *Antigone*. Apparently Sophocles coined the two verbs (*sunekthein* and *sumphilein*) to describe Antigone's feelings toward Creon: "οὔτοι συνέχθειν, ἀλλὰ συμφιλεῖν ἔφυν."[61] John D. B. Hamilton translates: "I was born not to share in hatred, but in 'nearness and dearness.'"[62] Woolf's allusive gesture is, I think, to equate the regime of Creon with the regime of Victoria, setting both regimes of hate against the promise of the "present day." There is no doubt where her sympathies lie.[63] *The Years* is a Manichaean history that records the destruction of the past for the sake of the good. In the chapter "1910," when human character changes, King Edward VII dies, symbolically taking the philandering Colonel Abel Pargiter with him – the last of the Victorians. The portrait of Rose Pargiter, Abel's wife and Eleanor's mother, gathers grime. Like the old-fashioned image of Mrs. Ramsay taking care of her boy, it is effaced. The mother is silenced. Eleanor sells off Pargiter House and gives the boot to old Crosby, still clutching the tokens of her Victorian servitude. Dr. Margaret (Peggy) Pargiter, who is childless like her Aunt Eleanor, will never need to know the horror and the hypocrisy of Pargiter House.[64]

All the while Woolf develops the Oedipal theme in her work, she makes an effort to present the artist as non-violent. The key is her hagiography of Shakespeare. Unlike Joyce, she invests Shakespeare with a power to create unsullied by gender or the neurotic ailments of buried sexuality. Like Jung, she imagines a biological basis for archetypal psychic androgyny. She literalizes Coleridge's poetical dictum "a great mind is androgynous" in order to analyze Shakespeare's "man-womanly mind," said to be "fully fertilised."[65] Her bardolatry centers on Shakespeare's "state of mind . . . when he wrote *Lear* and *Antony and Cleopatra*":

For though we say that we know nothing about Shakespeare's state of mind, even as we say that, we are saying something about Shakespeare's state of mind. The reason perhaps why we know so little of Shakespeare – compared with Donne or Ben Jonson or Milton – is that his grudges and spites and antipathies are hidden from us . . . All desire to protest, to preach, to proclaim an injury, to pay off a score, to make the world a witness of some hardship or grievance was fired out of him and consumed. Therefore his poetry flows from him free and unimpeded. If ever a human being got his work expressed completely, it was Shakespeare. If ever a mind was incandescent, unimpeded, I thought, turning again to the bookcase, it was Shakespeare's mind.[66]

Like the Pantheon, the passage is built in historical layers. First, there is Aristotle: "No activity is perfect when it is impeded [ἐμποδίζηται], and happiness is a perfect thing" (*Nic. Eth.* 1153b16).[67] Second, Sonnet 116 ("Let me not to the marriage of true minds / Admit impediments . . . "), which echoes the Marriage Service. And third, Pater on the alchemy of art: "Few artists . . . work quite cleanly, casting off all *débris*, and leaving us only what the heat of their imagination has wholly fused and trans-formed."[68] Woolf constructs a psychological model for destroying social and philosophical materialism: to follow Shakespeare is to cast off all *débris* from one's "state of mind." In effect, she purifies her ideal artist (Shakespeare) much as Lily purifies herself and Mrs. Ramsay. The artist relinquishes her ego, its "grudges and spites and antipathies," in order to achieve a higher, purer, impersonal self and – along with it – the goodness of art. Her violence therefore has a saintly justification. Woolf chooses an androgynous marriage with her own art, and alters the human brain to support a continual call to self-transcendence.

The novelist Bernard, whose name evokes the mystic St. Bernard of Clairvaux, manifests Woolf's ideal in *The Waves*. The writer's progress on his journey depends on his removing the last stumbling blocks of materi-alist illusion. Bernard can exploit the craft of a Victorian life and letters, but he cannot elude his own self-consciousness:

That is the biographic style, and it does to tack together torn bits of stuff, stuff with raw edges. After all, one cannot find fault with the biographic style if one begins letters 'Dear Sir,' ends them 'yours faithfully'; one cannot despise these phrases laid like Roman roads across the tumult of our lives, since they compel us to walk in step like civilised people with the slow measured tread of policemen though one may be humming any nonsense beneath one's breath at the same time – 'Hark, hark, the dogs do bark,' 'Come away, come away, death,' 'Let me not to the marriage of true minds,' and so on. 'He attained some success in his profession . . . He inherited a small sum of money from his uncle' – that is how the biographer continues . . .[69]

The biographer proses like Wells, Bennett, and Galsworthy. He is a materialist. He has a mind of fancy in the Coleridgean sense, of "fixities and definites." His job is to "tack together" the phrases of official corres-pondence, to ride the straight concrete Roman roads, amongst the "slow measured tread of policemen." Along with Shakespeare and Coleridge on the imagination, Woolf would seem to have in mind Conrad's Marlow, sitting cross-legged on the *Nellie*, contemplating murky old Britannia, before the civilizing influence of Caesar. For Conrad, the roads of civil-ization conceal the horror of a primitive darkness. For Woolf, they enter the mind and repress life and creativity. The artist, once more linked to Shakespeare and Sonnet 116, gains access to life, which emerges mysteriously as the "nonsense beneath one's breath." Seen from Bernard's ulterior perspective, the policemen stand on the alert, like Caesar's legions, like the Freudian censor, like the "dogs" that "bark" when "the beggars are coming to town . . ."[70] The saintly writer must "go alone"[71] in the midst of a worldly prison. And if going alone means having a deliberate will, it is the unconscious "nonsense" of an oracular threshold that renders the will passive and dependent. The revelation of art can suspend the ego, as often happens in the creative process. But the labor of the whole is not unconscious. The epitaph that Leonard Woolf chose for his wife, like Lily's final vision, relates a final assertiveness: "Against you I will fling myself, unvanquished and unyielding, O Death!"[72]

The beginning and the end of self-consciousness is unselfconsciousness. To transcend the self of conventional biography, Bernard must complete the almost impossible labor of "casting off" the ethical narratives that weave together the self. In the grip of "entire disillusionment,"[73] he awakes "one day"[74] in a state that William James would certainly have identified as madness. To quote James, Bernard becomes a man for whom "the present and the past . . . will not unite."[75] His *I* differs too much from his *me*. No longer a story-telling animal, he forsakes the bounding line of his already vague and dreamlike character. In return he gains numerous fluid lines, multiple and synchronous perspectives that yield a more thorough, harrowing knowledge of reality.

The Waves ends with Bernard as the witness and agent of apocalypse, uniting the contradictions and antinomies of "life" in a mystical revelation where real and unreal, being and non-being, unite.[76] To master necessity and rise above the contingency of a false world, Bernard ascends through his heightened, complex consciousness, his oracular selfless madness, to a world like a symbolist poem, a disembodied perception of pure form and pure sound, white and dark, sky and sea, uninhabited of men. At last there is nothing but inner relations, the condition of music, a symphony of the real:

Now the sun had sunk. Sky and sea were indistinguishable. The waves breaking spread their white fans far out over the shore, sent white shadows into the recesses of sonorous caves and then rolled by sighing over the shingle.[77]

The Waves returns with wavelike constancy to its consciousness of itself, to its own meticulously framed themes and symbols, in a supreme authorial effort to realize freedom in the necessity of the cosmos. In the choric chapter-preludes, the waves are described in the past tense, whereas a continuous present generally holds through the chapters proper. Yet his final resolution ("Against you I will fling myself, unvanquished and unyielding, O Death!") carries Bernard full circle through his projected future and back to the waves' past tense: *The waves broke on the shore.*[78] Time is englobed in his mind and in the novel. The last trace of the self is revealed as a wave, flinging itself at death, which is wave; the chapters themselves are waves in which past and future are present. And as the *débris* of biography is eliminated, the cosmic flux comes to an apotheosis, even as Bernard saves or salvages goodness and beauty in the complex whole of his formalized mind.

To attain the mystical revelation of the seer, Bernard offers himself as sacrifice. Likewise, through Bernard's martyrdom, Woolf presents the mystical labor of her own imagination without the corruptions of plot and narrative, convention and sex and history, that torture her thought and her work. The good of art transcends the negations of life simply by being good. Like Bernard, Woolf is saint and martyr for that goodness, which is her art.

I would like to leave it at that, but I must ask if there is not a touch of absurdity, of bathos even, in the ending of *The Waves.* Is there not a sinking from the sublime dance of metaphysical themes, of subject and object, being and non-being, identity and non-identity, into a poor self, a suicide that brings no resurrection, no redemption, no joy?[79] Bernard has ripped the veil of the temple from top to bottom, only to reveal what? Another wave, a repetition, another negation. He pursues and transforms his friend Percival's quest for wholeness, for the reality behind appearances, for "something very important, yet remote, to be just held in solitude."[80] But Woolf refuses the religious humanism of Tennyson's *Idylls of the King* and of Wagner's *Parsifal.* Tennyson and Wagner imagine, or hold on to, or attend to, a symbol from outside the self of God's compassionate knowledge. If "the love of art for its own sake"[81] is not enough, then one may feel Bernard's sacrifice to be a failure, a morbid collapse, if only because "something very important" was promised.

CHAPTER 5

Samuel Beckett: humanity in ruins

In 1945, after visiting with family in Ireland, Beckett took a position with the Irish Red Cross, who were planning to build a hospital in Saint-Lô.[1] The ruins of the town stood on the Vire River, in Normandy, close to Utah Beach, where the US Fourth Infantry Division came ashore on June 6, 1944. Returning to the continent, Beckett might have associated the name "Lô" with the archetypal Blakean poet, "Los," or "Los *demiurgos*," as Joyce has it (*Ulysses* 3.18). It is pleasing to think so, for Blake's Los represents the hope of fallen man for apocalyptic rebirth and universal brotherhood.

Beckett's experience at Saint-Lô is expressed in the bold new intimacy of his post-war writing. It is not that his ideas leapt off the track. The predominant philosophical themes, from Democritus, Descartes, Geulincx, Berkeley, and Schopenhauer, run through all stages of his work.[2] But the war deepened the spiritual longing behind his pessimism. It vindicated his apocalyptic ambition. In the dust and rubble of Saint-Lô, a ghastly setting of Dantean intensity, it revealed to him "a vision and sense of a time-honoured conception of humanity in ruins, and perhaps even an inkling of the terms in which our condition is to be thought again."[3]

Beckett wrote about his experience in Saint-Lô in a radio speech, which I have just quoted, and in a poem with versions in French and English. Composed for Radio Erin in June 1946, "The Capital of the Ruins" is epic in atmosphere from its title to its closing words.[4] Beckett alludes, for example, to the *Aeneid* in a reference to "the Irish bringing gifts."[5] The great questions of history were on the minds of his countrymen. The great writers, Yeats and Joyce, were dead. Eliot had addressed the English in *Four Quartets*, which echoes distantly in Beckett's speech. The time was ripe for reassessment, and Beckett's service with the Irish Red Cross afforded the proper occasion:

. . . The whole enterprise turned from the beginning on the establishing of a relation in the light of which the therapeutic relation faded to the merest of pretexts. What was important was not our having penicillin when they had none, nor the unregarding munificence of the French Ministry of Reconstruction (as it was then called), but the occasional glimpse obtained, by us in them and, who knows, by them in us (for they are an imaginative people), of that smile at the human conditions as little to be extinguished by bombs as to be broadened by the elixirs of Burroughes and Welcome, – the smile deriding, among other things, the having and the not having, the giving and the taking, sickness and health.[6]

One is immediately struck by the colossal scale of events, by the generous and confident tone, and only afterward, if one notices it at all, by the mystical direction that the speech takes. The mysterious smile, calm, detached from the push-pull of materialism, attends a moral threshold. Glimpsed by a company of altruists, it eludes the power of technology – exed out by the chiasmus of *extinguished . . . bombs . . . broadened . . . elixirs* – and reveals itself to "imaginative people." Beckett was seeking to instil in his compatriots a skepticism, aimed at civilization itself, for the sake of "deriding . . . the having and the not having, the giving and the taking, sickness and health." He had in mind all moral economies, systems of physics, and analyses of physiological and political life. For its enigmatic author, "The Capital of the Ruins" is singularly clear: its message is a mystical ethics based on an experience of spiritual sympathy beyond the pale of matter.

The 1946 poem that grew out of Beckett's Normandy experience is simply titled "Saint-Lô." It appeared that June in the *Irish Times*:

> Vire will wind in other shadows
> unborn through the bright ways tremble
> and the old mind ghost-forsaken
> sink into its havoc[7]

"Saint-Lô" is less hopeful than "The Capital of the Ruins." The poet suggests that nothing will be learned from the war, as time and mind take their course like the waters of the symbolical winding Vire. He alludes to Yeats, a fellow prophet, with "Vire" evoking "gyre," an etymological relation noted by Lawrence Harvey.[8] The fact that "the old mind" eventually will "sink into its havoc" may suggest a Viconian cycle, as in Yeats and Joyce, or a final, materialist collapse. In its delicate register of ambiguous meanings, what William James would call its "psychic over-tone" or "fringe,"[9] the poem "Saint-Lô" suggests a trembling birth – a paradoxical "unbirth" away from the world – which is much desired but unrealized: a vision of a world "unborn," a world that no sufferer must bear or be born into, a worldless vision.

"Three Dialogues," co-authored with French art critic Georges Duthuit and published in his journal *transition* in 1949, is as close as we come to getting a manifesto from Beckett. He had just written *En attendant Godot*, and was nearly done with the trilogy, *Molloy, Malone meurt*, and *L'Innommable*. In the pages of *transition*, he presents himself as an oracular clown. One of his tricks, or prophecies, is his obscure alternative to modern art: the "expression that there is nothing to express, nothing with which to express, nothing from which to express, no power to express, no desire to express, together with the obligation to express."[10] When Duthuit comments, "But that is a violently extreme and personal point of view," Beckett is silent: "B. – ." It is an unexpected reply, and oddly winning. It admits anxiety and defeat, but comically redeems them by exposing the poor self, with its burdens, drives, and incapacities. It offers refuge for Beckett's nihilistic willfulness – the charge of Duthuit. And if thought is puzzled by silence, one may sense a hidden purpose.

Praising the paintings of Bram van Velde, Beckett sweepingly dismisses all previous art and all attempts at "more authentic, more ample, less exclusive relations between representer and representee . . ."[11] Van Velde, a minor figure in the history of abstract art, serves as a proxy for Beckett, who denies the convenient answer, gamely supplied by Duthuit, "that the occasion of his [van Velde's] painting is his predicament, and that it is expressive of the impossibility to express." Beckett counters:

No more ingenious method could be devised for restoring him, safe and sound, to the bosom of Saint Luke. But let us for once, be foolish enough not to turn tail. All have turned wisely tail, before the ultimate penury, back to the mere misery where destitute virtuous mothers may steal bread for their starving brats. There is more than a difference of degree between being short, short of the world, short of self, and being without these esteemed commodities.[12]

Art about art is not the answer, not even the doleful testament of artistic poverty. "My case," Beckett elaborates, ". . . is that van Velde is . . . the first to submit wholly to the incoercible absence of relation, . . . the first to admit that to be an artist is to fail, as no other dare fail, that failure is his world and the shrink from it desertion, art and craft, good housekeeping, living."[13] Beckett's stance of ultimate aesthetic revolt takes the form of contempt for "the world," the "self," "commodities," "good housekeeping," and "living." His outlook exceeds the "realisation that art has always been bourgeois,"[14] since what foregoes matter must also forego dialectical materialism. He repudiates system and economy (i.e. "good house-keeping") by translating the mystical ethics of "humanity in ruins" into the paradox of anti-art.[15]

In retrospect, Beckett's early work serves as preparation for his post-war "dream of an art unresentful of its insuperable indigence and too proud for the farce of giving and receiving."[16] The farce had entered into *Murphy*, with its dark refrain: "The horse leech's daughter is a closed system. Her quantum of wantum cannot vary."[17] The eponymous hero of *Watt* grows "tired of adding, tired of subtracting to and from the same old things the same old things."[18] When he wrote *Waiting for Godot*, Beckett subjected the "quantum of wantum" to the demands of anti-art. In Act I, Estragon howls with pain after Lucky kicks him in the shins, and Beckett uses the occasion to question the public's taste. The stage directions say that Pozzo comments *lyrically*: "The tears of the world are a constant quantity. For each one who begins to weep somewhere else another stops. The same is true of the laugh."[19] The idea behind Pozzo's analysis of fortune goes back through Dante (*Inf.* VII) to Boethius. In Pozzo's case, however, the consolation of philosophy feeds an illusion of selfhood. The audience that enjoys the classic symmetry of tears and laughter may, on second thought, begin to suspect that Pozzo, as usual, is blowing smoke. Being tied so intimately to violence, its tastes suddenly savor of distaste. It wants off the whirligig.

To study Beckett's assault on ethics is to see its centrality to his work. *Godot* stands out for its intense, concise attack on the moral ambitions of the West. The concept of teleology is exposed as a psychological need directed at a dubious and receding good. Vladimir and Estragon shift erratically from mental state to mental state, defying all moral analysis. Theirs is a world without natural law, where they have "got rid" of their rights. Vladimir's version of the categorical imperative ("all mankind is us") ends in a rhetorical question about reason: "But has it not long been straying in the night without end of the abyssal depths?"[20] Pozzo rationalizes his master-slave morality, remarking of Lucky: "I might just as well have been in his shoes and he in mine. If chance had not willed otherwise. To each one his due."[21] Vladimir interprets this nonsense with a burst of babble, or glossolalia: "You waagerrim?" But Pozzo remains clueless, missing the lesson that each is due nothing. Each is the other – note the pun on "otherwise" – though the will of chance varies the shoes, or the hat, as the case may be. Molloy describes his lovers the same way: "another who might have been my mother, or even I think my grandmother, if chance had not willed otherwise."[22] The "will of chance" is an oxymoronic god-trope. Its deconstructive language enables Beckett to debunk moral agency. His characters expose and explore their hollowness by mouthing phrases that are the epiphenomenal shell of an impersonal fate.

Morality presumes a normal background of epistemological confidence to which Beckett, like the God of Barth, says his eternal No. The adverb *morally*, as it appears in *Watt*, obscures subject and predicate like a fog. According to the dictionary, the adjective *moral* can be "used to designate that kind of probable knowledge of the general tendencies of human nature, or of the character of particular individuals or classes of men."[23] This usage of *moral* has a likely connection with Aristotle's ἠθικὴ πίστις (ethical trust), a term from the *Rhetoric* that refers to the persuasive force of personal character, as opposed to the force either of logical argument or of emotional appeal. But this sense of *moral* started to drift around 1700. "Often in looser use," the dictionary reports, it is "applied to all evidence which is merely probable and not demonstrative." In *Tristram Shandy*, a novel Beckett knew well, Sterne uses the adverbial form in a breezy, witty fashion to make guesses about his reader: "and yet, my dear Sir, if I may presume to know your character, I am morally assured . . ."[24] Like Sterne, Beckett betrays an ironic lack of moral assurance. But he increases the irony, and the lack. He plies the looser usage amongst Cartesian dubieties: "Watt had not pressed a bell with any part of him, of that he was *morally* certain . . ."[25] In Watt's Cartesian world, moral probabilities dwindle into befuddled sensations about space and motion. No wonder Watt "had grown used to his loss of species."[26]

Justice, fortitude, prudence, and temperance (the cardinal virtues), in fact all the Aristotelian virtues, sink into the meaningless morass of "the eudemonistic slop," from which the police and other powerful liars retrieve them. While under arrest, Molloy describes virtuous action as state propaganda, and his "rocking" "on the handlebars" as an act of anti-virtue: "It is indeed a deplorable sight, a deplorable example, for the people, who so need to be encouraged, in their bitter toil, and to have before their eyes manifestations of strength only, of courage and of joy, without which they might collapse, at the end of the day, and roll on the ground."[27] Later he ridicules the public morality: "They wake up, hale and hearty, their tongues hanging out for order, beauty and justice, baying for their due."[28] And he ends by collapsing and rolling on the ground – a comment on humanity's true condition.

Good actions are not virtuous actions, but inexplicable occurrences in material reality. Molloy alludes to a passage from the *Ethics* of Geulincx: "I who had loved the image of old Geulincx . . . who left me free, on the black boat of Ulysses, to crawl towards the East, along the deck. That is a great measure of freedom for him who has not the pioneering spirit."[29] Whatever happens – and the westward itinerary of Ulysses's last voyage does not bode well – the embodied soul cannot take the credit or the blame. In the universe of Geulincx's *Ethics*, "I am nothing more than a spectator of the World."[30]

By denying moral agency, Beckett changes the imitation of morality and character into the abstraction of amorality and the soul. "Living souls," we read at the end of "The Expelled," "you will see how alike they are."[31] Murphy, Molloy, Malone: these are Irish Smiths and Joneses. Molloy is Adam, by way of his "great big Adam's apple."[32] Estragon literally names himself Adam. "People pass too," reflects Molloy, "hard to distinguish from yourself."[33] "Moral" is canceled out in the very name of Moran, plowed under by the force of a negating phoneme. Jacques Moran *fils* collects stamps and duplicates because he is one. Macmann is literally the son ("Mac") of man. Refusing the notion of earthly life as a moral crucible, such as we see in Dante's *Commedia* or in Keats's letters, Beckett accepts Schopenhauer's denial of any positive good or moral satisfaction tinctured by the earth. He renounces all joy in the unique destiny of individuals.

Beckett's response to the Christian virtues rewards close scrutiny because of his preoccupation with the soul. On the basis of scripture, Peter Geach suggests that charity "is love of God above all things in the world and of our neighbors for God's sake . . ."[34] False charity turns the office of holiness into a powerful weapon. "Against the charitable gesture, there is no defence," Molloy laments, laden by a "social worker" with a "little pile of tottering disparates."[35] This line of thought develops theologically in *Malone Dies*. Malone speculates about his efficient, elderly nurse: "it is conceivable that she does what she does out of sheer charity . . . Nothing is impossible."[36] An act of "sheer charity," if possible, would strip charity of its material dimension. Then spiritual depths might emerge, as in the ruins of Saint-Lô. But when Macmann, who "had eluded charity all his days," enters the House of Saint John of God, the staff regard him as their chattel: "Fear nothing, you are among friends . . . Take no thought for anything, it is we shall think and act for you, from now forward. We like it." Geach finds that charity "is incompatible with any gross defect" in the non-theological virtues, and that such "gross defect would mean a failure in charity too . . ."[37] Not only charity, but justice, temperance, and friendship, in quick succession, fall victim to the gross self-interest that characterizes the hospital staff. They continue in their welcoming address to Macmann: "In addition to the nourishment carefully calculated to keep you alive, and even well, you will receive, every Saturday, in honour of our patron, an imperial half-pint of porter and a plug of tobacco."[38] So much deadening stuff, the half-pint and the plug make a materialist of the sixteenth-century Portuguese Saint John of God, patron of the sick, of nurses, and of hospitals. It is only logical to ask whether the God of Saint John can inspire charity.

The Unnamable, looking back, acknowledges "having invented it all, in the hope it would console me." "All lies," he concludes.[39] Like Spenser's Despair (*Faerie Queene*, I. ix. 33–54), who dwells "low in an hollow caue/ . . . Darke, dolefull, drearie, like a greedie graue,"[40] the Unnamable is a story-teller fated to a living death. Despair's narrative of Redcrosse is not simply a lie, however. It is a recognizably true story that omits God's saving grace. By the same token, Despair's narrative is self-aggrandizing; hope is humbler, for it relies on something outside the self. It is Una, the Protestant church, who tears the "curséd knife" of self-slaughter from Redcrosse's hand.

For Beckett, despair is more real and authentic than Christian hope, at least if the object of Christian hope is nothing more than consolation, and not the *bonum arduum* that Redcrosse pursues, the "good possible of attainment, but only with difficulty and precariously."[41] Possibly, despair is Beckett's hope, for it is not without the paradoxical grace of a *via negativa*. Steeped in the fictions that are his "pretext" for not committing suicide, Malone approaches his object or end in "the true prayer at last, the one that asks for nothing." "And it is then," he continues, "a little breath of fulfillment revives the dead longings and a murmer (*sic*) is born in the silent world, reproaching you affectionately with having despaired too late. The last word in the way of viaticum."[42] *Fulfillment* is, I think, the word that surprises, though it is a fulfillment born of "nothing" and "silence."

The Unnamable's conception of Mahood is a sacrificial act of faith: "let me note that my next vice-exister will be a billy in the bowl, that's final, with his bowl on his head and his arse in the dust, plump down on thousand-breasted Tellus, it'll be softer for him. Faith that's an idea, yet another, mutilate, mutilate, and perhaps some day, fifteen generations hence, you'll succeed in beginning to look like yourself, among the passers-by."[43] Mahood is destined for his bowl, or jar, much as the lovers in *Play* are destined for their urns. It is hard going for all billies (*billy* is the Scots equivalent of the English *mate*) in the realm of Tellus, goddess of the earth, abode of "vice-existers." "Faith" (used interjectionally) is the expression of an "idea," the latest in a long series, more fodder for the scrap heap, another metonymy (part for the whole) of the vice-idea-creation-language-lie molecule. Faith keeps bad things happening. But that paradoxical phrase about "beginning to look like yourself" carries the hint of a goal or teleology, as Beckett reserves the virtue of some kind of faith as a way to the soul's fulfillment.

So far I have argued that Beckett's renunciation of "the closed system of the nothing new" extends from normative ethics to an ambiguous treatment of the Christian virtues. What emerges, then, is an arduous deliverance from false claims about morality and spirit. To fathom this deliverance from worldly entanglements, it will be helpful to consult Kierkegaard, beginning with *Stages on Life's Way*:

There are three existence-spheres: the esthetic, the ethical, the religious . . . The ethical sphere is only a transition sphere, and therefore its highest expression is repentance as a negative action. The esthetic sphere is the sphere of immediacy, the ethical sphere of requirement (and this requirement is so infinite that the individual always goes bankrupt), the religious the sphere of fulfillment, but, please note, not a fulfillment such as when one fills an alms box or a sack with gold, for repentance has specifically created a boundless space, and as a consequence the religious contradiction: simultaneously to be out on 70,000 fathoms of water and yet be joyful.[44]

Beckett is similarly wary of the "sack of gold" and the "alms box." Like Kierkegaard, he experiences spiritual truth as a *paradox*, which cannot be mediated.[45] In "Three Dialogues," it will be recalled, Beckett affirms "the obligation to express." In seeking to meet that obligation, he renounces the world of art, the aesthetic sphere. He pursues what Kierkegaard calls a religious "fulfillment." (In *Fear and Trembling*, Kierkegaard refers to such fulfillment as "absurd.") The passage from *Stages on Life's Way* clarifies the further point that, for Beckett, the "ethical sphere is only a transition sphere, and . . . its highest expression is repentance as a negative action." Abundant with self-denial, Beckett in the trilogy enters into what Kierkegaard in *Fear and Trembling* calls "a teleological suspension of the ethical."[46] A higher, spiritual *telos* replaces the *telos* of reason, duty, and "the giving and the taking."

Moran's journey is a recasting of the testing of Abraham, with *Fear and Trembling* giving Beckett his interpretive framework for Genesis 22.[47] The journey is a spiritual allegory for Beckett in the act of writing. The detective Moran is a writer himself, who is eventually revealed as the author of Beckett's other works. Gaber and Youdi are related to Gabriel and Yahweh, though they are more intimate – at least for Beckett. When

Moran protests to the messenger that the "chief" should send another "agent," Gaber gratifyingly replies, "He wants it to be you, God knows why . . . He said . . . that no one could do it but you."[48] Chosen by "God," Moran will supply his own sacrifice, none other than himself ("Youdi" = "You die"),[49] even as he sacrifices another.

In moments touched with satire, Christianity makes a poor appearance. From the first, "the job" intrudes on Moran's religious practices: "I who never missed mass, to have missed it on that Sunday of all Sundays! When I so needed it! To buck me up!"[50] His "eight minutes" with Father Ambrose, who evokes in name only the great Ambrose, Doctor of the Roman Church, go badly: "This interview with Father Ambrose left me with a painful impression. He was still the same dear man, and yet not. I seemed to have surprised, on his face, a lack, how shall I say, a lack of nobility. The host, it is only fair to say, was lying heavy on my stomach. And as I made my way home I felt like one who, having swallowed a pain-killer, is first astonished, then indignant, on obtaining no relief."[51] Ambrose lacks nobility because he is at best a well-meaning stooge. The host lies "heavy" on Moran's stomach because it is neither the real presence of Christ nor an opiate à la Marx. It is nothing but matter, bitter grist for the mill of life. Moran's unsteady narration should not obscure the fine line walked by Beckett, who asserts his own authenticity by avoiding the clichés of progress that could whisk him on his way. He is too severely honest a writer to debunk Christianity with the Enlightenment.

Committed to a mystical journey toward the absolute, Beckett is the knight of a nameless faith. He suffers the "absurd tribulations"[52] of Malone and the "fear and trembling"[53] of Macmann. He struggles to renounce everything, to come to nothing. Like Kierkegaard's Johannes de Silentio, the pseudonymous author of *Fear and Trembling*, he is an exile from God. Aching in spirit, he might well agree that "the highest passion in a person is faith."[54] But he is wary of all expressions of passion. He is the knight of a nameless faith, the origins of which may simply be his own godlike gifts and powers.[55] Moran answers increasingly to a daimonic voice: "For it is within me and exhorts me to continue to the end the faithful servant."[56] He is typecast ("the faithful servant") but irreducible to any known faith, and towards the end of *Molloy* he derides the Christian reward with a mock catechism: "Would we all meet in heaven one day, I, my mother, my son, his mother, Youdi, Gaber, Molloy, his mother, Yerk, Murphy, Watt, Camier and the rest?"[57] As satire, this seems fairly obvious. But the splintered self denies knowing any essential difference between itself and its personae, and promotes such ignorance before any reasoned explanation of good and evil. Paradoxically, then, Beckett's ignorance has the purgative effect of focusing his will on the absolute.

As a work of anti-art, the trilogy does not fit well with egotistical pleasures like artistic success. Its god-bent author sacrifices himself on the altar of reality, but he is comically aware of his duplicity, his incapacity for renunciation. He runs the risk of being Sexy Sadie. That is why *Molloy* is translated "from the French by Patrick Bowles in collaboration with the author."[58] In collaboration, not with a Nazi, but with a member of the Resistance. It is a prime example of Beckett's self-consciousness about his authorial egotism. To accuse himself of being the enemy is to accuse himself of art.

Certainly the massive force of Beckett's ego threatens to co-opt his spiritual intentions. But he may be justified, at least in part, by his asceticism, which is twofold in nature: he writes in an ordeal of self-denying isolation, and he writes as a "pretext" (the word connects "The Capital of the Ruins" to the trilogy) to something more important than art. The outcome of these circumstances hangs in the balance during one of Beckett's outright leaps into the spirit realm. His mission in jeopardy, Moran lies in a shelter in the wilderness, waiting for the return of his adolescent son (Abraham = Isaac), who has been dispatched to buy a bicycle. Supplies are short, catastrophe imminent, when Moran has a vision of the rarest intensity:

I . . . tried to remember what I was to do with Molloy, once I had found him. And on myself too I pored, on me so changed from what I was. And I seemed to see myself ageing as swiftly as a day-fly. But the idea of ageing was not exactly the one which offered itself to me. And what I saw was more like a crumbling, a frenzied collapsing of all that had always protected me from all I was always condemned to be. Or it was a kind of clawing toward a light and countenance I could not name, that I had once known and long denied. But what words can deny this sensation at first all darkness and bulk, with a noise like the grinding of stones, then suddenly as soft as water flowing. And then I saw a little globe swaying up slowly from the depths, through the quiet water, smooth at first, and scarcely paler than its escorting ripples, then little by little a face, with holes for the eyes and mouth and other wounds, and *nothing* to show if it was a man's face or a woman's face, a young face or an old face, or if its calm too was not an effect of the water trembling between it and the light. But I confess I attended but absently to these poor figures, in which I suppose my sense of disaster sought to contain itself. And that I did not labour more diligently was a further index of the great changes I had suffered and of my growing resignation to being dispossessed of self.[59]

We start with Milton's "O how fall'n! how changed / From him, who in the happy realms of light . . ." (*Paradise Lost*, I. 84–85),[60] which remembers

Virgil's "*Quantum mutatus ab illo . . .!*" (*Aeneid*, II. 274).[61] Being "so changed," Moran recognizes his and mankind's ruined state. He is ageing swiftly as the day-fly, one of the species that Shakespeare calls "time's flies." The "light and countenance I could not name, that I had once known and long denied" suggests a messianic countenance, like "the smile deriding, among other things, the having and the not having, the giving and the taking, sickness and health." The change from stone to water recalls *The Waste Land,* which itself partakes of romantic and spiritual waters, such as Beckett describes in his poem "Saint-Lô," such as Yeats describes in "The Philosophy of Shelley's Poetry," where water is "the great symbol of existence" and "an image" of the mind.[62] Introspection, a poring over the mind, yields an image of a "globe swaying up slowly from the depths": it is a skull, a world, with an allusion to Shakespeare's Globe, where "poor" players, or "figures," strut and fret their hour upon the stage. A counterpart of the nameless messianic face, it evokes Rousseau in *The Triumph of Life*: ". . . the holes it vainly sought to hide / Were or had been eyes."[63] But throughout the passage, the language of poetry is not the point. It serves as a pretext to the intuitions of the spirit. What I gain from "my growing resignation to being dispossessed of self" is, in precisely Kierkegaardian terms, "my eternal consciousness."[64] Beckett's eternal consciousness is the fountainhead of vision. It annuls the subject-object split. It reveals the other, spiritually, not as a thing in an economy. But Moran cannot sustain the vision. He continues his report, "And doubtless I should have gone from discovery to discovery, concerning myself, if I had persisted. But at the first faint light, I mean in these wild shadows gathering about me, dispensed by a vision or by an effort of thought, at the first light I fled to other cares. And all had been for nothing. And he who acted thus was a stranger to me too."[65] The shadowy "I" cannot persist. Therefore it cannot attend to itself through the wilderness of time.

Although Moran lacks Abraham's strength, described in *Fear and Trembling* as "the power to concentrate the whole substance of his life and the meaning of actuality into one desire,"[66] Beckett himself has this concentration, which is his faith. Moran's conclusion that "all had been for nothing" is an instance of dramatic irony, insofar as "nothing" might yield a paradoxical fulfillment. Though Moran fails to find Molloy, he comes to resemble and in a sense to reveal him. Though he has not made Abraham's "movement of faith by virtue of the absurd,"[67] he has made some such movement. And as it happens, things in the end go absurdly well for him and his son. Moran, though a murderer, passes the test and returns home to good weather: "They were the longest, loveliest days of all the year. I lived in the garden. I have spoken of a voice telling me things. I was getting to know it better now, to understand what it wanted."[68] He lives in uncertainties, mysteries, and doubts. His ego is traumatized, barely coherent, but its openness breaks through space and time like a sacred road.

Beckett's post-war writing proceeds from a breakdown of cause and effect: "I can't go on, I'll go on."[69] Rupert Wood refers to this "familiar Beckettian position" as an "ethical dilemma."[70] I am not sure that we can say even that much. To break out of the closed system, Beckett posits irrational situations that are intended to break, to disrupt, to dispel self and world. His frequent lapses of cause and effect include "the familiar Beckettian position"; the heavy rain bringing a resumption of outdoor activity in Chapter I of *Mercier and Camier*; the opening sentence of "The Calmative," "I don't know when I died";[71] bright streetlamps and empty streets in the same story; Molloy's remark, "I confuse east and west, the poles too, I invert them readily";[72] the use of "the mythological present" in *Molloy*, which renders space and time imaginary, and converts psychic experience into plot;[73] as well as Malone's description of Macmann: "the ideas of guilt and punishment were confused together in his mind, as those of cause and effect so often are in the minds of those who continue to think."[74] Spatial and temporal coordinates founder in *Godot*, and the window-eyes of *Endgame* look out on an apocalyptic landscape. Beckett learns from Rimbaud and others whom Jacques Barzun calls "the French Abolitionists," writers "bent on complete cultural destruction."[75] Viewing the English language as "a veil that must be torn apart in order to get at the things (or the Nothingness) behind it,"[76] Beckett expresses an enormous drive to slaughter the gods of reason and language. He galvanizes dead metaphors in an anatomical frenzy, and turns our attention to puns and paradoxes in order to snap us out of our reading habits. He digs into the mind, scrutinizing its illusions, archetypes, and myths. He answers the apocalypse of Europe, the Holocaust and the war, with an apocalypse of language and mind. But why he does so – whether his position is ethical – is beyond our grasp, just as his spiritual *telos* is beyond our moral calculus.

Since Beckett is a knight of faith, his authority cannot come from any communicable power or principle. The fierceness of his ascetic ordeal has the swarming air of madness. But if we understand anything about his position, it is that we cannot claim him as one of our own, as one who is morally known to us.

Not only is Beckett's art a pretext to the moments of breaking through, he views the great masterworks as a pretext to his arrival. Authorial presumption is certainly a factor. Beckett jokes about his monumental capacity for destruction in the Addenda of *Watt*. Amidst a dada-esque midden of language, lies the nugget *pereant qui ante nos nostra dixerunt*,[77] meaning "let them die who said our things before us." In good Latin, the author proclaims his nihilistic will, his royal ego on the rampage. Cartesian philosophy helps with the cultural demolition. Beckett treats the canon as *res extensa*, and regards only himself as *res cogitans*. This split divides the primary selves of the canon (the actual authors) from Beckett's authorial self. It is not just that the Dante is a "pretext," or that those who said our things before us should perish. Beckett criticism has begun to discover, and to put a rather fine spin upon, enormous wholesale borrowing by Beckett from a wide range of primary and secondary sources.[78] I am grateful to read Beckett, plagiarist or not. My point is that Beckett's view of the canon issues from his apocalyptic response to history. Only on this basis is Beckett a singular event. Otherwise, he is an artist vulnerable to charges of plagiarism.

Beckett's anti-art demands the sacrifice of the body. The dead affect of Molloy, Moran, Malone, et al. expresses the ordeal of a concentrated will intent on voiding the human form. Because Molloy is cut off from the habits and knowledge of his body, from any integration of thought and feeling, physical passion has no real claim upon him. His ironic distance from his lovers expresses a perverse Adamic innocence:

She went by the peaceful name of Ruth, I think, but I can't be certain. Perhaps the name was Edith. She had a hole between her legs, oh not the bunghole I had always imagined, but a slit, and in this I put, or rather she put, my so-called virile member, not without difficulty, and I toiled and moiled until I discharged or gave up trying or was begged by her to stop . . . She bent over the couch, because of her rheumatism, and in I went from behind. It was the only position she could bear, because of her lumbago. It seemed all right to me, for I had seen dogs, and I was astonished when she confided that you could go about it differently. I wonder what she meant exactly. Perhaps after all she put me in her rectum. A matter of complete indifference to me, I needn't tell you. But is it true love, in the rectum? That's what bothers me sometimes. Have I ever known true love, after all?[79]

Molloy's physical form has no capacity to explain his experience. His use of the words "differently" and "indifference" serve an abstract, barely human view. Encountering the mechanics of human sex for the first time, he is indifferent to things that matter to our animal nature. He is indifferent to things that touch our moral dignity, like the connection, extolled by

Dante on seeing Beatrice in the Earthly Paradise of *Purgatorio* XXX, between sex and love: *Conosco i segni dell' antica fiamma.*[80] Sex in Beckett is Dantescan parody: "And all I could see was her taut yellow nape which every now and then I set my teeth in, forgetting I had none, such is the power of instinct. We met in a rubbish dump . . ."[81] Suspecting that one of his lovers was "a man . . . or at least an androgyne," Molloy sensibly concludes, "man or woman, what does it matter?"[82] What does matter matter? To Beckett, there is no scandal in Molloy's failure to see the difference between marital relations and fornication, between intercourse and sodomy, between man and woman. He prods us to look behind such meaningless differences, to see through the rhetoric of romance and recognize the compulsions of matter.

Decomposition is Beckett's apt pun,[83] for his voice of disaffection sings to a theme of physical decay. Molloy says, "Tears and laughter, they are so much Gaelic to me."[84] Moran reminds himself, "No emotion, please."[85] Malone admits to "never having really evolved in the fields of affection and passion."[86] Bicycles, crutches, and sticks supply the physical defects of these fraying personae.[87] Mutilated and finally bodiless, the Unnamable describes itself as "devoid of feeling."[88] As Beckett unmakes the human form, he breaks down the body's mediating role as the site of emotion. The method is akin to shock therapy, inducing apocalypse by ungrounding the mind, which is anthropocentrically rooted in the body's warm earth. The *cogito* is rendered anti-foundational.

Beckett's moments of fulfillment are rare, their outcome ambiguous. Renunciation is boundless, redemption worldless. By his own account, the ordeal is "excavatory, immersive, a contraction of the spirit, a descent."[89] Into the trash go character, the body, and language itself, which is not only dependent on the principle of sufficient reason, but is a form of matter and the stuff of corpses. At the utmost limit of descent, the self crumbles. This is the ego's tragedy, when apocalypse begins. It is also a move central to our recent cultural history, from Schopenhauer to Beckett. For two centuries, men and women of genius have tried to yoke the oxen of Indic asceticism to the plow of western romanticism. Yeats, Eliot, and Woolf offer conspicuous examples of this ambitious turn. Beckett follows in kind when the Unnamable declares, ". . . the will has been opened, nothing for anybody . . ."[90] The author disowns the ego, plumbs the depths of mind, and reaches the pit where reality or the cosmic will dictates its terms of time and space. Being so dispossessed, the Unnamable might have inscribed the apocalyptic moment when self and other are saved. In Schopenhauer, we can see how the trilogy might have ended, for *The World as Will and Representation* offers a morsel of consolation, Schopenhauer's vision of the gnostic saint:

But we now turn our glance from our own needy and perplexed nature to those who have overcome the world, in whom the will, having reached complete self-knowledge, has found itself again in everything, and then freely denied itself, and who then merely wait to see the last trace of the will vanish with the body that is animated by that trace. Then, instead of the restless pressure and effort, instead of the constant transition from desire to apprehension and from joy to sorrow; instead of the never-satisfied and never-dying hope that constitutes the life-dream of the man who wills, we see that peace that is higher than all reason, that ocean-like calmness of spirit, that deep tranquility, that unshakable confidence and serenity, whose mere reflection in the countenance, as depicted by Raphael and Correggio, is a complete and certain gospel.[91]

The gnostic saint transcends the body (the epiphenomenal product of the cosmic will) to achieve a selfless joy. Schopenhauer goes on to compare this state to "the Prajna-Paramita of the Buddhists, the 'beyond all knowledge,' in other words, the point where subject and object no longer exist."[92] Beckett at Saint-Lô had glimpsed this type of "serenity." The "smile deriding, among other things, the having and the not having, the giving and the taking, sickness and health" is seen in faces painted by Raphael and Correggio, who translated to canvas their spiritual know-ledge of a path beyond "the human conditions."

Schopenhauer holds out the possibility that one can "recognize . . . the nature of the act of the will, and accordingly *eventualiter* will otherwise."[93] One can do this by returning to "the fountainhead itself, namely, compas-sion." "This truth is felt," writes Schopenhauer.[94] But where does that leave us? The waters of the noumenal fountainhead are murky. Schopenhauer's "complete and certain gospel" is by its very nature unreadable, beyond language, which cannot escape the principle of sufficient reason. There-fore the inside or ultimate reality consists precisely in what cannot be named, in the Unnamable. In the end, all that can be hoped of Scho-penhauer's ethics is that mystical communion with nothingness will lead us to compassion. As one of Schopenhauer's European disciples under-stands it, such mysticism will allow us to "glimpse 'the other,' sense its existence in the false, the untrue."[95] These words recall Beckett's epiphany at Saint-Lô and Moran's vision in the wilderness. But as an ethics, Schopenhauer's mysticism has no positive content. It is a nameless faith whose absurdity Beckett does not fail to insist upon. Beckett proves warier than Schopenhauer of saving acts of consciousness. He is a Ulysses who knows he has drowned.

The defensive tendency to appropriate Beckett to one's own ethics and tastes probably expresses some deep human need. When a critic praises "that fierce endeavour to bring the intellectual and the emotional into focus which characterizes Beckett's work," the critic, one must assume, has forgotten the alternatives to Cartesianism.[96] Likewise, Martha Nussbaum's "cognitive view" of the emotions repeats the engrained Cartesian bias. Ascribing to Beckett the idea that emotions take hold only as social constructs, Nussbaum cannot know or feel the full dehumanizing violence of Beckett's apocalyptic assault on the body. And then to describe emotion in the trilogy as "a construct out of stories" is to dismiss the source of Beckett's "obligation to express." That source, the final cause of an unknown or non-existent metaphysic, is like the God that summons Abraham in Genesis 22: it beckons from an inscrutable depth, and burdens its favorite with unspeakable dread. It is what inspires his commitment, as the knight of a nameless faith, to a paradoxical work of anti-art that is ultimately concerned with the human soul in the universal sense of "The Expelled": "Living souls, you will see how alike they are." To conclude that Moran's writing makes "us see that this assault on stories is just another story" is to restore Beckett, safe and sound, to the Enlightenment.[97]

The defensive tendency to appropriate Beckett to our ethics and our art probably expresses some deep human need – and I am no exception. There are at least two ways of objecting to my emphasis on Beckett's moral ideas. One way is to say that moral ideas do not really count for very much in Beckett's literary achievement. The other way is to say that they count for a great deal, but that I have not done them justice. I will consider the former objection first.

Vivian Mercier exemplifies the need to humanize Beckett, though Beckett is an author who defies humanism. In the recent *Beckett on Film*, narrator Jeremy Irons intones about "individuality" and "humanity," as if Beckett was a good European.[98] Irons makes Beckett sound like Ibsen. Mercier is clearer about his premises. He thoughtfully points out that Molloy confuses the name of his *inamorata*, Ruth or Edith, because "That hallmark of uniqueness, one's baptismal name, means nothing . . ."[99] But Mercier shares this insight only to ignore it. He goes on to profess a kind of faith:

I must insist, however, that the generalizations I have been making about the relations between the sexes in Beckett's work constitute . . . no more than a broad caricature, one that too neatly fits the stereotype of Beckett as a thinker imprisoned within a narrowly pessimistic world-view. When, recalling that Beckett is not in fact a philosopher but an artist, one looks at the individual work of art, the dangers inherent in critical generalization become evident. Every male and female character in Beckett's work differs subtly from every other, and *a fortiori*, every man-woman relationship is also different from all others. Whatever beliefs Beckett the man may claim to hold, whatever hypotheses Beckett the philosopher (entirely self-taught) may propose, Beckett the artist reveals that life and love are infinitely complex matters.[100]

The irony of Mercier's position is that it applies the standards of the aesthetic man to Beckett, who is spiritual. The aesthetic man in maturity develops into "a critic, a universal critic in all the branches of learning."[101] One recalls Estragon's withering retort, *"Crritic!"* The aesthetic truism that "life and love are infinitely complex matters" makes a mockery of Beckett. It sounds like Pozzo. It falls under the second part of Kierkegaard's observation: "The aesthetic choice is either altogether, immediate, and thus no choice, or it loses itself in a great multiplicity." Beckett's absurdist spiritual ethics define him, as their own ethics define the writers he admired, most of all Dante. I doubt that any great writer has ever held such a view of art as Mercier's.

Gabriel Josipovici takes Beckett's moral ideas quite seriously: "If we will give up our dreams of domination, of understanding, of fulfillment, of progress, our dreams even of the absurdity of life, then we will be able to attend to" our existence in time.[102] What Josipovici proposes that we "give up" is human nature itself. When a man asks me for so much, I cannot help wondering, do his saintly intentions possibly disguise a common condition? Why write if not to gratify some impulse, to scratch some egotistical itch? And if Josipovici is the voice of truth, we may want to reconsider the meaning of truth:

> The entire tradition of novel and autobiography depends on . . . sleight-of-hand, a voice murmuring "Yes, I remember." But even the most truthful of autobiographers omits to ask himself: "Even if the stories the voice tells me are familiar to me, how am I to know that they are stories about myself?" For what is a story about oneself? Is there a self even?[103]

Josipovici's is one of several recent challenges to ethical narrativity.[104] Clearly, the ideas being advanced are radical – they extend and amplify the apocalyptic mood of modernism. Josipovici appears ready to jettison "the entire tradition of novel and autobiography." All those books, in his Beckettian view, are made to serve as a pretext for a less hypocritical, more apperceptive something. But what could that something be, if Beckett failed to find it? Beckett attempted the boundless renunciation of the knight of faith, but his conclusions were highly ambiguous. In effect,

Josipovici promises a path to salvation among Beckett's thorns and lashes. He is the anti-humanistic version of Matthew Arnold.

Josipovici stays true to Beckett by refusing the personal and religious convictions that hold like locks on our sanity – at least for those of us who need locks. That is my way of saying that Josipovici has a point. But what American, coming out of William James, has ever subscribed to the notion of a complete and rational self, such as European thought has debated from Hegel to Derrida? We are story-telling animals.[105] That our personal fictions rely on flawed standards of truth I do not doubt. We weave our egos with a crazy thread, and memory is the mother of the Muses. Like you, I am prone to forgetting Beckett's epic sermon on the soul. Beckett chastens us – if we are so alike – with the knowledge that our moral and spiritual categories are always flawed, always liable to hypocrisy, falsehood, and inescapable ignorance.

Conclusion: technology and technique

The effort to transform human nature through the use of art is what I have called the modernist moral project. By this solemn phrase I mean to suggest only an important tendency within modernism. I am not proposing a monolithic model. Certainly it is true that the modernists played expressively with scientific concepts, exploiting opportunities for rhetorical advantage as they arose, and exploring new scientific vistas with the freedom of the imagination. But this combination of experiment, intuition, and risk, which makes the most subtle demands on our ears, is lost in the work of critical successors who put theory before literature. These successors lead the modernist moral project to a dangerous end: they legislate and enforce the perverse dogmas of pseudo-ethical anti-naturalism.

It should be borne in mind that modernism was contemporary with the eugenics movement, which prospered at major universities in the US and Europe.[1] The modernist moral project changes eugenics into an image of itself, as it fuses nature and art – ethics and aesthetics – into a technology of the void, a cosmic process that forgets humankind. Eugenic Man was only a more perfect version of the Yahoo. He was not a new species. In the words of its founder Francis Galton, the idea of modern eugenics was to "co-operate with the works of Nature by securing that humanity shall be represented by the fittest races."[2] Whether in its weeding or its fertilizing mode, eugenics sought only to recoup what had been lost. Because altruism and the conveniences of modern life had thwarted natural selection, the unfit were outbreeding the fit, and the resulting "differential birthrate" caused "degeneration." At least so ran the argument – complete with a bogus stamp of nature to seal its parody of justice.

Removing eugenics from the jurisdiction of nature, the modernists adapt it to art. The practice of eugenics has no limits under the militant stars of the imagination. For Aristotle, tragedy affirms the cosmic order, both in tragedy's religious origins and in its beneficial effects. For the modernists, art revises the cosmic order, by usurping the function and authority of religion. The modernist re-creates the cosmos as he re-creates man. Eugenics for Yeats is a type of the aspiration of art, an image of spiritual potency. *On the Boiler* unites the cause of eugenics with the cause of mysticism: "the whole nation must be convinced by some new argument that death is but passing from one room into another, for lacking that there can be no great lasting quality."[3] Yeats was already voicing this "new argument" in line after line. His faith is his own metaphysical concoction: it is more shockingly poetical than "the religion of the future" preached by George Bernard Shaw.[4]

In his book *Modernism and Eugenics: Woolf, Eliot, Yeats, and the Culture of Degeneration*, Donald Childs draws on the denatured theorizing of Foucault to explain modernist eugenics. Writes Childs:

Woolf, Eliot, and Yeats all appropriate the language of eugenical biology as a metaphor in aid of ostensibly non-biological cultural projects. In each case, however, the writer seems to serve as an agent – whether witting or unwitting – of what Foucault calls 'bio-power.' Each extends the imperial sway of the scientific discourse of the body into a realm long thought most different from it (if not most hostile to it): the realm of imagination.[5]

Given his premises, Childs is persuasive. But being of a realist temper, I would insist that the modernist writer "extends" the scientific discourse only metaphorically; and practical science is not a metaphor to the man who is getting his teeth drilled. Insofar as Woolf, Eliot, and Yeats "appropriate the language of eugenical biology as a metaphor in aid of ostensibly non-biological cultural projects," the metaphor is cut off from its referent, as happens in symbolist poetry. Modernism is not an exercise in "bio-power." Rather, modernism is a mutation of art in the direction of technology.

If I presume to refer to Yeats as a scientist, it is to place him in the tradition of Paracelsus. Yeats shared with his younger contemporaries a readiness to use art or *techne*, the knowledge of how to make things (*Nic. Eth.* 1140a), in order to transform human nature. A consummate stylist, he practiced verbal magic. And as C. S. Lewis has observed, magic and applied science are historically related:

There was very little magic in the Middle Ages: the sixteenth and seventeenth centuries are the high noon of magic. The serious magical endeavour and the serious scientific endeavour are twins: one was sickly and died, the other strong and throve . . . For magic and applied science alike the problem is how to subdue reality to the wishes of men: the solution is technique; and both, in the practice of technique, are ready to do things hitherto regarded as disgusting and impious – such as digging up and mutilating the dead.[6]

Yeats, the unweaver of "mummy-cloth," found his solution in "the elaborate technique of the arts . . . seeming to create out of itself a superhuman life."[7] To the "supreme masters of tragedy" he attributed "the birth of a new species of man."[8]

In "Under Ben Bulben," Yeats decries "the sort now growing up / All out of shape from toe to top / Base-born products of base beds."[9] These motley moderns lack the artistic purity of the ancient strains the poet celebrates, from "the peasantry" to "the lords and ladies gay." He urges his successors:

> Poet and sculptor do the work
> Nor let the modish painter shirk
> What his great forefathers did,
> Bring the soul of man to God,
> Make him fill the cradles right.[10]

The "modish painter" contrasts with the "great forefathers," the artists who served what for Yeats was the purpose of art: "Profane perfection of mankind" (line 52). Yeats asks the superior artist to use measurement and form (lines 42–44), the ancient means to Greece's victory over the "Asiatic vague immensities" described in "The Statues,"[11] so that the Irish may rival the Greeks. The pronoun "him," in the last line of the block quotation, could refer to the modish painter, who is being *forced* to improve his art; but it could also have "man" or "God" for antecedent ("God" would probably take "Him," but it nonetheless lingers in the oral atmosphere of the poem), in which case the poet's job is prophetically completed: the poem is a self-fulfilling prophecy. "Poet and sculptor" fill the cradles right, and Yeats's deployment of the verb "Make" lays stress on the poet's role as the divine maker (ὁ ποιητής) of man, God, or their superhuman progeny. As for the "cradles," Yeats's lunar symbolism (cradle = crescent) puts the eugenic sense in the context of the poet's metaphysical need, with Unity of Being as the essential interest.

By dramatizing a chemical reaction, which he (ironically) gets wrong, Eliot seeks to bolster the authority of the aesthetic per se:

There remains to define this process of depersonalization and its relation to the sense of tradition. It is in this depersonalization that *art may be said to approach the condition of science.* I shall, therefore, invite you to consider a suggestive analogy, the action which takes place when a bit of finely filiated platinum is introduced into a chamber containing oxygen and sulphur dioxide.[12]

Eliot alludes to Pater's memorable phrase: "*All art constantly aspires towards the condition of music.*"[13] As in impressionist and cubist art, Eliot wants the object of perception freed from convention and error. Impersonal clarity and precision demand that the artist, like the pure and amoral scientist, overcome the physiological link by which the body clouds the brain. "If the critic has performed his laboratory work well," Eliot writes, "his understanding will be evidence of appreciation; but his work is by the intelligence not the emotions."[14] In "Philip Massinger," he compares the "unique emotions" of Jacobean drama to "the properties of a chemical compound."[15] Once more he reveals himself to be a son of Pater, for whom the aesthetic critic regards a given virtue with the detachment of scientific analysis: "His end is reached when he has disengaged that virtue, and noted it, as a chemist notes some natural element, for himself and others . . ." Viewed aesthetically, art has an independent existence, like oxygen and sulphur dioxide. Insofar as Eliot differs from Pater, it is because he breaks more radically from the tradition of describing art in terms of its human content. The dehumanizing impulse is stronger.

Eliot looks at the relation of art to mankind as the relation of order to disorder. In "Dante," the last essay of *The Sacred Wood,* he calls the *Commedia* a "'moral education.'"[16] Art, not ethics or theology, supplies the substance of this education. According to Eliot, the artist's job is to provide "emotional structure."[17] More explicitly, if in Italian, he quotes the discourse on the soul from *Purgatorio* XVI: *Onde convenne legge per fren porre . . .*[18] which means roughly, "Therefore man needs to be checked by law." Eliot quotes the same line in his 1916 review of Paul More's *Aristocracy and Justice,* where it supports Moore's "distrust in undisciplined human nature."[19] Eliot's innovation lies in his means of investing the artist with power. The key is technique: "As for the verse of the present time," he writes, "the lack of curiosity in technical matters, of the academic poets of to-day (Georgian et caetera) is only an indication of their lack of curiosity in moral matters."[20] Similarly: "Georgian poetry . . . is inbred. It has developed a technique and a set of emotions all of its own."[21] Modernist poetry, by contrast, aims at a radical improvement of breeding by way of the best European technique, which has the power of structuring emotion and disciplining mankind. The task requires precision and efficiency: "A poet, like a scientist, is contributing towards the organic development of culture . . . It is exactly as wasteful for a poet to do what has been done already, as for a biologist to rediscover Mendel's discoveries."[22] This is to take Shelley's "unacknowledged legislators" and dress them up in lab coats.

Claiming "the importance of scientific discovery" for "the mythical method" of *Ulysses,* Eliot invokes Einstein.[23] The mythical method bears comparison to scientific method as "a way of controlling, of ordering, of giving a shape and a significance to the immense panorama of futility and anarchy which is contemporary history."[24] This line of thinking in Eliot well precedes his review of *Ulysses*: "science, as well as literature, is dependent upon the occasional appearance of a man of genius who discovers a new method."[25] Einstein had refashioned the cosmos through physics; modernist genius would refashion civilization through art.

Joyce, another exponent of artistic impersonality, builds *Ulysses* on the basis of "two temperaments," the "scientific" and the "artistic" (17.559). He seeks to integrate the new cosmic and evolutionary sciences with the structure of myth. How does this integration apply to the individual? Let us revisit the soul. For Joyce, as Maria Tymoczko explains, "reincarnation is a privilege and an affirmation of eternal verities, eternal values, eternal – archetypal, Jung would say – situations."[26] By laying bare the archetypal depths of the unconscious, science reveals the individual as epiphenomenal of these "eternal verities" and "situations."[27] The soul, as in Plato, passes under the throne of Necessity, and the grounds of moral agency disappear.

Joyce identifies biology with an immortal life-force, which, mimicking the style of T. H. Huxley in "Oxen of the Sun," he calls "the plasmic substance" (14.1281). He challenges Huxley, though, by indicating that the life-force is known to us, not only through science, but through the shaping power of myth. The synthesis of science and myth is not precisely worked out, but is left to speak for itself, somewhat along the lines of base and superstructure. The joint authority of science and myth precedes that of church, state, and family, much as fertility, conception, and birth precede civilization in "The Oxen of the Sun." Ordinary people fill their roles, unaware that authentic co-existence happens on a subconscious level, prior to the official social order. ("Fuck only time people really sincere," Joyce scribbled among his notesheets.)[28] Seeing the true situation, the artist proceeds to make the data of science habitable by overthrowing the old regime and giving human existence a superior new style. Joyce's dissent from eugenics (14.1243) therefore does not rule out his participation in the modernist moral project.

Woolf opens the soul – or subjects it – to technological improvements. One of her most daring comparisons equates spirit and matter: "in the drone of the aeroplane the voice of the summer sky murmured its fierce soul."[29] Mr. Bentley, a foretype of William Bankes, can see an airplane as "a symbol . . . of man's soul; of his determination . . . to get outside his body, beyond his house, by means of thought, Einstein, speculation, mathematics, Mendelian theory . . ."[30] Technology and art point to a new dispensation that unfurls like sky-writing on the visionary horizon: "the purity of . . . inspiration" triumphs over "the great clod of clay,"[31] and "scientifically speaking the flesh [is] melted off the world."[32] "Thanks to his scientific mind," William can understand Lily's "neglect of the significance of mother and son." Trading in the old lamp of wisdom, Nicholas Pomjalovsky uses "the light of modern science" to cast doubt on civilization: "If we do not know ourselves, how then can we make religions, laws, that . . . fit?"[33] In the minds of Nicholas and his friend Eleanor Pargiter, science creates utopian vistas of a "New World."

Possessing a deep sense of the English literary past and the wellsprings of its affections, Woolf felt pressed into an aggressive defense of her ideas against those who demanded loyalty to human nature:

> . . . we get another pleasure which comes when the mind is freed from the perpetual demand of the novelist that we shall feel with his characters. By cutting off the responses which are called out in actual life, the novelist frees us to take delight . . . in things in themselves . . . It is a pleasure somewhat akin, perhaps, to the pleasure of mathematics or the pleasure of music. Only, of course, since the novelist is using men and women as his subjects, he is perpetually exciting feelings which are opposed to the impersonality of numbers and sound; he seems, in fact, to ignore and repress their natural feelings, to be coercing them into a plan which we call with a vague resentment 'artificial' though it is probable that we are not so foolish as to resent artifice in art.[34]

The modernist writer views character and reader through a single lens. The focus in both cases is the difficult conflict between art and human material. Woolf resolves the conflict by redefining coercion as artifice. Force becomes art. But the move is not entirely persuasive, and so she bullies her reader, much as she imagines that "the art of fiction come alive . . . would undoubtedly bid us break and bully her."[35] If something like "the pleasure of mathematics" strikes the reader as a poor exchange for his "responses" to "actual life," he must be "foolish" and resentful. Put bluntly, he is threatened with the short end of a transvaluation of values. Woolf gives away what she negotiates with great subtlety in her fiction, namely, the means by which higher selves like Lily Briscoe and Eleanor Pargiter gain moral authority over their fleshier counterparts. In the end, it would appear, might makes right.

Beckett turns the modernist moral project on its head: he *deforms* human nature through the synthesis of art and technology. In *Endgame*, his masterpiece of the Cold War, a telescope creates an unhuman perspective, much as it does in *Paradise Lost*. Like Milton, Beckett is a poet of blindness and ruin, but he minimalizes the seductive effects of

Milton's "Tuscan artist" (*Paradise Lost* I. 288), even as he intensifies the old Puritan psychomachia of world versus soul. Looking out on the blighted sea and land, Clov reports to Hamm: "a multitude . . . in transports . . . of joy,"[36] which echoes Revelation 7:9–10.[37] Clov admits he is exaggerating, then describes the same view as "Zero" and "Corpsed." A moment later it is "Light black. From pole to pole." Telescope or H-bomb, technology is an angel of the void, cancelling our moral faculties. Hamm goes on to punctuate his "story time" with references to "the thermometer," "the heliometer," "the anemometer," and "the hygrometer."[38] Delivered in a "narrative tone," these references embellish the fragments of a wretched tale of moral blindness. They assert the darkness of man's self-dramatizing ethical nullity – the coefficient of his pointless science.

In *Krapp's Last Tape*, Beckett uses the technology of a tape recorder to demonstrate the collapse of man. Played by the author's invisible hand, the clownish Krapp *"switches off . . . switches on again."*[39] He rehearses the stock gestures of heroic modernist-romanticism: creative self, romantic love, lyric epiphany. He is psychologically vivisected to reveal a machine. His craving for the womb is expressed by his infantile confusion of "spoon" and "Spooool." His psychological drive for sex and death compels him to repeat himself, like a tape repeating, going around in circles. His being has no ethical structure. He is a kind of puppet, a framework of drawers and wires, his thoughts a patchwork of metonymic associations. Through his selection of magnetic tapes, he returns mechanically and unconsciously to the place of least pain, the dark north of womb and tomb.

The modernist moral project is currently alive and kicking in the form of new ethical theories, fed in part by the work of Emmanuel Levinas.[40] Joyce critic Derek Attridge offers a representative case in his efforts to adapt Levinas to an "urgent" program of "refashioning social, philosophical, cultural, and ethical tools."[41] Note the technological emphasis: "refashioning ethical tools." My sense is that Levinas has been misappropriated by theorists indifferent to the religious ground of his regard for the Other; so I will limit myself to stating just the root of my argument with Levinas, namely, that he denies the existence of human nature. Being an inheritor of phenomenological schools of thought, he neglects the body's physiological (non-intentional) contributions to mental activity. His ethics will elude those who cannot in practice extirpate "the gravity of the body" and its *conatus* or condition of striving.[42] Levinas asks us to strip the ego of "the protective mask of a character contemplating in the mirror of the world a reassured and self-positing portrait."[43] No doubt it is from time to time necessary to lay bare the pretensions of the ego, to put aside "the mask of character," insofar as character is a mask. But I would hesitate to build an entire ethics on such precarious and painful moments. Considered from the angle of practical living, Levinas does not speak adequately to the harsher elements of the embodied soul, for example, our need (even our sexual need) for social hierarchy.

In his book *Joyce Effects*, Attridge deconstructs the term *character*. Where character for Aristotle is natural and necessary, for Attridge it is an ideological construct or fiction that "bears a structural resemblance to" the Thomistic aesthetic of *integritas, consonantia,* and *claritas,* as discussed by Stephen Dedalus.[44] For Attridge, character and beauty are "historically and theoretically intertwined . . . They are both predicated upon a certain model of transcendence" that keeps faith with the "concept of human nature,"[45] which is yet another construct posing as "immutable" truth. The next move is to claim Joyce on behalf of the enlightened ones who see past the "illusory experience of unmediated access to knowable human nature."[46] (Here, by the way, is Pascal: "Instead of receiving ideas of these things in purity, we tinge them with our qualities, and stamp all the simple things that we contemplate [with] our own composite being.")[47]

Through Levinas and Derrida, if not more directly, Attridge is deeply indebted to Heidegger's critique of the history of metaphysics. Like the others, Attridge repeats what I take to be a blunder: Heidegger's failure to see how human nature helped shape the life of the *polis*. Heidegger sought to encounter truth as it existed before philosophy, art, and history covered naked being in their many-colored garments. But without Heidegger's ontology, Attridge falls into the pit of sophistry that Heidegger, for all his wordplay, manages to avoid.

Why sophistry? In the *Nicomachean Ethics*, Aristotle comments that the sophists consider politics to be "identical with rhetoric or even inferior to it" (1181a15). In other words, the sophists thought that speech itself (including laws) held all the power a ruler needed to persuade his subjects to obey. When Attridge enjoins "a suspension of . . . reading habits" when reading the other,[48] he recalls Levinas's demand for a stripping away of the ego and the *conatus* of the body. The reader must bow to the will of a text whose rhetoric is made good by the religious dimension that carries over from Levinas. But insofar as Attridge is not a religious writer, sophistry is all that remains.[49]

Using terms from Heidegger's analysis of technology, I would say that Attridge's deconstruction of character serves to "unlock and expose" the power in the field of the western tradition of thought, which he names as

such, while at the same time reaping "the maximum yield at the min-
imum expense" to the critic.[50] Attridge fulfills the technological model by
maintaining the "illusion . . . that everything man encounters exists only
insofar as it is his construct."[51] The construct of human "character" can be
harvested for the sake of maximum yield (Attridge cites twenty titles
under his own name in *Joyce Effects*), while the transformation of man
continues apace, right up to the present moment of hermeneutic enlightenment, when past evils are identified, at the cost of the enlightened
present, which slides into the unenlightened past, to be mined or exposed
by more hermeneutics.

Hélène Cixous in her essay "The Character of 'Character,'" cited by
Attridge in *Joyce Effects*, interprets modernist history along lines now
grown so familiar that they might be taken for orthodox: "How would
it be possible to study 'character' in Virginia Woolf's *The Waves* when the
vacillation of subjectivity between 'nobody' and all the possible individu-
alities discomposes the text by provoking it?"[52] Cixous is hammering away
at what she takes to be the constructs of bourgeois humanism (e.g.
"truth," "biography," "sense"), a way of life inspired to a wonderful extent
by Hegel. What she has really hit upon is Woolf's farewell to man in *The
Waves*, where the leading character, Bernard, must transcend nature and
the morbid despair it gives rise to: "Lord, how unutterably disgusting life
is! . . . Disorder, sordidity, and corruption surround us."[53] Debunking the
easy target of "an 'I' who is a *whole* subject,"[54] Cixous does not recognize
Woolf's novel as a meticulous and studied dehumanizing of character, an
assault on human nature in favor of the formal perfection of art. Bernard
is not a character so much as he is the spirit-medium of Woolf's formal
perfection.

Common readers, if they exist, can believe in character without
recourse to any "model of transcendence" – only intellectuals need drag
such heavy luggage around. Experience argues that immense practical
gains attach to believing in character, not the least of which is literature
itself. Put another way, human nature supports character because without
it we cannot flourish. In his *Psychology*, James addresses the phenomenon
of character in explaining why "ethical energy" is "the decisive issue of a
man's career":

When he debates, Shall I commit this crime? choose that profession? accept that
office, or marry this fortune? – his choice really lies between one of several equally
possible future Characters. What he shall *become* is fixed by the conduct of the
moment. Schopenhauer, who enforces his determinism by the argument that
with a given fixed character only one reaction is possible under given circumstances,

forgets that, in these critical ethical moments, what consciously *seems* to be in question is the complexion of the character itself. The problem with the man is less what act he shall now resolve to do than what being he shall now choose to become.[55]

James's answer to the arch-pessimist Schopenhauer revives an argument from the *Nicomachean Ethics*: "in purpose lies the essential element of virtue and character" (1163a22). Conscious purpose (aim or choice, moving toward the future) is an expression of free will. Without the twin supports of purpose and character, the moral agent will collapse entirely or, as in Schopenhauer, turn to mysticism in order to escape the prison of reality. But it is only partly the case that James defends what Cixous attacks as "the single, stable, socializable subject."[56] The Jamesian self is socializable (isn't that what we ask of children?), but its "constituents," "mutations" and "multiplications" are basic to our experience, the healthy attunement of which forms a good part of maturity.[57]

Goethe warns that the marriage of Faustus and Helen leads to the birth of the doomed and enchanting genius, Euphorion.[58] In the modernist period, the archpriest of this union of science and fine art is John Dewey. Dewey might be described as quasi-modernist. He shared feelings and practices with the writers whom we have discussed, including a powerful modernizing instinct, a belief in procedure over premises,[59] a jealous regard for private goods, and a revolutionary fusing of ethics and aesthetics through faith in the imagination. Further, he has a place in the anti-Arnoldian movement started by Pater, and he influenced Trilling. Dewey concedes the existence of human nature on an empirical basis, while arguing, "Intelligent action is not concerned with the bare consequences of the thing known, but with consequences *to be* brought into existence by action conditioned on the knowledge. Men may use their knowledge to induce conformity or exaggeration, or to effect change and abolition of conditions."[60] For Dewey, human nature, even as it exists, serves conservative bias more than it serves human happiness. He therefore argues against granting it any prescriptive force.

In *Art as Experience*, Dewey sniffs out the Aristotelian element in Arnold's reaction against romanticism:

Matthew Arnold's dictum that "poetry is a criticism of life" . . . suggests to the reader a moral intent on the part of the poet and a moral judgment on the part of the reader. It fails to see or at all events to state how poetry is a criticism of life; namely, not directly, but by disclosure, through imaginative vision addressed to imaginative experience (not to set judgment) of possibilities that contrast with actual conditions. A sense of possibilities that are unrealized and that might be realized are when they are put in contrast with actual conditions, the most penetrating "criticism" of the latter that can be made. It is by a sense of possibilities opening before us that we become aware of constrictions that hem us in and of burdens that oppress.[61]

In support of his case against Arnold, Dewey enlists Shelley's *Defense of Poetry*: "The imagination is the great instrument of moral good, and poetry administers to the effect by acting upon the causes."[62] Like the Shelley of the *Defense*, Dewey wants literature to enact a perpetual questing after the ideal, and to inspire a change in the actual by means of this quest. Change in the actual is a disburdening, an unhemming of the "closed world" of Aristotle. In *Reconstruction in Philosophy*, Dewey asks that "we advance to a belief in a plurality of changing, moving, individualized goods and ends, and to a belief that principles, criteria, laws are intellectual instruments for analyzing individual or unique situations."[63] To achieve this plurality, we must use instrumental reason, and address ourselves to unrealized possibilities. The fine arts and the applied sciences serve the same function in Dewey's broader project; only the reflective workings of poetry distinguish it from the material workings of a steam engine. In either case, we use our arts to improve our world. Art is *techne*, and morality is *techne* as well. Making and acting combine in the stride of power. It is no accident that, where James traces the pragmatic method to Aristotle, Dewey names Bacon "the prophet of a pragmatic conception of knowledge."[64] Bacon, Dewey's anti-Aristotle, stands for "power over nature."[65]

Laying out his progressive vision, Dewey faces a crucial test in trying to adjust the physical action of emotion to our aesthetic response. He exemplifies the modernist pattern:

Esthetic experience is imaginative. This fact . . . has obscured the larger fact that all *conscious* experience has of necessity some degree of imaginative quality. For while the roots of every experience are found in the interaction of a live creature with its environment, that experience becomes conscious, a matter of perception, only when meanings enter it that are derived from prior experiences. Imagination is the only gateway through which these meanings can find their way into a present interaction; or rather, as we have seen, the conscious adjustment of the new and old *is* imagination. Interaction of a living being with an environment is found in vegetative and animal life. But the experience enacted is human and conscious only as that which is given here and now is extended by meanings and values drawn from what is absent in fact and present only imaginatively.[66]

Though he works in the organismic tradition of James and C. S. Peirce, Dewey effectively breaks off the human from the animal when it comes to talking about imagination and aesthetic experience. He makes no allowance for the memory-work of habit or for the wisdom of the body. I do not agree with him that emotion "belongs of a certainty to the self"[67] if he means, as he appears to mean, that "emotion is entirely rooted in the self." It is right to characterize a blush as an expression of "shamed modesty." But it is wrong to say that shamed modesty in itself is not an "emotional state" because it is just an "automatic reflex."[68] There is always a social context for the blush. It is fine to say, "There is an element of passion in all esthetic perception." But it is foolish to talk about art in the following manner: "Yet when we are overwhelmed by passion . . . the experience is definitely non-esthetic."[69] Non-aesthetic, but we may be responding to great art just the same. Like the modernists, then, Dewey struggles against the social nature of our affections. He resists biology when it points to the idea of a species nature, which he finds politically unappealing. Having confined his ethical project and the fine arts to the aesthetic mind, he puts himself in the awkward position of demanding political progress on the basis of unreality.

Here is one of the riddles of modernity: in what sense does human nature translate (across the thick medium of human knowledge – remember Pascal) to being our reality, the only reality that we have? Dewey saw the limits of human nature as potentially changing, and not in any permanent sense "real," for the idea of a permanent reality conjured up in his mind a discredited metaphysics. But the imaginative science of biotechnology should prompt us to consider human nature not only in metaphysical terms, but in practical terms of the grounds of human flourishing.

Freeman Dyson is an English scientist who offers yet additional testimony that the modernist moral project continues. Like Dewey, Dyson preaches an imaginative faith in the technology of human transformation. He brings his speculative powers to bear on the genome, and he does so with enormous expertise and considerable eloquence. For Dyson, technology is our only hope on this bitch of an earth. He sees very plainly that artificial intelligence and biotech threaten our future, but he argues that we must embrace our fate of working intimately with advanced computers and altering the genome, through the science known as "reprogenetics," in order to better our natural inheritance.

Dyson predicts that we will see, at least in the near term, an emerging division between two new species of man: those who are genetically enriched, the "GenRich," and those unfortunates who are not, the "Naturals." Like geneticist Lee Silver, who first envisaged society's branching into these two species, Dyson confronts the problems created by technology in a market economy. His concerns parallel those of Joyce with the fate of the self in the world of mass culture. Devoted to social justice, Dyson believes that social and market forces will combine, at least for a time, to prevent our dividing into supermen and slaves. One fervently hopes so, but it could just as easily be the case that technology used in the name of equality will lead to the greatest inequalities possible, those of human gods and human excrement. The Aristotelian argument applies equally to Dyson and to Joyce: only a "shared vision of the good for man (as prior to and independent of any summing of individual interests), and a *consequent* shared practice of the virtues" will enable us, as a community, to guard against our own self-enslavement by the mechanisms of the market.[70] In this respect, *Ulysses* has more relevance to the new eugenics than *Brave New World* has. Biotech is propelled by consumers in the free market (and by scientists and corporations), not by the kind of events that Aldous Huxley describes: catastrophic war and the restoration of world order through massive government services.[71] The transformations of modernism appeal at the aesthetic level; Huxley's "College of Emotional Engineering" bypasses consciousness in favor of subliminal messages and infantile pleasure.

What is most fascinating about Dyson's scientific imagination is his prognosis for the more distant future. He agrees with Silver "that the technology of reprogenetics will ultimately split humanity into many species, and that the division will not be only between rich and poor." He continues: "The division will be between different philosophies of life and different ways of living. When desires for different ways of living can be translated into reality, the diversity of desires will be translated into a diversity of species."[72] Dyson answers the infinite private needs of modernity by promising their infinite fulfillment. It is a good selling point. More, it suggests why modernity is so much more strongly disposed to the future than to the past. "Science," says Nietzsche, ". . . seeks to abolish all limitations of horizon and launch mankind upon an infinite and unbounded sea of light whose light is knowledge of all becoming."[73] One thinks of the scientific imagination of Nicholas Pomjalovsky, entranced by "the light of modern science," and that of Leopold Bloom: "high vast irradiation everywhere all soaring around about the all, the endlessness-nessness . . ." (11.750). It is as if we were doomed to re-live the same future over and over again, to fade eternally into our own yearning. "When we have mastered the science of reprogenetics," Dyson predicts, "we shall be creating our own genetic barriers, not in opposition to nature, but enabling the natural processes of human evolution to continue."[74] Where

Galton aimed to "co-operate with the works of Nature," Dyson wants to cooperate with "the natural processes of human evolution," an oxymoronic god-trope that undoes the "human" by virtue of the blessed processes that it names. In his own fashion, then, Dyson is a knight of faith, concentrating his will toward a *telos* that he cannot communicate.

But at least this dilemma is known to us. If the history of modernism offers any indication of where science and imagination would lead the human race, Dyson's promised end may seem familiar:

Even if the division of humanity into several species is a division among equals and not a division between masters and slaves, it will still bring with it *intractable social and ethical problems*. It is difficult to imagine several human species coexisting peacefully on this small and crowded planet . . . To allow the diversification of human genomes and lifestyles on this planet to continue without restraint is a recipe for disaster. Sooner or later, the tensions between diverging ways of life must be relieved by emigration, some of us finding new places to live away from the Earth while others stay behind. In the end we must travel the high roads into space, to find new worlds to match our new capabilities. To give us room to explore the varieties of mind and body into which our genome can evolve, one planet is not enough.[75]

Dyson's *amor fati* leads him to the frozen regions that awaited Frankenstein and his monster: a colony of moons and asteroids, where he imagines human life will grow in a state of everlasting potentiality. It is the new moon of Yeats's cosmology: uttermost north where "man is submissive and plastic."[76] The dark end of Dyson's science and imagination is a boundless frontier of space that we can't get to, know little about, and would hate to the marrow of our bones. He resolves the problem of conflicting "lifestyles," of a species alienated from its species life, by launching us into the Kuiper Belt.

BON VOYAGE!

In his essay "Darwinism and Philosophy," Dewey remarks: "Old questions are solved by disappearing, evaporating, while new questions corresponding to the changed attitude of endeavor and preference take their place."[77] Beckett's Hamm has no such faith. He is not so happy a camper: "Ah the old questions, the old answers, there's nothing like them!"[78] Beckett's use of the word "nothing" is invariably pointed. The author of *Endgame* thought that humanity had run its course. But I would take up his suggestion that the fate of humanity is tied to the old questions. We will go with them if they go. In that case, nihilism will triumph. *No one* will be left on stage to report the tragedy.

Notes

INTRODUCTION: LITERATURE AND HUMAN NATURE

1 See Harold Fromm, "The New Darwinism in the Humanities, Part I: From Plato to Pinker," *Hudson Review* 56 (2003), 89–99; and Harold Fromm, "The New Darwinism in the Humanities, Part II: Back to Nature, Again," *Hudson Review* 56 (2003), 315–27.

2 See, for example, Joseph Carroll, *Evolution and Literary Theory* (Columbia: University of Missouri Press, 1995); Paul R. Gross and Norman Levitt, *Higher Superstition: The Academic Left and Its Quarrel with Science* (Baltimore: The Johns Hopkins University Press, 1994); Paul R. Gross, Norman Levitt, and Martin W. Lewis, eds., *The Flight from Science and Reason* (New York: The New York Academy of Sciences, 1996); and Alan Sokal and Jean Bricmont, *Fashionable Nonsense: Postmodern Intellectuals' Abuse of Science* (New York: Picador, 1999).

3 Virginia Woolf, *Collected Essays*, 4 vols. (London: Hogarth Press, 1966), vol. I, p. 320.

4 Steven Pinker, *The Blank Slate: The Modern Denial of Human Nature* (New York: Penguin Books, 2002), p. 404. Pinker misreads "human character" as "human nature," but corrects himself in a note. The mistake does not affect his argument.

5 Oscar Wilde, *Complete Works of Oscar Wilde*, ed. J. B. Foreman (New York: HarperCollins, 2001), p. 1015.

6 William Butler Yeats, *Autobiographies: Reveries Over Childhood and Youth* and *The Trembling of the Veil* (New York: Macmillan, 1927), p. 343.

7 José Ortega y Gasset, *The Dehumanization of Art and Other Essays on Art, Culture, and Literature* (Princeton: Princeton University Press, 1968), p. 8.

8 Ibid., p. 23.

9 For a rival view, see Jewel Spears Brooker, who places modernism, and Eliot in particular, in the context of "what the *Times Literary Supplement*, in a leading article in September 1926, called 'The Dethronement of Descartes.'" Brooker continues: "After describing the last three hundred years in western philosophy as a development of Cartesianism, the writer claims that Descartes and the great physicist-philosophers of the seventeenth century had been dethroned by the physicists and philosophers of the early twentieth,

ushering in a new dispensation in intellectual history." Jewel Spears Brooker, *Mastery and Escape: T. S. Eliot and the Dialectic of Modernism* (Amherst: University of Massachusetts Press, 1994), p. 173. I argue that the modernist moral project kept Descartes on his throne. More, the work of Damasio and Pinker would not be necessary if the "new dispensation" had taken hold.

10 See, for example, John Leofric Stocks, *Aristotelianism* (Bristol, England: Thoemmes Press, 1993), pp. 134–41.

11 Cowley quoted in T. S. Eliot, "A Note on Two Odes of Cowley," in John Purves, ed., *Seventeenth Century Studies Presented to Sir Herbert Grierson* (Oxford: Clarendon Press, 1938), p. 237.

12 William James, *Psychology: The Briefer Course*, ed. Gordon Allport (Notre Dame: University of Notre Dame Press, 1985), p. 247.

13 Georg Wilhelm Friedrich Hegel, *The Philosophy of History*, trans. J. Sibree (New York: Willey Book Co., 1944), p. 40 (his italics).

14 Karl Marx, *Selected Writings*, ed. David McLellan (Oxford: Oxford University Press, 1977), p. 134. For an informed rebuttal of the Marxist appropriation of Darwin, see Carroll, *Evolution and Literary Theory*.

15 Friedrich Nietzsche, *Basic Writings of Nietzsche*, ed. and trans. Walter Kaufmann (New York: Modern Library, 1992), p. 201.

16 Martin Heidegger, "Letter on Humanism," quoted in Alasdair MacIntyre, *Dependent Rational Animals: Why Human Beings Need the Virtues* (Chicago: Open Court, 1999), p. 43.

17 T. S. Eliot, *Knowledge and Experience in the Philosophy of F. H. Bradley* (New York: Columbia University Press, 1989), p. 132.

18 "In the case of the frightened child, I am not prepared to support the James-Lange theory . . ." Ibid., p. 116.

19 Woody Allen, *Annie Hall*, quoted in Pinker, *Blank Slate*, p. 190.

20 Pinker, *Blank Slate*, pp. 190–91.

21 Charles Baudelaire, *The Painter of Modern Life and Other Essays*, ed. and trans. Jonathan Mayne (London: Phaidon, 1965), p. 157.

22 Ibid.

23 Ibid.

24 Pinker, *Blank Slate*, p. 173.

25 John Stuart Mill, *Collected Works of John Stuart Mill*, Gen. ed. John M. Robson, 33 vols. (Toronto: University of Toronto Press, 1963–1991), vol. I, p. 141.

26 Three landmark works are Philippa Foot, *Virtues and Vices* (Berkeley: University of California Press, 1978); Peter Geach, *The Virtues* (Cambridge: Cambridge University Press, 1977); and Alasdair MacIntyre, *After Virtue*, 2nd edn. (Notre Dame: University of Notre Dame Press, 1984). My other sources in Aristotelian virtue ethics are Philippa Foot, *Natural Goodness* (Oxford: Clarendon Press, 2001); Rosalind Hursthouse, "Virtue Ethics," in *The Stanford Encyclopedia of Philosophy*, fall 2003 edition, ed. Edward N. Zalat, plato.stanford.edu/archives/fall 2003/entries/ethics-virtue; T. H. Irwin, "The Metaphysical and Psychological Basis of Aristotle's Ethics," in Amélie

Oksenberg Rorty, ed., *Essays on Aristotle's Ethics* (Berkeley: University of California Press, 1980), pp. 35–53; MacIntyre, *Dependent Rational Animals*; Martha C. Nussbaum, "Non-Relative Virtues: An Aristotelian Approach," in *Midwest Studies in Philosophy*, vol. 13, *Ethical Theory: Character and Virtue*, eds. Peter A. French, Theodore E. Uehling, Jr., and Howard K. Wettstein (Notre Dame: University of Notre Dame Press, 1988), 32–53; and Christine Swanton, *Virtue Ethics: A Pluralistic View* (Oxford: Oxford University Press, 2003). Of course, not everyone who writes well on Aristotle is a virtue ethicist.

27 The phrase is lifted wholesale from Carroll, *Evolution and Literary Theory*, p. 113.

28 Pinker, *Blank Slate*, pp. 235–36.

29 At least Aristotle discerned the limits of connecting ethics to biology: "There is no general integration of the causal dimensions of explanation of action, one that would link the logic of practical reasoning to the biology in which it is realized. The connection between *De Anima* and the theory of action developed in Aristotle's ethical works must, in the nature of the case, remain schematic because ethics is not, according to Aristotle, a psycho-biological science." Amélie Oksenberg Rorty, "Introduction B: *De Anima*: Its Agenda and Its Recent Interpreters," in Martha C. Nussbaum and Amélie Oksenberg Rorty, eds., *Essays on Aristotle's De Anima* (Oxford: Clarendon Press, 1992), p. 12. I have corrected a typo in Rorty's text ("ethnical"). For the relation between Aristotelian ethics and evolutionary biology, see Larry Arnhart, *Darwinian Natural Right: The Biological Ethics of Human Nature* (Albany: State University of New York Press, 1998); Foot, *Natural Goodness*, pp. 30–33; and Geach, *Virtues*, p. 11.

30 Quotations from Aristotle, including parenthetical references, are from *The Basic Works of Aristotle*, ed. Richard McKeon (New York: Random House, 1941).

31 See, for example, Hugh Lawson-Tancred, "Introduction," in Aristotle, *De Anima (On the Soul)*, ed. and trans. Hugh Lawson-Tancred (Harmondsworth: Penguin Books, 1986), pp. 112–13.

32 T. S. Eliot, "The Development of Leibniz's Monadism," *Monist* 26 (1916), 554.

33 Pinker, *Blank Slate*, pp. 176–77.

34 R. S. Crane, "Introduction," in R. S. Crane, W. R. Keast, Richard McKeon, Norman Maclean, Elder Olson, and Bernard Weinberg, *Critics and Criticism, Ancient and Modern*, ed. R. S. Crane (Chicago: University of Chicago Press, 1952), p. 2.

35 M. F. Burnyeat, "Is an Aristotelian Philosophy of Mind Still Credible? (A Draft)," in Nussbaum and Rorty, eds., *Essays on Aristotle's De Anima*, p. 25 (his italics).

36 Ibid., p. 17 (his italics).

37 To be fair, one cannot blame the computers. See the work of human being Charles Van Doren, *A History of Knowledge: Past, Present, and Future*

(New York: Ballantine Books, 1991), pp. 377–83. Both the philosophical background of the *mind=brain=computer* school of thought, and the linguistic sleight of hand that makes a computer of the mind, are addressed by Raymond Tallis, *Why the Mind Is Not a Computer: A Pocket Lexicon of Neuromythology* (Charlottesville, VA: Imprint Academic, 2004).

38 Antonio Damasio, *Descartes' Error: Emotion, Reason, and the Human Brain* (New York: Quill, 2000).

39 James, *Psychology: Briefer Course*, p. 247.

40 W. B. Yeats, *Ideas of Good and Evil*, 2nd edn. (A. H. Bullen: London, 1903), p. 299.

41 Samuel Beckett, *Three Novels: Molloy, Malone Dies, The Unnamable* (New York: Grove Press, 1965), p. 55.

42 Woolf, *Collected Essays*, I:10.

43 Damasio, *Descartes' Error*, p. 129.

44 Nussbaum, "Non-Relative Virtues," 45.

45 J. O. Urmson, *Aristotle's Ethics* (Oxford: Blackwell, 1988), p. 32.

46 For an attempt in virtue ethics to coordinate the "narrow reflective equilibrium" of Aristotle and the "wide reflective equilibrium" of Nietzsche, see Swanton, *Virtue Ethics*.

47 For the usage of *man*, see Jacques Barzun, *From Dawn to Decadence: 500 Years of Cultural Life, 1500 to the Present* (New York: HarperCollins, 2000), pp. 82–85.

48 MacIntyre, *After Virtue*, p. 204.

49 See Woolf, *Collected Essays*, I:191–94.

50 Charles Dickens, *The Pickwick Papers* (Oxford: Oxford University Press, 1948), p. 11.

51 "In Latin, *persona* refers originally to a device of transformation and concealment on the theatrical stage." Robert C. Elliott, *The Literary Persona* (Chicago: University of Chicago Press, 1982), p. 21.

52 I have never heard anyone mention the phonograph in Eliot's "Portrait of a Lady." To my ear, "windings" and "cracked" suggest an old-fashioned 78 rpm. But Grover Smith says the music is "the yearning music of her voice." Grover Smith, *T. S. Eliot's Poetry and Plays: A Study in Sources and Meaning* (Chicago: University of Chicago Press, 1956), p. 11.

53 Wilde, *Complete Works*, p. 1078.

54 William Butler Yeats, *Mythologies* (New York: Macmillan, 1969), p. 334.

55 T. S. Eliot, review of *Per Amica Silentia Lunae*, by William Butler Yeats, *Egoist* 5 (June/July 1918), 87.

56 See Hursthouse, "Virtue Ethics," 3–4.

57 It is helpful to compare Ronald Bush's discussion of Eliotic impersonality with Richard Ellmann's discussion of Yeatsian personality. Both critics discern an underlying paradox in how the poet conveys, to quote Bush, "his authentically personal emotion." See Ronald Bush, *T. S. Eliot: A Study in Character and Style* (New York: Oxford University Press, 1983), pp. 44–47; and Richard Ellmann, *Yeats: The Man and the Masks* (New York: E. P. Dutton,

1948), pp. 236–37. Less helpfully, R. F. Foster sees Eliot and Yeats as diametrically opposed: "When Richard Ellmann remarked that for T. S. Eliot the creative process was an escape from personality, the contrast with WBY must have been in his mind." R. F. Foster, *W. B. Yeats: A Life*, 2 vols. (New York: Oxford University Press, 1998–2003), vol. II, p. xxiii.

58 W. B. Yeats, "Friends of My Youth," quoted in Gale Schricker, *A New Species of Man: The Poetic Persona of W. B. Yeats* (Lewisburg: Bucknell University Press, 1982), p. 13.

59 T. S. Eliot, *The Sacred Wood: Essays on Poetry and Criticism* (London: Methuen, 1960), p. 53.

60 Ibid., p. 139.

61 T. S. Eliot, *On Poetry and Poets* (London: Faber and Faber, 1957), p. 95.

62 T. S. Eliot, *Collected Poems: 1909–1962* (New York: Harcourt, 1988), p. 72.

63 Virginia Woolf, *To the Lighthouse* (San Diego: Harcourt, 1989), p. 98.

64 Beckett, *Three Novels*, p. 343.

65 I am indebted to Amélie Rorty, "A Literary Postscript," in Amélie Oksenberg Rorty, ed., *The Identities of Persons* (Berkeley: University of California Press, 1976), p. 317.

66 Matthew Arnold, *Complete Prose Works of Matthew Arnold*, ed. R. H. Super, 11 vols. (Ann Arbor, MI: University of Michigan Press, 1961–1977), vol. I, pp. 1–2.

67 I marvel at Henry Ebel's gross slander: "Much of the Preface stumbles along under the weight of Aristotle's *Poetics*, a work to whose principles Arnold swears implicit allegiance . . ., but whose gist Arnold conveys to the reader through an often dishonest medley of straight paraphrase, loose recapitulation, and outright but unacknowledged embroidery." Henry Ebel, "Matthew Arnold and Classical Culture," *Arion* 4 (1965), 198. Ebel betrays no knowledge of Greek.

68 MacIntyre, *Dependent Rational Animals*, p. 116.

69 Arnold, *Complete Prose Works*, I:4.

70 Ibid., V: 126–27. Warren Anderson notes that Arnold, as an undergraduate at Oxford, was responsible for reading (in Greek) all of the *Nicomachean Ethics* and "at the least the first two books of the *Rhetoric*." However, Anderson contends, the "greatest single influence of ancient thought upon Matthew Arnold was exerted by Stoicism and Epicureanism, post-Hellenic ethical systems whose spokesmen made no significant contribution to literature." Warren Anderson, "Arnold and the Classics," in Kenneth Allott, ed., *Matthew Arnold* (Athens, OH: University of Ohio Press, 1976), p. 278. Anderson's summary accounts neither for Arnold's concern with "primary affections" and "elementary feelings," nor for Arnold's political and cultural views. In one of his letters to Clough, Arnold quotes the *Nicomachean Ethics* apparently from memory. See the letter dated September 23, 1849, in Matthew Arnold, *The Letters of Matthew Arnold to Arthur Hugh Clough*, ed. Howard Lowry (London: Oxford University Press, 1932), p. 111.

71 Arnold, *Complete Prose Works*, V:225.

72 Ibid., III:258.

73 Ibid., III:12–13.

74 Ibid., III:261.

75 Ibid., X:57.

76 Ibid., X:63.

77 Ibid., X:70.

78 Thomas H. Huxley, *Science and Education: Essays* (New York: D. Appleton, 1896), p. 150.

79 Ibid.

80 Thomas H. Huxley, *Evolution and Ethics* (New York: D. Appleton, 1896), p. 83. Like Huxley, J. S. Mill finds no warrant for natural teleology. See Mill's essay "Nature," from the posthumously published *Three Essays on Religion* (1874), in *Collected Works*, X: 369–489.

81 Virginia Woolf, *Mrs. Dalloway* (New York: Harcourt, 1925), p. 117.

82 Ibid.

83 Thomas Nagel, *The Last Word* (New York: Oxford University Press, 1997), p. 133.

84 Arnold, *Complete Prose Works*, X:68.

85 See, for example, Irwin, "The Metaphysical and Psychological Basis."

86 John Locke, *An Essay Concerning Human Understanding*, 2 vols. (Mineola, NY: Dover, 1959), vol. I, p. 122.

87 Discussing the second paragraph of the Conclusion to the *Renaissance* ("Or if we begin . . ."), Carolyn Williams addresses Pater's Lockean background:

> Behind the words of this paragraph lie the empiricist epistemologies of Locke and Hume, but also more immediately the critiques of Berkeley and Kant. Pater seems to grapple here with the difficult notion that the long tradition of empiricist epistemology has undergone a dialectical reversal: a discourse instituted to counteract the classical form of idealism by relying on the evidence of the senses seems to have circled back to enunciate another, subjectivist form of it. The empiricist sense-impression has been replaced by a subjectivist, idealist "impression" that has only a "relic" of "a sense" left in it, a distant reminder of the sensory experience that stimulated it in the first place. The difference between the empiricist "impression" and the subjectivist "impression" has to do with the one's relative attention to the object and the other's relative absorption in the mind's own processes.

> Carolyn Williams, *Transfigured World: Walter Pater's Aesthetic Historicism* (Ithaca: Cornell University Press, 1989), pp. 20–21.

88 Walter Pater, *Works*, library edition, 10 vols. (London: Macmillan, 1912–1915), vol. I, p. viii.

89 Ibid., I:ix–x.

90 *OED* sense 9.

91 Pater, *Works*, V:5.

92 Ibid., II:99.

93 Ibid., II:99–100.

94 Yeats, *Autobiographies*, pp. 386–87.

95 T. S. Eliot, *To Criticize the Critic and Other Writings* (Lincoln: University of Nebraska Press, 1991), p. 40.

96 Arnold, *Complete Prose Works*, III:109.

97 Ibid., I:174 (his italics).

98 Ibid., IX:43.

99 Frank Kermode, *Romantic Image* (London: Routledge, 1957), p. 20.

100 See Graham Hough, *The Last Romantics* (London: Methuen, 1961), pp. 134–74; Harold Bloom, "Introduction," in Walter Pater, *Selected Writings of Walter Pater*, ed. Harold Bloom (New York: Columbia University Press, 1974), pp. vii–xxxi; and David Bromwich, *A Choice of Inheritance* (Cambridge: Harvard University Press, 1989), pp. 106–32.

101 Arnold, *Complete Prose Works*, V:242.

102 Ibid., V:254.

103 Ibid., V:96.

104 Ibid., V:127.

105 Pater, *Works*, V:61 (his italics).

106 Ibid., V:62.

107 Ibid., II:243.

108 Ibid., I:239.

109 Ibid., VIII:183.

110 Ibid., VIII:186.

111 Ibid., I:235.

112 Ibid., VIII:187–88.

113 Ibid., VIII:182–83.

114 Edmund Burke, *Reflections on the Revolution in France*, ed. Conor Cruise O'Brien (New York: Penguin, 1968), p. 170.

115 Pater, *Works*, VIII:180–81.

116 Virginia Woolf, *The Years* (San Diego: Harcourt, 1939), p. 276.

117 Woolf, *To the Lighthouse*, p. 51.

118 Virginia Woolf, *Between the Acts* (San Diego: Harcourt, 1970), p. 187 (her italics).

119 Arnold, *Complete Prose Works*, V:150.

120 Ibid., V:175.

121 Pater, *Works*, I:237–38.

122 Thomas Carlyle, *Carlyle's Complete Works*, 20 vols. (Boston: Estes and Lauriat, 1885), vol. I, pp. 195–96.

123 Pater, *Works*, I:236–37.

124 Wilde, *Complete Works*, p. 973.

125 Ibid., p. 1040, quoted in Bromwich, *Choice of Inheritance*, p. 131.

126 Woolf, *Between the Acts*, p. 90.

127 Wilde, *Complete Works*, p. 1030.

128 Ibid., p. 1027.

129 Ibid.

130 Aristotle says "the poet's function is to describe . . . a kind of thing that might happen, i.e. what is possible as being probable or necessary" (*Poet.* 1451a36).

131 Wilde, *Complete Works*, p. 925.

132 Ibid., p. 56.

133 Ibid., p. 161.

134 Yeats, *Autobiographies*, p. 320.

135 Yeats, *Mythologies*, p. 359.

136 Yeats, "Friends of My Youth," quoted in Schricker, *New Species of Man*, p. 13.

137 Quotations from *Ulysses*, including parenthetical references, are from James Joyce, *Ulysses*, ed. Hans Walter Gabler (New York: Vintage, 1986).

138 Woolf, *Collected Essays*, I:239.

139 Ibid., I:243.

140 Virginia Woolf, *The Waves* (New York: Harcourt), p. 134.

141 W. B. Yeats, "Introduction," in W. B. Yeats, ed., *The Oxford Book of Modern Verse 1892–1935* (New York: Oxford University Press, 1935), p. xxi.

142 Eliot, *Collected Poems*, p. 14.

143 James Joyce, *Dubliners* (New York: Viking Press, 1968), p. 49.

144 Harry Levin, *James Joyce* (Norfolk, CT: New Directions, 1941), p. 5.

145 One finds the same idea in Bergson. See Henri Bergson, *Matter and Memory*, trans. Nancy Margaret Paul and W. Scott Palmer (Garden City, NY: Doubleday, 1959), p. 68.

146 Samuel Beckett, *Proust* (New York: Grove Press, 1931), pp. 8–9, quoted in Christopher Ricks, *Beckett's Dying Words* (Oxford: Oxford University Press, 1993), p. 72.

147 Beckett, *Proust*, pp. 7–8.

148 "Disgust (*dégoût*), a productive force in the arts since Baudelaire, is insatiable in Beckett's historically mediated impulses." Theodor W. Adorno, "Trying to Understand *Endgame*," trans. Michael T. Jones, *New German Critique* 26 (1982), 121.

149 Samuel Beckett, *Waiting for Godot: A Tragicomedy in Two Acts* (New York: Grove Press, 1956), p. 58.

150 "Ultimately," writes Virgil Nemoianu, "the dilemmas of general aesthetics *rediviva* cannot be hidden. An aesthetic model that wants to be consistent with itself must sooner or later turn against itself . . ." Virgil Nemoianu, *A Theory of the Secondary: Literature, Progress, and Reaction* (Baltimore: Johns Hopkins University Press, 1989), p. 82.

151 Arnold, *Complete Prose Works*, I:8.

152 Charles Taylor describes modern art as "a crucial terrain for the ideal of authenticity," and the modern artist as "the paradigm case of the human being, as agent of original self-definition." Charles Taylor, *The Ethics of Authenticity* (Cambridge: Harvard University Press, 1991), p. 82 and p. 62.

153 MacIntyre, *Dependent Rational Animals*, p. 164.

154 Wilde quoted in Richard Ellmann, *Oscar Wilde* (New York: Alfred A. Knopf, 1988), p. 469.

155 Virginia Woolf, *Jacob's Room* (San Diego: Harcourt, 1978), p. 72.

156 Woolf, *Collected Essays*, I:361.

157 Samuel Beckett and Georges Duthuit, "Three Dialogues," in Martin Esslin, ed., *Samuel Beckett: A Collection of Critical Essays* (Englewood Cliffs, NJ: Prentice-Hall, 1965), p. 19.

CHAPTER 1: W. B. YEATS: OUT OF NATURE

1 Yeats, *Ideas of Good and Evil,* p. 198.
2 Ibid., p. 199.
3 Ibid., p. 198.
4 Ibid., pp. 306–307.
5 Ibid., p. 198.
6 Ibid., p. 206.
7 Ibid., pp. 198–99.
8 Ibid., p. 203.
9 Ibid., p. 215.
10 Ibid., p. 200.
11 Ibid., p. 204.
12 Pater, *Works,* I:54.
13 Ibid., V:61.
14 Ibid., VI:142.
15 Yeats, "Introduction," p. ix.
16 Ibid., p. xii.
17 Yeats, *Autobiographies,* p. 127.
18 Yeats, *Ideas of Good and Evil,* p. 340.
19 Arthur Symons, *The Symbolist Movement in Literature* (New York: E. P. Dutton, 1958), p. 5.
20 Yeats, *Ideas of Good and Evil,* pp. 239–40.
21 Ibid., p. 128.
22 Symons, *Symbolist Movement,* p. 49.
23 Yeats, *Ideas of Good and Evil,* p. 240.
24 W. B. Yeats, *The Collected Poems of W. B. Yeats,* ed. Richard J. Finneran (New York: Macmillan, 1989), p. 81.
25 Yeats, *Ideas of Good and Evil,* pp. 67–68.
26 Yeats, *Collected Poems,* p. 9.
27 Samuel Taylor Coleridge, *The Collected Works of Samuel Taylor Coleridge,* ed. Kathleen Coburn, 16 vols. (Princeton: Princeton University Press, 1971–2000), vol. VI, p. 30.
28 Yeats, *Ideas of Good and Evil,* p. 69.
29 Ibid., p. 247.
30 Ibid., p. 304.
31 In his letter to George Russell (AE) of May 14, 1903, Yeats writes: "I am no longer in much sympathy with an essay like 'The Autumn of the Body,' not that I think the essay untrue." W. B. Yeats, *The Letters of W. B. Yeats,* ed. Allan Wade (New York: Macmillan, 1955), p. 402. He had started reading Nietzsche.

32 Yeats, *Ideas of Good and Evil*, p. 243.

33 Ibid., p. 188.

34 Yeats, *Mythologies*, p. 285.

35 Pater, *Works*, I:53–54.

36 Yeats, *Ideas of Good and Evil*, p. 327.

37 Yeats, *Collected Poems*, p. 28.

38 Ibid., p. 327.

39 Ibid., p. 320.

40 Ibid., p. 241.

41 Friedrich Nietzsche, *Thus Spoke Zarathustra: A Book for All and None*, trans. Walter Kaufmann (New York: Modern Library, 1995), p. 34.

42 W. B. Yeats, *Essays and Introductions* (New York: Macmillan, 1961), p. 271.

43 Ibid., p. 297.

44 Ibid., p. 293.

45 Denis Donoghue discusses the influence of Nietzsche's master-slave morality on Yeats in Denis Donoghue, *William Butler Yeats* (New York: Ecco Press, 1988), pp. 52–61; see also Richard Ellmann, *The Identity of Yeats* (New York: Oxford University Press, 1954), pp. 91–98; Vereen Bell, "Yeats's Nietzschean Idealism," *Southern Review* 29 (1993), 491–513; and the famous letter of September 1902 from Yeats to Lady Gregory: ". . . you have a rival in Nietzsche, that strong enchanter. I have read him so much that I have made my eyes bad again . . . Nietzsche completes Blake and has the same roots." Yeats, *Letters of W. B. Yeats*, p. 379. For the chronology of Yeats's reception of Nietzsche, in primary and secondary sources, see Foster, *W. B. Yeats*, I: passim.

46 William Blake, *Blake's Poetry and Designs*, ed. Mary Lynn Johnson and John E. Grant (New York: W. W. Norton, 1979), p. 90.

47 Nietzsche, *Basic Writings of Nietzsche*, p. 299.

48 Percy Bysshe Shelley, "Preface" to *Frankenstein; or, The Modern Prometheus*, in M. H. Abrams, Gen. ed., *The Norton Anthology of English Literature*, 7th edn., 2 vols. (New York: W. W. Norton, 2000), II:907.

49 Yeats, *Mythologies*, p. 361.

50 Arnold, *Complete Prose Works*, IX:237.

51 Percy Bysshe Shelley, *Shelley's Poetry and Prose*, eds. Donald H. Reiman and Sharon B. Powers (New York: Norton, 1977), p. 74.

52 Nietzsche, *Thus Spoke Zarathustra*, p. 36.

53 Wilde, *Complete Works*, p. 1029.

54 Yeats, *Ideas of Good and Evil*, p. 282.

55 Nietzsche, *Thus Spoke Zarathustra*, p. 25 (my italics).

56 Nietzsche, *Basic Writings*, p. 488 (his italics). For Goethe and Nietzsche, see Walter Kaufmann, *Nietzsche: Philosopher, Psychologist, Antichrist* (New York: Meridian, 1956), p. 132.

57 Yeats, *Mythologies*, p. 357.

58 Nietzsche, *Thus Spoke Zarathustra*, p. 37 (his italics).

59 Yeats, *Essays and Introductions*, p. 509.

60 Nietzsche, *Basic Writings*, p. 73.

61 Yeats, *Autobiographies*, p. 338.

62 Yeats, *Mythologies*, p. 356.

63 Nietzsche, *Basic Writings*, p. 73 (I have removed his italics from the word *could*).

64 Yeats, *Autobiographies*, p. 338.

65 Yeats, *Essays and Introductions*, p. 515.

66 W. B. Yeats, *Dramatis Personae* (New York: Macmillan, 1936), p. 95.

67 S. H. Butcher, *Aristotle's Theory of Poetry and Fine Art, with a Critical Text and Translation of the Poetics*, 4th edn. (Mineola, NY: Dover, 1951), p. 123.

68 Nietzsche, *Basic Writings*, p. 64.

69 Yeats, *Essays and Introductions*, p. 470.

70 In *The Cutting of an Agate*, Yeats advances by way of the Noh drama: "No 'naturalistic' effect is sought. The players wear masks and found their movements upon those of puppets . . ." Ibid., p. 230. His theories of daimonism, tragedy, and character are joined by his attempt to overcome nature through artistic technique.

71 See, for example, George Bornstein, *Transformations of Romanticism in Yeats, Eliot, and Stevens* (Chicago: University of Chicago Press, 1976), p. 71; C. K. Stead, *The New Poetic: Yeats to Eliot* (Philadelphia: University of Pennsylvania Press, 1987), p. 191; and Thomas Whitaker, *Swan and Shadow: Yeats's Dialogue with History* (Chapel Hill: University of North Carolina Press, 1964), pp. 163–87. Donoghue voices a thoughtful objection to his contemporaries' "faith" in "the primacy of the creative imagination," in *William Butler Yeats*, pp. 132–34. The "Unity of Being" tradition continues in an intelligent essay by Kevin J. Porter, "The Rhetorical Problem of Eternity in Yeats's Byzantium Poems," *Yeats Eliot Review* 14 (1996), 10–17.

72 Aldous Huxley, *End and Means: An Inquiry into the Nature of Ideals and into the Methods Employed for Their Realization* (New York: Harper and Brothers, 1937), p. 291.

73 Yeats, *Autobiographies*, p. 241.

74 Yeats elaborates his Neoplatonic theory of the emotions in *Autobiographies*, pp. 324–26.

75 Ibid., p. 324.

76 Ibid., p. 403.

77 Yeats, *Collected Poems*, p. 294.

78 Ibid., p. 203.

79 Ibid., p. 259.

80 Brian Atkins puts it this way: "what we find in the poetry is that Platonism is either accepted or is rejected through the mechanism of inverting Platonic doctrine." Brian Atkins, "Yeats: Platonist, Gnostic or What?," in *Yeats: An Annual of Critical and Textual Studies*, vol. 7, *1989*, ed. Richard J. Finneran (Ann Arbor, MI: University of Michigan Press, 1990), 10 (I have removed his italics).

81 W. B. Yeats, *A Vision* (New York: Macmillan, 1966), p. 19.

82 Ibid., pp. 279–80.
83 Nietzsche, *Basic Writings*, p. 22.
84 Yeats, *Autobiographies*, pp. 325–26.
85 W. B. Yeats, *W. B. Yeats and T. Sturge Moore: Their Correspondence, 1901–1937*, ed. Ursula Bridge (New York: Oxford University Press, 1953), p. 162.
86 For a review of this tradition, and a persuasive resolution to its disagreements, see David Peters Corbett, "T. Sturge Moore's 'Do We or Do We Not, Know It' and the Writing of 'Byzantium,'" *Yeats Annual No. 10*, ed. Warwick Gould (London: Macmillan, 1993), 241–49.
87 Yeats, *W. B. Yeats and T. Sturge Moore*, p. 162.
88 Ibid., p. 164.
89 Kermode, *Romantic Image*, p. 88.
90 Yeats, *Collected Poems*, pp. 248–49.
91 Ibid., p. 460.
92 Wyndham Lewis, *Time and Western Man* (Boston: Beacon Press, 1957), p. 442 (his italics).
93 Ibid., p. 242.
94 Yeats, *W. B. Yeats and T. Sturge Moore*, p. 122.
95 Lewis, *Time and Western Man*, p. 457.
96 Yeats, *Essays and Introductions*, p. 405.
97 Yeats, *W. B. Yeats and T. Sturge Moore*, p. 121.
98 Ibid., p. 74.
99 Ibid., p. 95.
100 Yeats, *Essays and Introductions*, p. 400.
101 Yeats, *Collected Poems*, p. 238.
102 Lewis, *Time and Western Man*, p. 456.
103 Yeats, *Collected Poems*, p. 248.
104 Ibid., p. 436.
105 Ibid., p. 461.
106 Ibid., p. 481.
107 Ibid.
108 Ibid., p. 482.
109 Yeats, *Vision*, pp. 24–25.
110 Nietzsche, *Basic Writings*, p. 52.
111 Ibid., p. 135.
112 Yeats, *Vision*, p. 126.
113 Ibid., p. 300.
114 Ibid., pp. 301–302 (his italics), quoted in Ellmann, *Yeats*, p. 282.
115 Ellmann, *Identity of Yeats*, p. 162.
116 Harold Bloom, *Yeats* (New York: Oxford University Press, 1970), p. 470.
117 Yeats, *Collected Poems*, p. 214.
118 Nietzsche, *Basic Writings*, pp. 582–83 (his italics).
119 Ibid., p. 18 (his italics).
120 Alfred North Whitehead, *Science and the Modern World*, (New York: The Free Press, 1967), p. 194.

121 James quoted in Whitehead, *Science and the Modern World*, p. 3.
122 Ibid.
123 Ibid., pp. 195–96.

CHAPTER 2: T. S. ELIOT: THE MODERNIST ARISTOTLE

1 T. S. Eliot, *Inventions of the March Hare: Poems 1909–1917*, ed. Christopher Ricks (New York: Harcourt, 1996), p. 11.
2 Ibid.
3 Herbert Howarth, *Notes on Some Figures Behind T. S. Eliot* (Boston: Houghton Mifflin, 1964), pp. 107–108. For Eliot and Laforgue, see pp. 101–108.
4 Jules Laforgue, *Poems of Jules Laforgue* (London: Anvil Press Poetry, 1986), p. 220.
5 Symons, *Symbolist Movement*, p. 57.
6 Jules Laforgue, *Derniers Vers* X, quoted in T. S. Eliot *Selected Essays*, new edition (New York: Harcourt, 1950), p. 249.
7 T. S. Eliot, *The Varieties of Metaphysical Poetry*, ed. Ronald Schuchard (New York: Harcourt, 1993), p. 215.
8 Arthur Schopenhauer, *The World as Will and Representation*, trans. E. F. J. Payne, 3rd edn., 2 vols. (New York: Dover, 1966), vol. II, p. 406.
9 For Laforgue, "life was *consciously* divided into thought and feeling . . ." Eliot, *Varieties*, p. 212 (his italics). Accordingly, Laforgue's irony is a "*dédoublement* of the personality." T. S. Eliot, "A Commentary," *Criterion* 12 (April 1933), 469.
10 See the indispensable essay by William Blissett, "Wagner in *The Waste Land*," in Jane Campbell and James Doyle, eds., *The Practical Vision: Essays in English Literature in Honour of Flora Roy* (Waterloo, Ontario: Wilfrid Laurier University Press, 1978), pp. 71–85.
11 Eliot, *Inventions*, p. 17. The poem is dated November 1909.
12 Eliot, *Varieties*, p. 212.
13 Laforgue, "Dimanches" (*"Bref, j'allais me donner d'un ≪Je vous aime≫"*), quoted in Eliot, *Varieties*, p. 214.
14 Jules Laforgue, *Derniers Vers* XI (*Sur une Défunte*), quoted in Eliot, *Selected Essays*, p. 249.
15 Symons, *Symbolist Movement*, p. 61.
16 Eliot, *Varieties*, p. 215.
17 Ibid., p. 219.
18 Arnold, *Complete Prose Works*, I:2–3. For Arnold's understanding of suffering in his emergence from dandyism, see James Najarian, *Victorian Keats: Manliness, Sexuality, and Desire* (New York: Palgrave Macmillan: 2002), pp. 76–81.
19 Arnold, *Complete Prose Works*, I:8.
20 Ibid., I:4.
21 Arnold, "The Function of Criticism at the Present Time," quoted in Eliot, *Sacred Wood*, p. xii.

22 Ibid., p. 49.
23 Eliot, *Collected Poems*, p. 56.
24 Ibid., p. 69.
25 Ibid.
26 Eliot, *Sacred Wood*, pp. 49–50.
27 Eliot, *Selected Essays*, p. 21.
28 Ibid., p. 19.
29 Arnold, *Complete Prose Works*, IX:171.
30 T. S. Eliot to Sydney Schiff, September [10?], 1920. T. S. Eliot, *The Letters of T. S. Eliot*, vol. I, *1898–1922*, ed. Valerie Eliot (San Diego: Harcourt, 1988), p. 406.
31 Ezra Pound, "Historical Survey," *Little Review* 8 (Autumn 1921), 39.
32 Eliot, *Sacred Wood*, p. 12, but see the critique of Arnold on pp. 24–25.
33 Ibid., p. 15.
34 Ibid., p. 1.
35 Following Richard Shusterman's *T. S. Eliot and the Philosophy of Criticism*, a number of critics have addressed the subject of Eliot and Aristotle, often drawing on Eliot's unpublished papers at Harvard and Oxford, where he studied the Greek philosopher under Bradley's disciple Harold Joachim. Shusterman argues that Eliot connected Aristotle to American pragmatism. See Richard Shusterman, *T. S. Eliot and the Philosophy of Criticism* (New York: Columbia University Press, 1988). For an overview of the subject, see Benjamin Lockerd, Jr., *Aethereal Rumours: T. S. Eliot's Physics and Poetics* (Lewisburg, PA: Bucknell University Press, 1998), pp. 46–52.
36 Eliot, *Sacred Wood*, p. 13.
37 Ibid., p. 11.
38 Ibid., p. 73.
39 Eliot's early papers at Harvard show his commitment to a "search for reality by the analysis of grammar." He remarks: "It is only the persistent faith in a difference between thought and reality which prevents Aristotle from explicitly handling metaphysics as the investigation into the ultimate meaning of thought as expressed in the forms of language. He conducts himself as if he were analysing things and not ideas." See Jeffrey Perl, "The Language of Theory and the Language of Poetry: The Significance of T. S. Eliot's Philosophical Notebooks, Part Two," *Southern Review* 21 (October 1985), 1012–23.
40 Eliot, *Sacred Wood*, p. 10.
41 Ibid.
42 William Hazlitt, *Complete Works of William Hazlitt*, ed. P. P. Howe, 21 vols. (London, 1930–1934), V:53.
43 A watershed in the history of aesthetics, *The Critique of Judgment* inspires rival readings. Charles Taylor holds that in Kant the beautiful, as "a symbol of the morally good" (Kant's phrase), is "related and firmly subordinated to our moral destiny." Charles Taylor, *Sources of the Self: The Making of Modern Identity* (Cambridge: Harvard University Press, 1989), p. 423. Discussing the

same key passage in Kant, David Ellison writes: "Kant's style, his poetics of harmonization and elevation, in which the ethical *becomes beautiful* in its 'noble' loftiness, performs the opposite: namely, a rhetorically subtle aestheticization of the moral" (his italics). David Ellison, *Ethics and Aesthetics in European Modernist Literature: From the Sublime to the Uncanny* (Cambridge: Cambridge University Press, 2001), p. 8.

44 Bernard Bosanquet, *A History of Aesthetic: From the Greeks to the Twentieth Century*, 2nd edn. (New York: Meridian, 1957).

45 James, *Psychology: Briefer Course*, p. 251.

46 For James's legacy in the study of emotion and feeling, see Damasio, *Descartes' Error*, p. 129f.

47 Eliot, *Sacred Wood*, p. 11.

48 Ibid., p. 23.

49 T. S. Eliot, "Reflections on Contemporary Poetry [II]," *Egoist* 4 (October 1917), 133.

50 T. S. Eliot, "Modern Tendencies in Poetry," *Shama'a* 1 (April 1920), 11, quoted in Ronald Schuchard, *Eliot's Dark Angel: Intersections of Life and Art* (New York: Oxford University Press, 1999), p. 74. I have not seen the original, which is rare.

51 "So far as we can distinguish the enjoyment of art from our theory about it, there is no reason why the Naturalist and the Theist should not be equally sensitive; when they value different things they will be valuing on grounds not purely aesthetic." T. S. Eliot, review of *Theism and Humanism*, by A. J. Balfour, *International Journal of Ethics* 26 (January 1916), 286.

52 For analysis of Eliot's wavering distinction between "emotion" and "feeling," see René Wellek, *A History of Modern Criticism*, 7 vols. (New Haven: Yale University Press, 1955–1986), V:184–85.

53 Cyril Tourneur, *The Revenger's Tragedy*, quoted in Eliot, *Sacred Wood*, pp. 56–57.

54 Ibid., p. 58.

55 See Alasdair MacIntyre, *Whose Justice? Which Rationality?* (Notre Dame: University of Notre Dame Press, 1988), p. 26.

56 Peter Ackroyd, *T. S. Eliot: A Life* (New York: Simon and Schuster, 1984), p. 155. But the principal influence on Eliot's Clark Lectures is George Santayana, *Three Philosophical Poets* (Garden City, NY: Doubleday, 1938), esp. pp. 71–123; originally published in 1910.

57 Eliot, *Varieties*, p. 216.

58 T. S. Eliot, *Selected Prose of T. S. Eliot*, ed. Frank Kermode (New York: Harcourt, 1975), p. 177.

59 Eliot, *Sacred Wood*, p. xvi.

60 T. S. Eliot, *For Lancelot Andrewes: Essays on Style and Order* (Garden City, NY: Doubleday, 1929), p. vii.

61 For Bradley and Eliot, see, for example, Brooker, *Mastery and Escape*, pp. 191–206; Sanford Schwartz, *The Matrix of Modernism: Pound, Eliot, and Early Twentieth-Century Thought* (Princeton: Princeton University

Press, 1985), pp. 156–60 and 165–66; and Eric Sigg, *The American T. S. Eliot: A Study of the Early Writings* (Cambridge: Cambridge University Press, 1989), pp. 46–58.

62 Eliot, *For Lancelot Andrewes*, p. 88.

63 Ibid., p. 87.

64 F. H. Bradley, *Ethical Studies*, 2nd edn. (Oxford: Clarendon Press, 1927), p. 80.

65 Ibid., p. 230. The good will is "the will that realizes an end which is above this or that man [i.e. as merely this or that man], superior to them, and capable of confronting them in the shape of a law or an ought." Ibid., p. 162.

66 Ibid., p. 80.

67 Ibid., p. 170.

68 Ibid., p. 192.

69 Ibid., p. 201.

70 I discuss the Aristotelian tension between practical happiness and divine happiness – with respect to Moore's critique of Aristotle – in Chapter 4. I agree that Aristotle "fails to bring out sufficiently the bond between the meditative or religious life that he describes at the end of his 'Ethics' and the humanistic life . . . to which most of this work is dedicated." Irving Babbitt, *Rousseau and Romanticism* (New York: Meridian, 1959), p. 288.

71 Bradley, *Ethical Studies*, p. 325.

72 Eliot, *For Lancelot Andrewes*, p. 84.

73 Bradley, *Ethical Studies*, p. 326.

74 Ibid., pp. 318–19.

75 Eliot, *For Lancelot Andrewes*, p. 82.

76 Eliot, *Selected Essays*, p. 390.

77 Ibid., p. 391.

78 A. E. Housman, *Introductory Lecture, Delivered before the Faculties of Arts and Laws and of Science in University College, London, October 3, 1892* (New York: Macmillan, 1937), pp. 24–25.

79 Eliot, *Selected Essays*, p. 387.

80 Ibid.

81 I agree in this instance with Graham Hough. See Hough, *Last Romantics*, p. 135.

82 In "Second Thoughts about Humanism," Eliot makes an allowance for naturalism in ethics, but he appears to have Freud and not Aristotle or Arnold in mind: "I can understand, though I do not approve, the naturalistic system of morals based upon biology and analytical psychology (what is valid in these consists largely of things that were always known) . . ." *Selected Essays*, p. 432. Eliot's understanding of emotion reveals the Puritan side of his character: "the difficult discipline is the discipline and training of emotion; this the modern world has great need of; so great need that it hardly understands what the word means; and this I have found is only attainable through dogmatic religion." T. S. Eliot, "Religion Without Humanism," in Norman Foerster, ed., *Humanism and America: Essays on the Outlook of Modern Civilisation* (New York: Farrar and Rinehart, 1930), p. 110. On the other hand, in his 1934 lecture "Religion and Literature,"

Eliot works from the humanistic premise that literature can contribute, in a healthy if secondary sense, to one's moral formation: "Knowledge of life obtained through fiction is only possible through another stage of self-consciousness. That is to say, it can only be knowledge of other people's knowledge of life, not of life itself." Eliot develops his argument with respect to Dickens, Thackeray, George Eliot, and Balzac: "these authors are only really helping us when we can see, and allow for, their differences from ourselves." T. S. Eliot, *Essays Ancient and Modern* (New York: Harcourt, 1936), pp. 104–105.

83 T. S. Eliot, "Introduction," in Josef Pieper, *Leisure: The Basis of Culture* (New York: Mentor, 1963), p. 14.

84 Bradley, *Essays on Truth and Reality*, quoted in Frederick Coplestone, S.J., *A History of Philosophy*, 9 vols. (New York: Doubleday, 1985), VIII:200.

85 T. S. Eliot, *The Use of Poetry and the Use of Criticism* (Cambridge: Harvard University Press, 1964), p. 108.

86 Ibid., p. 98.

87 Ibid., p. 103.

88 Arnold, *Complete Prose Works*, IX:202, quoted in Eliot, *Use of Poetry*, p. 110.

89 Ibid., p. 137.

90 T. S. Eliot, *Notes towards the Definition of Culture*, reprinted with *The Idea of a Christian Society*, in *Christianity and Culture* (San Diego: Harcourt, 1977), p. 103.

91 Lionel Trilling, *Matthew Arnold* (New York: Harcourt, 1979), p. 358. Trilling is roughly quoting Bradley's *Ethical Studies*, p. 318n2.

92 Walter Jackson Bate, ed., *Criticism: The Major Texts* (San Diego, Harcourt, 1970), p. 438.

93 Trilling, *Matthew Arnold*, p. 346.

94 "William James . . . is perfectly at one with Arnold on the matter of objectification . . ." Ibid., p. 348.

95 Housman, *Introductory Lecture*, p. 24.

96 Butcher, *Aristotle's Theory*, p. 402.

97 Trilling, *Matthew Arnold*, p. 153.

98 Arnold, *Complete Prose Works*, I:6.

99 Eliot, *Selected Essays*, p. 385.

100 Trilling, *Matthew Arnold*, p. 342.

101 Ibid., p. 347. Arnold writes: ". . . Aristotle will undervalue knowing: 'In what concerns virtue,' says he, 'three things are necessary – knowledge, deliberate will, and perseverance; but whereas the last two are all-important, the first is a matter of little importance.'" Arnold, *Complete Prose Works*, V:166. R. H. Super helpfully refers us to the *Nicomachean Ethics* (1105a31).

102 Trilling accepts the influence of the *Poetics* on Arnold, but he places Arnold in the "dangerous tradition of absolute moralists, of Bonald, Carlyle, and Newman, all of whom argued against a rationalistic conception of morality on the ground of an *a priori* morality intuitively perceived . . ." Trilling, *Matthew Arnold*, p. 357. This is an odd remark, given that the classical morality that Arnold adopts from Aristotle is broadly "rationalistic."

103 Arnold, *Complete Prose Works*, VI:181, quoted in Trilling, *Matthew Arnold*, p. 357.

104 Bradley, *Ethical Studies*, p. 318, quoted in Trilling, *Matthew Arnold*, p. 358.

105 *OED* sense 8 (1755 Johnson). Arnold derives his maxim from Proverbs (11:19): "'Conduct brings *happiness*,' or, 'Righteousness tendeth to *life*.'" Arnold, *Complete Prose Works*, VI:205 (his italics). Bravo for the King James! "Tendeth" is the happiest choice imaginable.

106 Ibid., VI:296 (his italics).

107 Michael H. Levenson, *A Genealogy of Modernism: A Study of English Literary Doctrine 1908–1922* (Cambridge: Cambridge University Press, 1984), p. 179.

108 James Wood, *The Broken Estate: Essays on Literature and Belief* (New York: Random House, 1999), pp. 242–48.

109 For the tension between Eliot's critical program and his poetry, see Ronald Bush, "T. S. Eliot and Modernism at the Present Time: A Provocation," in Ronald Bush, ed., *T. S. Eliot: The Modernist in History* (Cambridge: Cambridge University Press, 1991), pp. 191–202.

110 T. S. Eliot, *The Idea of a Christian Society*, reprinted with *Notes towards the Definition of Culture* in *Christianity and Culture*, p. 14.

111 Ibid., p. 22.

112 Ibid., p. 27.

113 Francis Fergusson argues that Eliot based the characterization of *Murder in the Cathedral* on Pascal's theological doctrine of the three discontinuous orders: the order of nature, the order of the mind, and the order of charity. See Francis Fergusson, *The Idea of a Theater: The Art of Drama in Changing Perspective* (Garden City, NY: 1953), p. 229.

114 T. S. Eliot, *The Complete Poems and Plays: 1909–1950* (San Diego: Harcourt, 1950), pp. 363–64.

115 Eliot, *For Lancelot Andrewes*, p. 7.

116 "Humanism makes for breadth, tolerance, equilibrium and sanity. It operates against fanaticism." Eliot, *Selected Essays*, p. 436.

117 Lyndall Gordon, *Eliot's New Life* (New York: Farrar, Straus and Giroux, 1988), p. 176.

118 Eliot, *Complete Poems and Plays*, p. 360.

119 Eliot, *Varieties*, pp. 91–92 (see also pp. 80–81 and p. 262).

120 Eliot, *Complete Poems and Plays*, p. 381.

CHAPTER 3: JAMES JOYCE: LOVE AMONG THE SKEPTICS

1 James Joyce, *The Critical Writings*, eds. Ellsworth Mason and Richard Ellmann (New York: Viking Press, 1964), p. 65.

2 James Joyce, *Stephen Hero*, eds. Theodore Spencer, John J. Slocum, and Herbert Cahoon (New York: New Directions, 1963), p. 78. Compare Joyce, *Critical Writings*, pp. 73–75.

3 Joyce's differences from Pater, alluded to in my Introduction, are of course important; see, for example, Jacques Aubert, *The Aesthetics of James Joyce*

(Baltimore: Johns Hopkins University Press, 1992), pp. 112–14. For Joyce and Flaubert, see Richard K. Cross, *Flaubert and Joyce: The Rite of Fiction* (Princeton: Princeton University Press, 1971).

4 Pater, *Works*, V:27.
5 James Joyce, *Portrait of the Artist as a Young Man* (New York: Viking Press, 1964), p. 215.
6 Wilde, *Complete Works*, p. 17.
7 Eliot, *Letters*, p. 197.
8 T. S. Eliot, *After Strange Gods* (New York: Harcourt, 1934), p. 39. Having joined the Anglican communion, the author of *The Waste Land* rejected I. A. Richards' suggestion that he had accomplished "a complete severance between poetry and *all* beliefs." Eliot, *Use of Poetry*, pp. 122–23. But Richards had simply grasped the fact that modernism was built on romantic irony and aesthetic distance.
9 The term "romantic irony" goes back at least to Herman Hettner's *Die romantische Schule in ihrem inneren Zusammenhange mit Goethe und Schiller* (1850). See Joseph Dane, *The Critical Mythology of Irony* (Athens: The University of Georgia Press, 1991), p. 83.
10 G. W. F. Hegel, *Hegel's Philosophy of Right*, trans. T. M. Knox (London: Oxford University Press, 1967), p. 103.
11 Babbitt, *Rousseau and Romanticism*, p. 193.
12 Ibid., p. 190.
13 See Norman Davies, *Europe: A History* (New York: Oxford University Press, 1996), pp. 15–16.
14 Plato, *The Collected Dialogues*, eds. Edith Hamilton and Huntington Cairns (Princeton: Princeton University Press, 1963), p. 180 (*Euth.* 11b).
15 Joyce, *Critical Writings*, p. 100.
16 Joyce quoted in Richard Ellmann, *James Joyce* (Oxford: Oxford University Press, 1983), p. 163.
17 Joyce quoted in the invaluable work by Kevin Sullivan, *Joyce among the Jesuits* (New York: Columbia University Press, 1958), p. 2. See also Robert Boyle, S. J., *James Joyce's Pauline Vision: A Catholic Exposition* (Carbondale: Southern Illinois University Press, 1978), pp. 59–83.
18 Joyce, *Portrait*, pp. 246–47.
19 Theodore Spencer, "Introduction," in Joyce, *Stephen Hero*, p. 12.
20 Joyce, *Portrait*, p. 214.
21 Joyce, *Stephen Hero*, p. 103.
22 Ibid., p. 104.
23 Joyce interprets Aristotle along similar "theoretic" lines: "Aristotle's consideration of man as a political animal interested Joyce far less than his metaphysics and aesthetics." Mason and Ellmann, eds., Joyce, *Critical Writings*, p. 110n1. See also R. J. Schork, *Greek and Hellenic Culture in Joyce* (Gainesville, FL: University Press of Florida, 1998), pp. 157–77; and Aubert, *Aesthetics of James Joyce*.
24 Joyce, *Portrait*, p. 184.
25 Ibid., p. 8.

26 Ibid., p. 214.

27 So far as I know, this reading is original with me. For other Trinitarian influences in Joyce, including the "Trinitarian strands in the 'Shakespeare' art theory" of "Scylla and Charybdis," see William T. Noon, *Joyce and Aquinas: A Study of the Religious Elements in the Writings of James Joyce* (New Haven: Yale University Press, 1957); see also Boyle, *James Joyce's Pauline Vision*, e.g. p. 22 and p. 82.

28 Joyce, *Portrait*, p. 172.

29 William Wordsworth, *Poetical Works*, eds., Thomas Hutchinson and Ernest de Selincourt (Oxford: Oxford University Press, 1936), p. 750 (his italics).

30 Joyce, *Portrait*, p. 247.

31 Ibid., pp. 124–25.

32 Levin, *James Joyce*, p. 41.

33 Stendhal, *The Life of Henry Brulard*, trans. Jean Stewart and B. C. J. C. Knight (Minerva Press, 1968), p. 55.

34 Joyce, *Portrait*, p. 134.

35 Ibid., p. 127.

36 Regarding the *Portrait*, David Hayman says that "shaded allusions to birds" and "figurative labyrinths" . . . "must be seen not only as part of the controlling and unifying mechanism but also as a commentary on the hero that is not entirely negative though it is certainly ironic." David Hayman, *Ulysses: The Mechanics of Meaning* (Madison: University of Wisconsin Press, 1982), p. 18. I agree, at least if Hayman is referring to dramatic irony, which would be perfectly appropriate for looking back from later experience to earlier naiveté.

37 See R. B. Kershner, "A Critical History of *A Portrait of the Artist as a Young Man*," in James Joyce, *A Portrait of the Artist as a Young Man*, ed. R. B. Kershner (Boston: St. Martin's Press, 1993), pp. 221–34.

38 Joyce quoted in Frank Budgen, *James Joyce and the Making of "Ulysses"* (Bloomington: Indiana University Press, 1960), p. 60.

39 Joyce, *Portrait*, p. 224.

40 See the fine comments on style in the *Portrait* in Sidney Bolt, *Joyce*, 2nd edn. (Harlow, England: Longman, 1992), pp. 76–86. One problem in interpreting the relation between Joyce and Stephen is gauging the sincerity of writing such as the following: "It was the windless hour of dawn when madness wakes and strange plants open to the light and the moth flies forth silently." Joyce, *Portrait*, p. 217. Bolt cites the sentence as an example of "cosmetic aestheticism." To my ear, it is an example of rich Joycean badness – and there is more to be said for badness in art than is commonly recognized.

41 Ibid., p. 246 (my italics).

42 Ibid., pp. 252–53.

43 Ibid., p. 159.

44 Ibid., pp. 168–69.

45 Essential to Aristotle, friendship is "the greatest good of states" and the glue that keeps the community together. It is a glue that has been dissolving since

Stephen's farewell to Cranly. Linking arms with Mulligan, Stephen remembers "Cranly's arm" (1. 159).

46 Beckett, *Proust*, pp. 46–47.

47 Hugh Kenner, *Ulysses: revised edition* (Baltimore: Johns Hopkins University Press, 1987), p. 60.

48 For Bloom as the "necessary complement" for Stephen's artistic growth, see Daniel R. Schwarz, *Reading Joyce's Ulysses* (New York: St. Martin's Press, 1987), p. 225.

49 G. K. Chesterton, *Heretics* (New York: John Lane, 1909), p. 32.

50 Joyce, *Critical Writings*, pp. 74–75.

51 Ibid., p. 219.

52 Joyce quoted in Levin, *James Joyce*, p. 30.

53 Donald T. Torchiana reaches a similar conclusion, then proposes a darker alternative, in *Backgrounds for Joyce's Dubliners* (Boston: Allen and Unwin, 1986), pp. 36–51.

54 Joyce, *Dubliners*, p. 27.

55 Ellmann, *James Joyce*, p. 47.

56 Joyce, *Dubliners*, p. 203.

57 Compare the following passage from Joyce's letter to his brother Stanislaus, dated September 25, 1906, when he was working on "The Dead": "Sometimes thinking of Ireland it seems to me that I have been unnecessarily harsh. I have reproduced (in *Dubliners* at least) none of the attraction of the city for I have never felt at ease in any city since I left it except in Paris. I have not reproduced its ingenuous insularity and its hospitality. The latter 'virtue' so far as I can see does not exist elsewhere in Europe." Joyce quoted in Ellmann, *James Joyce*, p. 231.

58 Joyce, *Dubliners*, p. 223.

59 Eliot, *After Strange Gods*, pp. 40–41.

60 Joyce, *Portrait*, p. 205. For the "Paris Notebook," see Joyce, *Critical Writings*, pp. 143–44.

61 Hayman defines Joyce's epiphanies as "secular illuminations." Hayman, *Ulysses*, p. 128. Aubert is wrong to insist that Joyce's revision of Aristotle's theory of tragedy is no more radical than "Bernays's famous commentary echoed by Butcher. . ." Aubert, *Aesthetics of James Joyce*, p. 85. There is a major difference between deriving from Aristotle a purely cognitive theory of tragedy (as in Joyce) and ascribing to Aristotle a theory of catharsis (as in Bernays and Butcher) that admits the body's emotional contribution. Joyce's Bernays-influenced 1904 satire "The Holy Office" is a better guide to the meaning of "Katharsis-Purgative." See Joyce, *Critical Writings*, pp. 149–52.

62 John Carey makes this important point about *Ulysses*: "The complexity of the novel, its avant-garde technique, its obscurity . . . exclude people like Bloom from its readership." John Carey, *The Intellectuals: Pride and Prejudice among the Literary Intelligentsia, 1880–1939* (New York: St. Martin's Press, 1992), p. 20.

63 See Bate, *From Classic to Romantic*, pp. 48–58.

64 Alasdair MacIntyre, *A Short History of Ethics* (New York: Macmillan, 1966), p. 197.

65 Ellmann, *James Joyce*, pp. 5–6.

66 Joyce, *Portrait*, p. 11.

67 G. M. Young, *Victorian England: Portrait of an Age*, 2nd edn. (London: Oxford University Press, 1960), pp. 158–59. See also Cyril Pearl, *Dublin in Bloomtime: The City James Joyce Knew* (London: Angus and Robertson, 1969).

68 MacIntyre, *Dependent Rational Animals*, pp. 116–18.

69 Joseph Heininger, "Molly Bloom's Ad Language and Goods Behavior: Advertising as Social Communication in *Ulysses*," in Richard Pearce, ed., *Molly Blooms: A Polylogue on "Penelope" and Cultural Studies* (Madison: University of Wisconsin Press, 1994), p. 171.

70 Ibid.

71 Fritz Senn's discussion of "romantic *kitsch*" in *Ulysses*, especially Nausicaa, is closer to the mark respecting Joyce's general intentions. But I want to give more attention to the moral framework of what Senn calls "the intricacies of structure and tone" and the "complexity of response that is closely tied up with human motivation." Fritz Senn, "Nausicaa," in Clive Hart and David Hayman, eds., *James Joyce's Ulysses* (Berkeley: University of California Press, 1974), pp. 310–11.

72 Jennifer Wicke, "'Who's She When She's at Home?': Molly Bloom and the Work of Consumption," in *Molly Blooms*, p. 193.

73 Larry McShane (Associated Press), "Stern sees freedom in satellite broadcasts," Worcester Telegram and Gazette, October 7, 2004, p. C3. Stern has signed a "five-year, multimillion dollar deal" with Sirius Satellite Radio; as this book goes to press (January 2006), Stern is launched.

74 I adopt these terms from MacIntyre, *After Virtue*, p. 119.

75 Bromwich, *Choice of Inheritance*, p. 160.

76 Joyce, *Critical Writings*, p. 109.

77 John Burnet, *Aristotle on Education* (Cambridge: Cambridge University Press, 1913), p. 136.

CHAPTER 4: VIRGINIA WOOLF: ANTIGONE TRIUMPHANT

1 Woolf, *Collected Essays*, I:321.

2 Samuel Butler, *The Way of All Flesh* (London: J. M. Dent, 1933), p. 293.

3 Young, *Victorian England*, p. 4.

4 Ibid., pp. 18–25. "Hardy and Rider Haggard, observers of unquestioned competence, agreed that village tradition came to an end about 1865." Ibid., p. 166n.

5 For Hume's law as historically marking the breakdown of traditional morality in England, see MacIntyre, *Short History of Ethics*, p. 173.

6 G. E. Moore, *Principia Ethica* (Cambridge: Cambridge University Press, 1960), pp. 6–15.

7 Ibid., p. 9.

8 Keynes quoted in MacIntyre, *After Virtue*, p. 17.
9 Strachey quoted in MacIntyre, *After Virtue*, p. 16.
10 Foot, *Virtues and Vices*, p. 8.
11 J. L. Ackrill, "Aristotle on *Eudaimonia*," in Rorty, ed., *Essays on Aristotle's Ethics*, p. 33.
12 Moore, *Principia Ethica*, p. 177. The influence of the *Principia Ethica* lies in the direction of emotivism. See MacIntyre, *After Virtue*, pp. 17–22.
13 Keynes quoted in MacIntyre, *After Virtue*, p. 14.
14 Moore, *Principia Ethica*, p. 188.
15 Ibid., p. 189 (his italics).
16 For Moore and utilitarianism, see MacIntyre, *After Virtue*, p. 15.
17 See Hermione Lee, *Virginia Woolf* (New York: Alfred A. Knopf, 1997), pp. 204–208.
18 Virginia Woolf, *The Letters of Virginia Woolf*, eds. Nigel Nicolson and Joanne Trautmann, 6 vols. (New York: Harcourt, 1980), VI:400.
19 In observing the influence of Moore, I am preceded by numerous scholars, including Gabriel Franks, "Virginia Woolf and the Philosophy of G. E. Moore," *The Personalist* 50 (Spring 1969), 222–40; Penelope Ingram, "'One Drifts Apart': *To the Lighthouse* as Art of Response," *Philosophy and Literature* 23 (April 1999), 78–95; S. P. Rosenbaum, *Victorian Bloomsbury: The Early History of the Bloomsbury Group*, vol. 1. (New York: St. Martin's Press, 1987); and Wellek, *History of Modern Criticism*, VI:66. For Woolf on Moore and "Old Bloomsbury," see Woolf, *Moments of Being*, ed. Jeanne Schulkind, 2nd edn. (San Diego: Harcourt, 1985), p. 190. The rival view, which sees Woolf as largely uninterested in philosophy, descends from Clive Bell, *Old Friends* (New York: Harcourt, 1957), p. 132. It is extended in Erwin R. Steinberg, "G. E. Moore's Table and Chair in *To the Lighthouse*," *Journal of Modern Literature* 15 (Summer 1988), 161–68.
20 "Of the men who go to make up the perfect novelist and should live in amity under his hat, two – the poet and the philosopher – failed to come when Dickens called them." Woolf, *Collected Essays*, I:193.
21 Woolf, *Jacob's Room*, p. 149. In the 1935 version of *Freshwater*, the Acropolis receives the same ironical treatment as Dante, Petrarch, and the Victorians, with their dated views of women and love. See Virginia Woolf, *Freshwater: A Comedy*, ed. Lucio Ruotolo (New York: Harcourt, 1976), pp. 27–28.
22 Woolf, *Jacob's Room*, p. 150 and p. 138.
23 Ibid., p. 139.
24 Virginia Woolf, *A Room of One's Own* (New York: Harcourt, 1929), p. 113.
25 Virginia Woolf, *Orlando* (San Diego: Harcourt, 1928), p. 322.
26 Virginia Woolf, *The Voyage Out* (San Diego: Harcourt, 1920), p. 374.
27 Woolf, *Moments of Being*, p. 72.
28 In his 1904 essay "Does 'Consciousness' Exist?," James takes issue with G. E. Moore's belief that consciousness "can be distinguished, if we look attentively enough, and know that there is something to look for." Moore quoted in William James, *Writings 1902–1910* (New York: Library of America, 1987),

p. 1143. Consciousness per se is a "nonentity" for James: it is a function. "Let the case be what it may in others," he writes, "I am as confident as I am of anything that, in myself, the stream of thinking (which I recognize emphatically as a phenomenon) is only a careless name for what, when scrutinized, reveals itself to consist chiefly of the stream of my breathing." Ibid., p. 1157.

29 Todd Avery, "*Three Guineas* and the Aesthetic Ethics of Cultural Dissent," *Virginia Woolf Miscellany* 60 (Spring 2002), 6–7.

30 Moore, *Principia Ethica*, p. 43.

31 James Naremore observes: "Throughout Mrs. Woolf's work, the chief problem for her and for her characters is to overcome the space between things, to attain an absolute unity with the world . . ." James Naremore, *The World Without a Self: Virginia Woolf and the Novel* (New Haven: Yale University Press, 1973), p. 242.

32 In a 1909 essay, Roger Fry faces this formalist quandary by arguing "We must . . . give up the attempt to judge the work of art by its reaction on life, and consider it as an expression of emotions regarded as ends in themselves." Roger Fry, *Vision and Design* (London: Chatto and Windus, 1923), p. 29, quoted in Donald J. Watt, "G. E. Moore and the Bloomsbury Group," in *English Literature in Transition* 12 (1969), 119–34.

33 Moore, *Principia Ethica*, p. 190 (his italics).

34 Woolf, *Voyage Out*, p. 374.

35 Woolf, *Room of One's Own*, p. 74.

36 Ibid., p. 75.

37 See Henry B. Veatch, *For an Ontology of Morals: A Critique of Contemporary Ethical Theory* (Evanston: Northwestern University Press, 1971), pp. 101–105.

38 Woolf, *Collected Essays*, I:326.

39 Virginia Woolf, *Three Guineas* (San Diego: Harcourt, 1966), p. 170n39.

40 Woolf, *Collected Essays*, I:324.

41 Woolf, *To the Lighthouse*, p. 193.

42 Woolf, *Collected Essays*, II:106.

43 Ibid., II:110.

44 Pater, *Works*, I:134–35.

45 The influence of cubism on Woolf points in the same direction. See Maurice Géracht, "Cubism and Points of View in Virginia Woolf's *To the Lighthouse*," *Interfaces* 13 (*Juin* 1998), 119–37.

46 Woolf, *To the Lighthouse*, p. 192.

47 Ibid., p. 145.

48 Ibid., p. 146.

49 Woolf, *Moments of Being*, p. 72.

50 Woolf, *To the Lighthouse*, p. 176.

51 Ibid., pp. 175–76.

52 Franks, "Virginia Woolf and the Philosophy of G. E. Moore," p. 230. See also *Principia Ethica*, pp. 203–205.

53 Woolf, *To the Lighthouse*, p. 176.

54 Ibid., pp. 62–63.

55 Ibid., p. 51.

56 Ibid., p. 52.

57 Ibid., p. 202.

58 Ibid., p. 185.

59 *To the Lighthouse* is often read as elegy, with less attention to Woolf's contempt for the Victorians. This elegiac reading finds support in Woolf, *Moments of Being*, pp. 80–81, and in Woolf's diary, where she considers "elegy" as more appropriate than "novel" for *To the Lighthouse*. Virginia Woolf, *The Diary of Virginia Woolf*, ed. Anne Olivier Bell, 5 vols. (New York: Harcourt, 1977–84), III:34. Among the elegizing critics, see Maria DiBattista, *Virginia Woolf's Major Novels: The Fables of Anon* (New Haven: Yale University Press, 1980), pp. 64–110; Lee, *Virginia Woolf*, pp. 471–77; John Mepham, "Mourning and Modernism," in Patricia Clements and Isabel Grundy, eds., *Virginia Woolf: New Critical Essays* (London: Vision Press Limited, 1983), pp. 137–54; and Randall Stevenson and Jane Goldman, "'But What Elegy?': Modernist Readings and the Death of Mrs. Ramsay," *The Yearbook of English Studies* 26 (1996), 173–86. I find support for my reading in Woolf's self-confessed murder of the "Angel in the House" (Coventry Patmore's phrase) in "Professions for Women," a paper originally delivered in 1931. Woolf, *Collected Essays*, II:284–89. I find some precedent in Nicole Ward Jouve, "Virginia Woolf and Psychoanalysis," in Sue Roe and Susan Sellers, eds., *The Cambridge Companion to Virginia Woolf* (Cambridge: Cambridge University Press, 2000), pp. 245–72; and in John R. Maze, *Virginia Woolf: Feminism, Creativity, and the Unconscious* (Westport, CT: Greenwood Press, 1997), pp. 85–118.

60 Woolf, *To the Lighthouse*, p. 175.

61 Virginia Woolf, *The Years* (San Diego: Harcourt, 1939), p. 414.

62 John D. B. Hamilton, "Antigone: Kinship, Justice, and the Polis," in Dora C. Pozzi and John M. Wickersham, eds., *Myth and the Polis* (Ithaca, New York: Cornell University Press, 1991), p. 92.

63 Compare the famous remark of E. M. Forster: ". . . if I had to choose between betraying my country and betraying my friend, I hope I should have the guts to betray my country." E. M. Forster, *Two Cheers for Democracy* (London: Edward Arnold, 1951), p. 78.

64 For Woolf as "anti-Victorian," with special reference to *The Years*, see A. D. Moody, *Virginia Woolf* (Edinburgh: Oliver and Boyd, 1963), pp. 70–82.

65 Woolf, *Room of One's Own*, p. 102.

66 Ibid., pp. 58–59.

67 Likewise: "not all pleasures have an end different from themselves, but only the pleasures of persons who are being led to the perfecting of their nature. This is why . . . pleasure . . . should . . . be called activity of the natural state, and . . . 'unimpeded'" (*Nic. Eth.* 1153a12).

68 Pater, *Works*, I:x–xi.

69 Woolf, *The Waves*, p. 259 (her ellipses after the word "profession").

70 "Hark, hark, / The dogs do bark, / The beggars are coming to town . . ." Iona and Peter Opie, eds., *The Oxford Dictionary of Nursery Rhymes* (Oxford: Oxford University Press, 1951), p. 152.

71 Woolf, *Room of One's Own*, p. 118.

72 Woolf, *The Waves*, p. 297.

73 Ibid., p. 285.

74 Ibid., p. 283.

75 James, *Psychology: Briefer Course*, p. 76.

76 For Woolf's unique sense of "non-being," see Woolf, *Moments of Being*, p. 70.

77 Woolf, *The Waves*, p. 236 (her italics).

78 Ibid., p. 297 (her italics).

79 On the failure of *The Waves*, see J. W. Graham, "Manuscript Revision and the Heroic Theme of *The Waves*," *Twentieth Century Literature* 29 (Fall 1983), pp. 312–32.

80 Woolf, *The Waves*, p. 263.

81 Pater, *Works*, I: 239.

CHAPTER 5: SAMUEL BECKETT: HUMANITY IN RUINS

1 See James Knowlson, *Damned to Fame: The Life of Samuel Beckett* (New York: Simon and Schuster, 1997), pp. 309–22.

2 See Ruby Cohn, "Philosophical Fragments in the Works of Samuel Beckett," in Martin Esslin, ed., *Samuel Beckett: A Collection of Critical Essays* (Englewood Cliffs, NJ: Prentice-Hall, 1965), pp. 169–77; and Rubin Rabinovitz, *The Development of Samuel Beckett's Fiction* (Urbana: University of Illinois Press, 1984), esp. pp. 8–9.

3 Samuel Beckett, *The Complete Short Prose: 1929–1989*, ed. S. E. Gontarski (New York: Grove Press, 1995), p. 278.

4 See the editorial notes in Beckett, *Complete Short Prose*, pp. 285–86. It now appears doubtful that the address was actually broadcast, but John Harrington is surely right to notice how Beckett used his Irish rhetorical platform to reflect on the human condition. See John P. Harrington, *The Irish Beckett* (Syracuse: Syracuse University Press, 1991), pp. 144–45.

5 Beckett, *Complete Short Prose*, p. 276.

6 Ibid., pp. 276–77. "Burroughes and Welcome" is a pharmaceutical brand.

7 Samuel Beckett, *Collected Poems in English and French* (New York: Grove Press, 1977), p. 32.

8 Lawrence E. Harvey, *Samuel Beckett: Poet and Critic* (Princeton: Princeton University Press, 1970), p. 180.

9 James, *Psychology: Briefer Course*, p. 33.

10 Beckett and Duthuit, "Three Dialogues," p. 17.

11 Ibid., p. 21.

12 Ibid., p. 20.

13 Ibid., p. 21.

14 Ibid.

15 Richard Coe distills from "Three Dialogues" the paradoxical essence of Beckett: "Beckett's own art . . . is by definition trying to do something that it cannot conceivably do – to create and to define that which, created and defined, ceases to be what it must be if it is to reveal the truth of the human situation: Man as Nothing in relation to all things which themselves are Nothing." Coe goes on to characterize Beckett's "ideal of art and 'reality'" as "quasi-mystical." Richard N. Coe, *Beckett* (Edinburgh: Oliver and Boyd, 1964), pp. 2–5. In his fine essay "God and Samuel Beckett," Coe concludes by way of Tertullian: Beckett's "philosophy is at bottom that of the mystic: *Credo quia impossibile est. . .*" Richard N. Coe, "God and Samuel Beckett," in J. D. O'Hara, ed., *Twentieth Century Interpretations of Molloy, Malone Dies, The Unnamable: A Collection of Critical Essays* (Englewood Cliffs, NJ: Prentice-Hall, 1970), p. 112. As James Knowlson observes, it may be that "few readers" will identify Beckett with a deeply mystical sense of life and art, but the newly unearthed German diaries (from the 1930s) should help correct that misconception. See Knowlson, *Damned to Fame*, p. 222.

16 Beckett and Duthuit, "Three Dialogues," p. 18.

17 Samuel Beckett, *Murphy* (New York: Grove Press, 1957), p. 57.

18 Samuel Beckett, *Watt* (New York: Grove Press, 1959), p. 212.

19 Beckett, *Waiting for Godot*, p. 22.

20 Ibid., p. 51.

21 Ibid., p. 21.

22 Beckett, *Three Novels*, p. 56.

23 *OED* sense 11.

24 Laurence Sterne, *The Life and Opinions of Tristram Shandy* (Oxford: Oxford University Press, 1983), p. 43.

25 Beckett, *Watt*, p. 121 (my italics).

26 Ibid., p. 85.

27 Beckett, *Three Novels*, p. 24.

28 Ibid., p. 67.

29 Ibid., p. 51. The passage is quoted in Cohn, "Philosophical Fragments," p. 171. See also Eugene Webb, *Samuel Beckett: A Study of His Novels* (Seattle: University of Washington Press, 1970), p. 112.

30 Arnold Geulincx, *Metaphysics*, trans. Martin Wilson (Wisbech, England: Christoffel Press, 1999), p. 128. Wilson includes a key section of Geulincx's *Ethics* in an appendix, which I have quoted.

31 Beckett, *Complete Short Prose*, p. 60.

32 Beckett, *Three Novels*, p. 22.

33 Ibid., p. 8.

34 Geach, *Virtues*, p. 17.

35 Beckett, *Three Novels*, pp. 23–24.

36 Ibid., p. 185.

37 Geach, *Virtues*, p. 169.

38 Beckett, *Three Novels*, p. 256.

39 Ibid., p. 314.

40 Edmund Spenser, *The Faerie Queene*, ed. Thomas P. Roche, Jr. (London: Penguin Books, 1987), p. 154.
41 Geach, *Virtues*, p. 45.
42 Beckett, *Three Novels*, p. 277.
43 Ibid., p. 315.
44 Soren Kierkegaard, *The Essential Kierkegaard*, eds. Howard V. Hong and Edna H. Hong (Princeton: Princeton University Press, 2000), p. 182.
45 The following passage, from the "Concluding Unscientific Postscript" to *Philosophical Fragments*, bears significantly on Beckett: "When the paradox itself is the paradox, it thrusts away by virtue of the absurd, and the corresponding passion of inwardness is faith." *Essential Kierkegaard*, p. 211.
46 Soren Kierkegaard, *Fear and Trembling* and *Repetition*, eds. and trans. Howard V. Hong and Edna H. Hong (Princeton: Princeton University Press, 1983), p. 66.
47 In discussing Kierkegaard and the Moran narrative, I am preceded by Paul A. Bové, who writes during the heyday of deconstruction: "Simply put, the trilogy is an ironic dialectical inversion of fiction's traditional attempt to fill or cover-up the void. It is a repetitive deconstruction which discloses the habit of western consciousness to distance Nothing in a fiction which hopes to augment or complete the real world." Paul A. Bové, "Beckett's Dreadful Postmodern: The Deconstruction of Form in *Molloy*," in Leonard Orr, ed., *De-Structing the Novel: Essays in Applied Postmodern Hermeneutics* (Troy, New York: Whitston Publishing, 1982), p. 210. Bové has a point, but he misses the spirit of Beckett's anti-art.
48 Beckett, *Three Novels*, p. 94.
49 I am indebted to Martha C. Nussbaum, *Love's Knowledge: Essays on Philosophy and Literature* (New York: Oxford University Press, 1990), p. 298.
50 Beckett, *Three Novels*, p. 95.
51 Ibid., pp. 101–102.
52 Ibid., p. 224.
53 Ibid., p. 240.
54 Kierkegaard, *Fear and Trembling*, p. 121.
55 I am following some suggestions of Kierkegaard, *Fear and Trembling*, pp. 106–107.
56 Beckett, *Three Novels*, p. 132.
57 Ibid., pp. 167–68.
58 Ibid., p. 5.
59 Ibid., pp. 148–49.
60 John Milton, *Paradise Lost*, ed. Scott Elledge (New York: W. W. Norton, 1975), pp. 8–9.
61 Virgil, *Virgil's Aeneid: Books I–VI*, eds. H. R. Fairclough and Seldon L. Brown (Chicago: Benj. H. Sanborn & Co., 1925), p. 41.
62 Yeats, *Essays and Introductions*, p. 85.
63 *Shelley's Poetry and Prose*, p. 460.

64 Kierkegaard, *Fear and Trembling*, p. 48.

65 Beckett, *Three Novels*, p. 149.

66 Kierkegaard, *Fear and Trembling*, p. 43.

67 Ibid., p. 119.

68 Beckett, *Three Novels*, pp. 175–76.

69 Ibid., p. 414.

70 Rupert Wood, "An Endgame of Aesthetics: Beckett as Essayist," in John Pilling, ed., *The Cambridge Companion to Beckett* (Cambridge: Cambridge University Press, 1994), p. 11.

71 Beckett, *Complete Short Prose*, p. 61.

72 Beckett, *Three Novels*, p. 19.

73 See J. D. O'Hara, "Jung and the Narratives of *Molloy*," in S. E. Gontarski, ed., *The Beckett Studies Reader* (Gainesville, FL: University Press of Florida, 1993), pp. 129–45.

74 Beckett, *Three Novels*, pp. 240, quoted in Nussbaum, *Love's Knowledge*, p. 287.

75 Jacques Barzun, *An Essay on French Verse: For Readers of English Poetry* (New York: New Directions, 1990), pp. 109–111; and Barzun, *From Dawn to Decadence*, pp. 619–20.

76 Samuel Beckett, 1937 letter to Axel Kaun, translated by Martin Esslin, quoted in Ricks, *Beckett's Dying Words*, p. 56.

77 Beckett, *Watt*, p. 250.

78 See S. E. Gontarski, "Preface," in C. J. Ackerley, *Demented Particulars: The Annotated Murphy* (Tallahassee, FL: Journal of Beckett Studies Books, 1998), pp. v–viii.

79 Beckett, *Three Novels*, pp. 56–57.

80 Dante Alighieri, *La Divina Commedia*, ed. C. H. Grandgent (Boston: D. C. Heath, 1913), *Purgatorio*, p. 204.

81 Beckett, *Three Novels*, p. 57.

82 Ibid., p. 56.

83 Ibid., p. 254.

84 Ibid., p. 37.

85 Ibid., p. 132.

86 Ibid., p. 248.

87 See Hugh Kenner, *Samuel Beckett: A Critical Study* (New York: Grove Press, 1961), pp. 117–32.

88 Beckett, *Three Novels*, p. 293.

89 Beckett, *Proust*, p. 51.

90 Beckett, *Three Novels*, p. 375.

91 Schopenhauer, *World as Will and Representation*, I:411.

92 Ibid., I:412n.

93 Ibid., II:646.

94 Arthur Schopenhauer, *Philosophical Writings*, ed. Wolfgang Schirmacher (New York: Continuum, 1998), p. 211.

95 Martin Hielscher, quoted in Wolfgang Schirmacher, "Introduction," in Schopenhauer, *Philosophical Writings*, p. xvii.

96 "That fierce endeavour to bring the intellectual and the emotional into focus which characterizes Beckett's work is reflected in his poetry as much as in his theater and prose." Roger Little, "Beckett's Poems and Verse Translations or: Beckett and the Limits of Poetry," in *Cambridge Companion to Beckett*, p. 184.

97 Nussbaum, *Love's Knowledge*, pp. 291–313. Writes Nussbaum: "emotions do not give us a bedrock of reliable 'natural' evidence that stands apart from what society makes." Ibid., p. 310. Bedrock is hard to come by, but emotions do in fact give us reliable natural evidence. See, for example, Carroll, *Evolution and Literary Theory*, pp. 291–97.

98 Jeremy Irons, *Beckett on Film*, produced by Michael Colgan and Alan Moloney, Blue Angel Films, Tyrone Productions, London: Clarence Pictures, 2001.

99 Vivian Mercier, *Beckett/Beckett* (New York: Oxford University Press, 1977), p. 190.

100 Ibid., p. 190.

101 Kierkegaard, *Essential Kierkegaard*, p. 73.

102 Gabriel Josipovici, *On Trust: Art and the Temptations of Suspicion* (New Haven: Yale University Press, 1999), p. 250.

103 Ibid., p. 251.

104 See, for example, Galen Strawson, "A fallacy of our age," *Times Literary Supplement* no. 5288 (Oct. 15, 2004), 13–15.

105 See MacIntyre, *After Virtue*, p. 216.

CONCLUSION: TECHNOLOGY AND TECHNIQUE

1 For a knowledgeable contemporary in reaction against eugenics, see G. K. Chesterton, *Eugenics and Other Evils* (London: Cassell and Company, 1922). For eugenics and its modernist confluences, see David Bradshaw, "The Eugenics Movement in the 1930s and the Emergence of *On the Boiler*," in *Yeats Annual No. 9*, ed. Deirdre Toomey (London: Macmillan, 1992), pp. 189–215; Carey, *Intellectuals*, pp. 12–15; Donald J. Childs, *Modernism and Eugenics: Woolf, Eliot, Yeats, and the Culture of Degeneration* (Cambridge: Cambridge University Press, 2001); and Juan Leon, "Meeting Mr. Eugenides," *Yeats Eliot Review* 9 (Summer–Fall 1988), 169–77.

2 Galton quoted in Childs, *Modernism and Eugenics*, p. 3.

3 W. B. Yeats, *The Collected Works of W. B. Yeats*, eds. Richard J. Finneran and George Mills Harper, 14 vols. (New York: Charles Scribner's Sons, 1989–), V:243.

4 Shaw quoted in Childs, *Modernism and Eugenics*, p. 7.

5 Ibid., p. 14.

6 C. S. Lewis, *The Abolition of Man* (New York: Simon and Schuster, 1996), pp. 83–84.

7 Yeats, *Essays and Introductions*, p. 235.

8 Yeats, *Autobiographies*, p. 338.

9 Yeats, *Collected Poems*, p. 327.

10 Ibid., p. 326.

11 Ibid., p. 337.

12 Eliot, *Sacred Wood*, p. 53 (my italics).

13 Pater, *Works*, I:135 (his italics).

14 T. S. Eliot, "Studies in Contemporary Criticism [I]," *Egoist* 5 (October 1918), 113.

15 Eliot, *Sacred Wood*, p. 133.

16 Ibid., p. 164.

17 Ibid., p. 168.

18 Dante quoted in Eliot, *Sacred Wood*, p. 170.

19 T. S. Eliot, "An American Critic," *New Statesman* 7 (June 24, 1916), 284.

20 T. S. Eliot, "The Lesson of Baudelaire," *Tyro* 1 (Spring 1921), 4.

21 T. S. Eliot, "Verse Pleasant and Unpleasant," *Egoist* 5 (March 1918), 43.

22 T. S. Eliot, "Contemporanea," *Egoist* 5 (June/July 1918), 84.

23 Eliot, *Selected Prose*, p. 177.

24 Ibid.

25 Eliot, "Studies in Contemporary Criticism [I]," 113.

26 Maria Tymoczko, *The Irish Ulysses* (Berkeley: University of California Press, 1994), p. 46. Tymoczko adopts the term "deep structure" from Mieke Bal to show how Joyce "uses myth as an architectural substructure to the realistic surface of the story." Ibid., p. 29.

27 I am drawing on Lewis, *Time and Western Man*, pp. 324–25.

28 James Joyce, *Joyce's Ulysses Notesheets in the British Museum*, ed. Phillip F. Herring (Charlottesville: University Press of Virginia, 1972), p. 429.

29 Virginia Woolf, *The Complete Shorter Fiction of Virginia Woolf*, ed. Susan Dick (San Diego: Harcourt, 1985), p. 89.

30 Woolf, *Mrs. Dalloway*, p. 41.

31 Woolf, *Collected Essays*, II:104.

32 Woolf, *Mrs. Dalloway*, p. 102.

33 Woolf, *The Years*, p. 281.

34 Woolf, *Collected Essays*, II:82.

35 Ibid., II:110.

36 Samuel Beckett, *Endgame* and *Act without Words* (New York: Grove Press, 1958), p. 29.

37 Abrams, Gen. ed., *Norton Anthology*, II: 2482n9.

38 Beckett, *Endgame*, pp. 51–53.

39 Samuel Beckett, *The Collected Shorter Plays of Samuel Beckett* (New York: Grove Press, 1984), p. 61.

40 For example, see Michael Beehler, "'Riddle the Inevitable': Levinas, Eliot, and the Critical Moment of Ethics," in Kathryne V. Lindberg and Joseph Kronick, eds., *America's Modernisms* (Baton Rouge: Louisiana State University Press, 1996), pp. 118–34; and Marian Eide, *Ethical Joyce* (Cambridge: Cambridge University Press, 2002). For an introduction to the work of Levinas, see Robert Bernasconi, "The Ethics of Suspicion," *Research in Phenomenology*

20 (1990), 3–18. For another version of the modernist moral project, based on the "cognitive emotions" of the modernist Aristotle and therefore designed to override what is given in our emotional nature, see Nussbaum, *Love's Knowledge.*

41 Derek Attridge, *Joyce Effects: On Language, Theory, and History* (Cambridge: Cambridge University Press, 2000), p. 20.

42 Emmanuel Levinas, *Basic Philosophical Writings*, eds. Adrian Peperzak, Simon Critchley, and Robert Bernasconi (Bloomington: Indiana University Press, 1996), p. 102.

43 Emmanuel Levinas, *The Levinas Reader*, ed. Seán Hand (Oxford: Basil Blackwell, 1989), p. 81.

44 Attridge, *Joyce Effects*, p. 53.

45 Ibid.

46 Ibid., p. 54.

47 Blaise Pascal, *The Thoughts, Letters, and Opuscules of Blaise Pascal*, trans. O. W. Wright (Boston: Houghton, Mifflin and Company, 1893), p. 166.

48 Derek Attridge, "Innovation, Literature, Ethics: Relating to the Other," *PMLA* 114 (1999), 25.

49 Lawrence Buell sees in Attridge a "readiness to push . . . the image of engagement with text . . . as encounter with virtual person." Lawrence Buell, "In Pursuit of Ethics," *PMLA* 114 (1999), 13. I agree with Buell that Attridge's "ethical hermeneutics" is characterized by a "temptation to reify the metaphor" and by an implication that "reader resistance is unethical." Ibid.

50 Martin Heidegger, *Basic Writings*, ed. David Krell (San Francisco: Harper Collins, 1993), pp. 320–21.

51 Ibid., p. 332.

52 Hélène Cixous, "The Character of 'Character,'" *New Literary History* 5 (1974), 388–89.

53 Woolf, *The Waves*, p. 291.

54 Cixous, "Character of 'Character,'" 385 (her italics).

55 James, *Psychology: Briefer Course*, p. 41 (his italics).

56 Cixous, "Character of 'Character,'" 389.

57 See James, *Psychology: Briefer Course*, pp. 43–83.

58 Eliot picks up on this theme in his Gloucester notebook: "Euphorion of the modern time / Improved and up to date – sublime. . ." Eliot, *Inventions*, p. 35.

59 See Louis Menand, *The Metaphysical Club: A Story of Ideas in America* (New York: Farrar, Straus & Giroux, 2001), p. 432.

60 John Dewey, *Human Nature and Conduct: An Introduction to Social Psychology* (New York: Modern Library, 1930), pp. 274–75 (his italics).

61 John Dewey, *Art as Experience* (New York: G. P. Putnam's Sons, 1958), p. 346.

62 *Shelley's Poetry and Prose*, p. 488.

63 John Dewey, *Reconstruction in Philosophy*, enlarged edition (Boston: Beacon Press, 1948), pp. 162–63.

64 Ibid., p. 38.

65 Ibid., p. 37.

66 Dewey, *Art as Experience*, p. 272 (his italics).
67 Ibid., p. 42.
68 Ibid.
69 Ibid., p. 49.
70 MacIntyre, *After Virtue*, p. 236.
71 For Huxley's lack of relevance in the world of consumers, see Yuval Levin, review of *Consumer's Guide to a Brave New World*, by Wesley J. Smith, *Weekly Standard* 10 (November 29, 2004), 39.
72 Freeman Dyson, *The Sun, the Genome, and the Internet: Tools of Scientific Revolutions* (New York: Oxford University Press, 1999), p. 112.
73 Friedrich Nietzsche, "On the Uses and Disadvantages of History for Life," in Daniel Breazeale, ed., *Untimely Meditations* (Cambridge: Cambridge University Press, 1997), p. 120.
74 Dyson, *Sun*, p. 113.
75 Ibid. (my italics).
76 Yeats, *Vision*, p. 82.
77 John Dewey, *The Influence of Darwin on Philosophy and Other Essays in Contemporary Thought* (Bloomington: University of Indiana Press, 1965), p. 19.
78 Beckett, *Endgame*, p. 38.

Works Cited

Abrams, M. H., Gen. ed., *The Norton Anthology of English Literature*, 7th edn., 2 vols., New York: W. W. Norton, 2000

Ackrill, J. L., "Aristotle on *Eudaimonia*," in Amélie Oksenberg Rorty, ed., *Essays on Aristotle's Ethics*, Berkeley: University of California Press, 1980, 15–33

Ackroyd, Peter, *T. S. Eliot: A Life*, New York: Simon and Schuster, 1984

Adorno, Theodor W., "Trying to Understand *Endgame*," trans. Michael T. Jones, *New German Critique* 26 (1982), 119–50

Anderson, Warren, "Arnold and the Classics," in Kenneth Allott, ed., *Matthew Arnold*, Athens, OH: University of Ohio Press, 1976, 259–85

Aristotle, *The Basic Works of Aristotle*, ed. Richard McKeon, New York: Random House, 1941

Arnhart, Larry, *Darwinian Natural Right: The Biological Ethics of Human Nature*, Albany: State University of New York Press, 1998

Arnold, Matthew, *Complete Prose Works of Matthew Arnold*, ed. R. H. Super, 11 vols., Ann Arbor, MI: University of Michigan Press, 1961–77

   The Letters of Matthew Arnold to Arthur Hugh Clough, ed. Howard Lowry, London: Oxford University Press, 1932

Atkins, Brian, "Yeats: Platonist, Gnostic or What?," in *Yeats: An Annual of Critical and Textual Studies*, vol. 7, 1989, ed. Richard J. Finneran, Ann Arbor, MI: University of Michigan Press, 1990, 3–16

Attridge, Derek, "Innovation, Literature, Ethics: Relating to the Other," PMLA 114 (1999), 20–31

   Joyce Effects: On Language, Theory, and History, Cambridge: Cambridge University Press, 2000

Aubert, Jacques, *The Aesthetics of James Joyce*, Baltimore: Johns Hopkins University Press, 1992

Avery, Todd, "*Three Guineas* and the Aesthetic Ethics of Cultural Dissent," *Virginia Woolf Miscellany* 60 (2002), 6–7

Babbitt, Irving, *Rousseau and Romanticism*, New York: Meridian, 1959

Barzun, Jacques, *An Essay on French Verse: For Readers of English Poetry*, New York: New Directions, 1990

   From Dawn to Decadence: 500 Years of Cultural Life, 1500 to the Present, New York: HarperCollins, 2000

Bate, Walter Jackson, *From Classic to Romantic: Premises of Taste in Eighteenth Century England*, New York: Harper and Row, 1961
    ed., *Criticism: The Major Texts*, San Diego, Harcourt, 1970
Baudelaire, Charles, *The Painter of Modern Life and Other Essays*, ed. and trans. Jonathan Mayne, London: Phaidon, 1965
Beckett, Samuel, *Collected Poems in English and French*, New York: Grove Press, 1977
    The Collected Shorter Plays of Samuel Beckett, New York: Grove Press, 1984
    The Complete Short Prose: 1929–1989, ed. S. E. Gontarski, New York: Grove Press, 1995
    Endgame and *Act without Words*, New York: Grove Press, 1958
    Mercier and Camier, New York: Grove Press, 1975
    Murphy, New York: Grove Press, 1957
    Proust, New York: Grove Press, 1931
    Three Novels: Molloy, Malone Dies, The Unnamable, New York: Grove Press, 1965
    Waiting for Godot: A Tragicomedy in Two Acts, New York: Grove Press, 1956
    Watt, New York: Grove Press, 1959
Beckett, Samuel and Georges Duthuit, "Three Dialogues," in Martin Esslin, ed., *Samuel Beckett: A Collection of Critical Essays*, Englewood Cliffs, NJ: Prentice-Hall, 1965, 16–22
Beehler, Michael, "'Riddle the Inevitable': Levinas, Eliot, and the Critical Moment of Ethics," in Kathryne V. Lindberg and Joseph Kronick, eds., *America's Modernisms*, Baton Rouge: Louisiana State University Press, 1996, 118–34
Bell, Clive, *Old Friends*, New York: Harcourt, 1957
Bell, Vereen, "Yeats's Nietzschean Idealism," *Southern Review* 29 (1993), 491–513
Bergson, Henri, *Matter and Memory*, trans. Nancy Margaret Paul and W. Scott Palmer, Garden City, NY: Doubleday, 1959
Bernasconi, Robert, "The Ethics of Suspicion," *Research in Phenomenology* 20 (1990), 3–18
Blake, William, *Blake's Poetry and Designs*, eds. Mary Lynn Johnson and John E. Grant, New York: W. W. Norton, 1979
Blissett, William, "Wagner in *The Waste Land*," in Jane Campbell and James Doyle, eds., *The Practical Vision: Essays in English Literature in Honour of Flora Roy*, Waterloo, Ontario: Wilfrid Laurier University Press, 1978, 71–85
Bloom, Harold, "Introduction," in Walter Pater, *Selected Writings of Walter Pater*, ed. Harold Bloom, New York: Columbia University Press, 1974, vii–xxxi
    Yeats, New York: Oxford University Press, 1970
Bolt, Sidney, *Joyce*, 2nd edn., Harlow, England: Longman, 1992
Bornstein, George, *Transformations of Romanticism in Yeats, Eliot, and Stevens*, Chicago: University of Chicago Press, 1976
Bosanquet, Bernard, *A History of Aesthetic: From the Greeks to the Twentieth Century*, 2nd edn., New York: Meridian, 1957
Bové, Paul A., "Beckett's Dreadful Postmodern: The Deconstruction of Form in *Molloy*," in Leonard Orr, ed., *De-Structing the Novel: Essays in Applied Postmodern Hermeneutics*, Troy, NY: Whitston Publishing, 1982, 185–221

Boyle, Robert, S. J., *James Joyce's Pauline Vision: A Catholic Exposition*, Carbondale: Southern Illinois University Press, 1978

Bradley, F. H., *Ethical Studies*, 2nd edn., Oxford: Clarendon Press, 1927

Bradshaw, David, "The Eugenics Movement in the 1930s and the Emergence of *On the Boiler*," in *Yeats Annual No. 9*, ed. Deirdre Toomey, London: Macmillan, 1992, 189–215

Bromwich, David, *A Choice of Inheritance*, Cambridge: Harvard University Press, 1989

Brooker, Jewel Spears, *Mastery and Escape: T. S. Eliot and the Dialectic of Modernism*, Amherst: University of Massachusetts Press, 1994

Budgen, Frank, *James Joyce and the Making of "Ulysses,"* Bloomington: Indiana University Press, 1960

Buell, Lawrence, "In Pursuit of Ethics," PMLA 114 (1999), 7–19

Burke, Edmund, *Reflections on the Revolution in France*, ed. Conor Cruise O'Brien, New York: Penguin, 1968

Burnet, John, *Aristotle on Education*, Cambridge: Cambridge University Press, 1913

Burnyeat, M. F., "Is an Aristotelian Philosophy of Mind Still Credible? (A Draft)," in Martha C. Nussbaum and Amélie Oksenberg Rorty, eds., *Essays on Aristotle's De Anima*, Oxford: Clarendon Press, 1992, 15–26

Bush, Ronald, "T. S. Eliot and Modernism at the Present Time: A Provocation," in Ronald Bush, ed., *T. S. Eliot: The Modernist in History*, Cambridge: Cambridge University Press, 1991, 191–202

   T. S. Eliot: A Study in Character and Style, New York: Oxford University Press, 1983

Butcher, S. H., *Aristotle's Theory of Poetry and Fine Art, with a Critical Text and Translation of the Poetics*, 4th edn., Mineola, NY: Dover, 1951

Butler, Samuel, *The Way of All Flesh*, London: J. M. Dent, 1933

Carey, John, *The Intellectuals and the Masses: Pride and Prejudice among the Literary Intelligentia, 1880–1939*, New York: St. Martin's, 1992

Carlyle, Thomas, *Carlyle's Complete Works*, 20 vols., Boston: Estes and Lauriat, 1885

Carroll, Joseph, *Evolution and Literary Theory*, Columbia: University of Missouri Press, 1995

Chesterton, G. K., *Eugenics and Other Evils*, London: Cassell, 1922

   Heretics, New York: John Lane, 1909

Childs, Donald, J., *Modernism and Eugenics: Woolf, Eliot, Yeats, and the Culture of Degeneration*, Cambridge: Cambridge University Press, 2001

Cixous, Hélène, "The Character of 'Character,'" *New Literary History* 5 (1974), 383–402

Coe, Richard N., *Beckett*, Edinburgh: Oliver and Boyd, 1964

   "God and Samuel Beckett," in J. D. O'Hara, ed., *Twentieth Century Interpretations of Molloy, Malone Dies, The Unnamable: A Collection of Critical Essays*, Englewood Cliffs, NJ: Prentice-Hall, 1970, 91–113

Cohn, Ruby, "Philosophical Fragments in the Works of Samuel Beckett," in Martin Esslin, ed., *Samuel Beckett: A Collection of Critical Essays*, Englewood Cliffs, NJ: Prentice-Hall, 1965, 169–77

Coleridge, Samuel Taylor, *The Collected Works of Samuel Taylor Coleridge*, ed. Kathleen Coburn, 16 vols., Princeton: Princeton University Press, 1971–2000

Copleston, Frederick, S. J., *A History of Philosophy*, 9 vols., New York: Doubleday, 1985

Corbett, David Peters, "T. Sturge Moore's 'Do We or Do We Not, Know It' and the Writing of 'Byzantium,'" in Warwick Gould, ed., *Yeats Annual No. 10*, London: Macmillan, 1993, 241–49

Crane, R. S., "Introduction," in R. S. Crane, W. R. Keast, Richard McKeon, Norman Maclean, Elder Olson, and Bernard Weinberg, *Critics and Criticism, Ancient and Modern*, ed. R. S. Crane, Chicago: University of Chicago Press, 1952, 1–24

Cross, Richard K., *Flaubert and Joyce: The Rite of Fiction*, Princeton: Princeton University Press, 1971

Damasio, Antonio, *Descartes' Error: Emotion, Reason, and the Human Brain*, New York: Quill, 2000

Dane, Joseph, *The Critical Mythology of Irony*, Athens: The University of Georgia Press, 1991

Dante Alighieri, *La Divina Commedia*, ed. C. H. Grandgent, Boston: D. C. Heath, 1913

Davies, Norman, *Europe: A History*, New York: Oxford University Press, 1996

Dewey, John, *Art as Experience*, New York: G. P. Putnam's Sons, 1958
  Human Nature and Conduct: An Introduction to Social Psychology, New York: Modern Library, 1930
  The Influence of Darwin on Philosophy and Other Essays in Contemporary Thought, Bloomington: Indiana University Press, 1965
  Reconstruction in Philosophy, enlarged edition, Boston: Beacon Press, 1948

DiBattista, Maria, *Virginia Woolf's Major Novels: The Fables of Anon*, New Haven: Yale University Press, 1980

Dickens, Charles, *The Pickwick Papers*, Oxford: Oxford University Press, 1948

Donoghue, Denis, *William Butler Yeats*, New York: Ecco Press, 1988

Dyson, Freeman, *The Sun, the Genome, and the Internet: Tools of Scientific Revolutions*, New York: Oxford University Press, 1999

Ebel, Henry, "Matthew Arnold and Classical Culture," *Arion* 4 (1965), 188–220

Eide, Marian, *Ethical Joyce*, Cambridge: Cambridge University Press, 2002

Eliot, T. S., *After Strange Gods*, New York: Harcourt, 1934
  "An American Critic," *New Statesman* 7 (June 24, 1916), 284
  Collected Poems 1909–1962, New York: Harcourt, 1988
  "A Commentary," *Criterion* 12 (1933), 468–73
  The Complete Poems and Plays: 1909–1950, San Diego: Harcourt, 1950
  "Contemporanea," *Egoist* 5 (June/July 1918), 84–85
  "The Development of Leibniz's Monadism," *Monist* 26 (1916), 534–56
  Essays Ancient and Modern, New York: Harcourt, 1936
  For Lancelot Andrewes: Essays on Style and Order, Garden City, New York: Doubleday, 1929

The Idea of a Christian Society, reprinted with *Notes Towards the Definition of Culture*, in *Christianity and Culture*, San Diego: Harcourt, 1977

"Introduction," in Josef Pieper, *Leisure: The Basis of Culture*, New York: Mentor, 1963, 11–16

Inventions of the March Hare, ed. Christopher Ricks, New York: Harcourt, 1996

Knowledge and Experience in the Philosophy of F. H. Bradley, New York: Columbia University Press, 1989

"The Lesson of Baudelaire," *Tyro* 1 (1921), 4

The Letters of T. S. Eliot, vol. I, *1898–1922*, ed. Valerie Eliot, San Diego: Harcourt, 1988

"Modern Tendencies in Poetry," *Shama'a* 1 (April 1920), 9–18

"A Note on Two Odes of Cowley," in John Purves, ed., *Seventeenth Century Studies Presented to Sir Herbert Grierson*, Oxford: Clarendon Press, 1938, 235–42

Notes Towards the Definition of Culture, reprinted with *The Idea of a Christian Society*, in *Christianity and Culture*

On Poetry and Poets, London: Faber, 1957

"Reflections on Contemporary Poetry [II]," *Egoist* 4 (October 1917), 133–34

"Religion Without Humanism," in Norman Foerster, ed., *Humanism and America: Essays on the Outlook of Modern Civilisation*, New York: Farrar and Rinehart, 1930, 105–12

Review of *Per Amica Silentia Lunae*, by William Butler Yeats, *Egoist* 5 (June/July 1918), 87

Review of *Theism and Humanism*, by A. J. Balfour, *International Journal of Ethics* 26 (1916), 284–89

The Sacred Wood: Essays on Poetry and Criticism, London: Methuen, 1960

Selected Essays, new edition, New York: Harcourt, 1950

Selected Prose of T. S. Eliot, ed. Frank Kermode, New York: Harcourt, 1975

"Studies in Contemporary Criticism [I]," *Egoist* 5 (October 1918), 113–14

To Criticize the Critic and Other Writings, Lincoln: University of Nebraska Press, 1991

"Turgenev," *Egoist* 6 (December 1917), 167

The Use of Poetry and the Use of Criticism, Cambridge: Harvard University Press, 1964

The Varieties of Metaphysical Poetry, ed. Ronald Schuchard, New York: Harcourt, 1993

"Verse Pleasant and Unpleasant," *Egoist* 5 (March 1918), 43–44

Elliott, Robert, C., *The Literary Persona*, Chicago: University of Chicago Press, 1982

Ellison, David, *Ethics and Aesthetics in European Modernist Literature: From the Sublime to the Uncanny*, Cambridge: Cambridge University Press, 2001

Ellmann, Richard, *The Identity of Yeats*, New York: Oxford University Press, 1954

James Joyce, Oxford: Oxford University Press, 1983

Oscar Wilde, New York: Alfred A. Knopf, 1988

Yeats: The Man and the Masks, New York: E. P. Dutton, 1948

Ellmann, Richard and Ellsworth Mason, eds., James Joyce, *The Critical Writings*, New York: Viking Press, 1964

Fergusson, Francis, *The Idea of a Theater: The Art of Drama in Changing Perspective*, Garden City, NY: Doubleday, 1953

Foot, Philippa, *Natural Goodness*, Oxford: Clarendon Press, 2001

Virtues and Vices, Berkeley: University of California Press, 1978

Forster, E. M., *Two Cheers for Democracy*, London: Edward Arnold, 1951

Foster, R. F., *W. B. Yeats: A Life*, 2 vols., Oxford: Oxford University Press, 1998–2003

Franks, Gabriel, "Virginia Woolf and the Philosophy of G. E. Moore," *The Personalist* 50 (1969), 222–40

Fromm, Harold, "The New Darwinism in the Humanities, Part I: From Plato to Pinker," *Hudson Review* 56 (2003), 89–99

"The New Darwinism in the Humanities, Part II: Back to Nature, Again," *Hudson Review* 56 (2003), 315–27

Fry, Roger, *Vision and Design*, London: Chatto and Windus, 1923

Geach, Peter, *The Virtues*, Cambridge: Cambridge University Press, 1977

Géracht, Maurice, "Cubism and Points of View in Virginia Woolf's *To the Lighthouse*," *Interfaces* 13 (*Juin* 1998), 119–37

Geulincx, Arnold, *Metaphysics*, trans. Martin Wilson, Wisbech, England: Christoffel Press, 1999

Gontarski, S. E., "Preface," in C. J. Ackerley, *Demented Particulars: The Annotated Murphy*, Tallahassee, FL: Journal of Beckett Studies Books, 1998, v–viii

Gontarski, S. E., ed., Samuel Beckett, *The Complete Short Prose: 1929–1989*, New York: Grove Press, 1995

Gordon, Lyndall, *Eliot's New Life*, New York: Farrar, Straus and Giroux, 1988

Graham, J. W., "Manuscript Revision and the Heroic Theme of *The Waves*," *Twentieth Century Literature* 29 (Fall 1983), 312–32

Gross, Paul R. and Norman Levitt, *Higher Superstition: The Academic Left and Its Quarrel with Science*, Baltimore: The Johns Hopkins University Press, 1994

Gross, Paul R., Norman Levitt, and Martin W. Lewis, eds., *The Flight from Science and Reason*, New York: The New York Academy of Sciences, 1996

Hamilton, John D. B., "Antigone: Kinship, Justice, and the Polis," in Dora C. Pozzi and John M. Wickersham, eds., *Myth and the Polis*, Ithaca, NY: Cornell University Press, 1991, 86–98

Harrington, John P., *The Irish Beckett*, Syracuse, NY: Syracuse University Press, 1991

Harvey, Lawrence, E., *Samuel Beckett: Poet and Critic*, Princeton: Princeton University Press, 1970

Hayman, David, *Ulysses: The Mechanics of Meaning*, Madison: University of Wisconsin Press, 1982

Hayman, David and Clive Hart, eds., *James Joyce's Ulysses*, Berkeley: University of California Press, 1974

Hazlitt, William, *Complete Works of William Hazlitt*, ed. P. P. Howe, 21 vols., London: J. M. Dent, 1930–34

Hegel, G. W. F., *Hegel's Philosophy of Right*, trans. T. M. Knox, London: Oxford University Press, 1967

The Philosophy of History, trans. J. Sibree, New York: Willey Book Company, 1944

Heidegger, Martin, *Basic Writings*, ed. David Krell, San Francisco: HarperCollins, 1993

Heininger, Joseph, "Molly Bloom's Ad Language and Goods Behavior: Advertising as Social Communication in *Ulysses*," in Richard Pearce, ed., *Molly Blooms: A Polylogue on "Penelope" and Cultural Studies*, Madison: University of Wisconsin Press, 1994, 155–73

Hough, Graham, *The Last Romantics*, London: Methuen, 1961

Housman, A. E., *Introductory Lecture, Delivered before the Faculties of Arts and Laws and of Science in University College, London, October 3, 1892*, New York: Macmillan, 1937

Howarth, Herbert, *Notes on Some Figures Behind T. S. Eliot*, Boston: Houghton Mifflin, 1964

Hursthouse, Rosalind, "Virtue Ethics," in Edward N. Zalat, ed., *The Stanford Encyclopedia of Philosophy*, fall 2003 edition, URL= <*http://plato.stanford. edu/archives/fall 2003/entries/ethics-virtue/*>

Huxley, Aldous, *End and Means: An Inquiry into the Nature of Ideals and into the Methods Employed for Their Realization*, New York: Harper and Brothers, 1937

Huxley, Thomas H., *Evolution and Ethics*, New York: D. Appleton, 1896
Science and Education: Essays, New York: D. Appleton, 1896

Ingram, Penelope, "'One Drifts Apart': *To the Lighthouse* as Art of Response," *Philosophy and Literature* 23 (1999), 78–95

Irons, Jeremy, *Beckett on Film*, produced by Michael Colgan and Alan Moloney, Blue Angel Films, Tyrone Productions, London: Clarence Pictures, 2001

Irwin, T. H., "The Metaphysical and Psychological Basis of Aristotle's Ethics," in Amélie Oksenberg Rorty, ed., *Essays on Aristotle's Ethics*, Berkeley: University of California Press, 1980, 35–53

James, William, *Psychology: The Briefer Course*, ed. Gordon Allport, Notre Dame: University of Notre Dame Press, 1985
Writings 1902–1910, New York: Library of America, 1987

Josipovici, Gabriel, *On Trust: Art and the Temptations of Suspicion*, New Haven: Yale University Press, 1999

Jouve, Nicole Ward, "Virginia Woolf and Psychoanalysis," in Sue Roe and Susan Sellers, eds., *The Cambridge Companion to Virginia Woolf*, Cambridge: Cambridge University Press, 2000, 245–72

Joyce, James, *The Critical Writings*, eds. Ellsworth Mason and Richard Ellmann, New York: Viking Press, 1964
Dubliners, New York: Viking Press, 1968
Joyce's Ulysses Notesheets in the British Museum, ed. Phillip F. Herring, Charlottesville: University Press of Virginia, 1972
Portrait of the Artist as a Young Man, New York: Viking Press, 1964
Stephen Hero, eds. Theodore Spencer, John J. Slocum, and Herbert Cahoon, New York: New Directions, 1963

Ulysses, ed. Hans Walter Gabler, New York: Vintage, 1986

Kaufmann, Walter, *Nietzsche: Philosopher, Psychologist, Antichrist*, New York: Meridian, 1956

Kenner, Hugh, *Samuel Beckett: A Critical Study*, New York: Grove Press, 1961

Ulysses, revised edition, Baltimore: Johns Hopkins University Press, 1987

Kermode, Frank, *Romantic Image*, London: Routledge, 1957

Kershner, R. B., "A Critical History of *A Portrait of the Artist as a Young Man*," in James Joyce, *A Portrait of the Artist as a Young Man*, ed. R. B. Kershner, Boston: St Martin's Press, 1993, 221–34

Kierkegaard, Soren, *The Essential Kierkegaard*, eds. Howard V. Hong and Edna H. Hong, Princeton: Princeton University Press, 2000

Fear and Trembling and *Repetition*, eds. and trans. Howard V. Hong and Edna H. Hong, Princeton: Princeton University Press, 1983

Knowlson, James, *Damned to Fame: The Life of Samuel Beckett*, New York: Simon and Schuster, 1997

Lawson-Tancred, Hugh, "Introduction," in Aristotle, *De Anima (On the Soul)*, ed. and trans. Hugh Lawson-Tancred, Harmondsworth: Penguin Books, 1986, 11–116

Lee, Hermione, *Virginia Woolf*, New York: Alfred A. Knopf, 1997

Leon, Juan, "Meeting Mr. Eugenides," *Yeats Eliot Review* 9 (Summer-Fall 1988), 169–77

Levenson, Michael H., *A Genealogy of Modernism: A Study of English Literary Doctrine 1908–1922*, Cambridge: Cambridge University Press, 1984

Levin, Harry, *James Joyce*, Norfolk, CT: New Directions, 1941

Levin, Yuval, review of *Consumer's Guide to a Brave New World*, by Wesley J. Smith, *Weekly Standard* 10 (November 29, 2004), 39

Levinas, Emmanuel, *Basic Philosophical Writings*, eds. Adrian Peperzak, Simon Critchley, and Robert Bernasconi, Bloomington: Indiana University Press, 1996

The Levinas Reader, ed. Seán Hand, Oxford: Basil Blackwell, 1989

Lewis, C. S., *The Abolition of Man*, New York: Simon and Schuster, 1996

Lewis, Wyndham, *Time and Western Man*, Boston: Beacon Press, 1957

Little, Roger, "Beckett's Poems and Verse Translations or: Beckett and the Limits of Poetry," in John Pilling, ed., *The Cambridge Companion to Beckett*, Cambridge: Cambridge University Press, 1994, 184–95

Locke, John, *An Essay Concerning Human Understanding*, 2 vols., Mineola, NY: Dover, 1959

Lockerd, Benjamin G., Jr., *Aethereal Rumours: T. S. Eliot's Physics and Poetics*, Lewisburg, PA: Bucknell University Press, 1998

MacIntyre, Alasdair, *After Virtue*, 2nd edn., Notre Dame: University of Notre Dame Press, 1984

Dependent Rational Animals: Why Human Beings Need the Virtues, Chicago: Open Court, 1999

A Short History of Ethics, New York: Macmillan, 1966

Whose Justice? Which Rationality?, Notre Dame: University of Notre Dame Press, 1988

Marx, Karl, *Selected Writings*, ed. David McLellan, Oxford: Oxford University Press, 1977

Maze, John R., *Virginia Woolf: Feminism, Creativity, and the Unconscious*, Westport, CT: Greenwood Press, 1997

McShane, Larry, "Stern sees freedom in satellite broadcasts" (Associated Press), *Worcester Telegram and Gazette* (October 7, 2004), C3

Menand, Louis, *The Metaphysical Club: A Story of Ideas in America*, New York: Farrar, Straus & Giroux, 2001

Mepham, John, "Mourning and Modernism," in Patricia Clements and Isabel Grundy, eds., *Virginia Woolf: New Critical Essays*, London: Vision Press Limited, 1983, 137–54

Mercier, Vivian, *Beckett/Beckett*, New York: Oxford University Press, 1977

Mill, John Stuart, *Collected Works of John Stuart Mill*, Gen. ed. John M. Robson, 33 vols., Toronto: University of Toronto Press, 1963–91

Milton, John, *Paradise Lost*, ed. Scott Elledge, New York: W. W. Norton, 1975

Moody, A. D., *Virginia Woolf*, Edinburgh: Oliver and Boyd, 1963

Moore, G. E., *Principia Ethica*, Cambridge: Cambridge University Press, 1960

Nagel, Thomas, *The Last Word*, New York: Oxford University Press, 1997

Najarian, James, *Victorian Keats: Manliness, Sexuality, and Desire*, New York: Palgrave Macmillan, 2002

Naremore, James, *The World Without a Self: Virginia Woolf and the Novel*, New Haven: Yale University Press, 1973

Nemoianu, Virgil, *A Theory of the Secondary: Literature, Progress, and Reaction*, Baltimore: Johns Hopkins University Press, 1989

Nietzsche, Friedrich, *Basic Writings of Nietzsche*, ed. and trans. Walter Kaufmann, New York: Modern Library, 1992

"On the Uses and Disadvantages of History for Life," in Daniel Breazeale, ed., *Untimely Meditations*, Cambridge: Cambridge University Press, 1997, 57–123

Thus Spoke Zarathustra: A Book for All and None, trans. Walter Kaufmann, New York: Modern Library, 1995

Noon, William T., *Joyce and Aquinas: A Study of the Religious Elements in the Writings of James Joyce*, New Haven: Yale University Press, 1957

Nussbaum, Martha, C., *Love's Knowledge: Essays on Philosophy and Literature*, New York: Oxford University Press, 1990

"Non-Relative Virtues: An Aristotelian Approach," in *Midwest Studies in Philosophy*, vol. 13, *Ethical Theory: Character and Virtue*, eds. Peter A. French, Theodore E. Uehling, Jr., and Howard K. Wettstein, Notre Dame: University of Notre Dame Press, 1988, 32–53

Nussbaum, Martha C. and Amélie Oksenberg Rorty, eds., *Essays on Aristotle's De Anima*, Oxford: Clarendon Press, 1992

O'Hara, J. D., "Jung and the Narratives of *Molloy*," in S. E. Gontarski, ed., *The Beckett Studies Reader*, Gainesville, FL: University Press of Florida, 1993, 129–45

ed., *Twentieth Century Interpretations of Molloy, Malone Dies, The Unnamable: A Collection of Critical Essays*, Englewood Cliffs, NJ: Prentice-Hall, 1970

Opie, Iona and Peter, eds., *The Oxford Dictionary of Nursery Rhymes*, Oxford: Oxford University Press, 1951

Ortega Y Gasset, José, *The Dehumanization of Art and Other Essays on Art, Culture, and Literature*, Princeton: Princeton University Press, 1968

Pascal, Blaise, *The Thoughts, Letters, and Opuscules of Blaise Pascal*, trans. O. W. Wright, Boston: Houghton, Mifflin and Company, 1893

Pater, Walter, *Works*, library edition, 10 vols., London: Macmillan, 1912–15

Pearl, Cyril, *Dublin in Bloomtime: The City James Joyce Knew*, London: Angus and Robertson, 1969

Perl, Jeffrey, "The Language of Theory and the Language of Poetry: The Significance of T. S. Eliot's Philosophical Notebooks, Part Two," *Southern Review* 21 (1985), 1012–23

Pinker, Steven, *The Blank Slate: The Modern Denial of Human Nature*, New York: Penguin Books, 2002

Plato, *The Collected Dialogues*, eds. Edith Hamilton and Huntington Cairns, Princeton: Princeton University Press, 1963

Porter, Kevin J., "The Rhetorical Problem of Eternity in Yeats's Byzantium Poems," *Yeats Eliot Review* 14 (1996), 10–17

Pound, Ezra, "Historical Survey," *Little Review* 8 (Autumn 1921), 39–42

Rabinovitz, Rubin, *The Development of Samuel Beckett's Fiction*, Urbana: University of Illinois Press, 1984

Ricks, Christopher, *Beckett's Dying Words*, Oxford: Oxford University Press, 1993

ed., T. S. Eliot, *Inventions of the March Hare*, New York: Harcourt, 1996

Rorty, Amélie Oksenberg, "Introduction B: *De Anima*: Its Agenda and Its Recent Interpreters," in Martha C. Nussbaum and Amélie Oksenberg Rorty, eds., *Essays on Aristotle's De Anima*, Oxford: Clarendon Press, 1992, 7–13

"A Literary Postscript," in Amélie Oksenberg Rorty, ed., *The Identities of Persons*, Berkeley: University of California Press, 1976, 301–23

ed., *Essays on Aristotle's Ethics*, Berkeley: University of California Press, 1980

ed., *The Identities of Persons*, Berkeley: University of California Press, 1976

Rosenbaum, S. P., *Victorian Bloomsbury*, vol. 1, *The Early History of the Bloomsbury Group*, New York: St. Martin's Press, 1987

Santayana, George, *Three Philosophical Poets*, Garden City, NY: Doubleday, 1938

Schirmacher, Wolfgang, "Introduction," in Arthur Schopenhauer, *Philosophical Writings*, ed. Wolfgang Schirmacher, New York: Continuum, 1998, vii–xvii

Schopenhauer, Arthur, *Philosophical Writings*, ed. Wolfgang Schirmacher, New York: Continuum, 1998

The World as Will and Representation, trans. E. F. J. Payne, 3rd edn., 2 vols., New York: Dover, 1966

Schork, R. J., *Greek and Hellenic Culture in Joyce*, Gainesville: University Press of Florida, 1998

Schricker, Gale, *A New Species of Man: The Poetic Persona of W. B. Yeats*, Lewisburg, PA: Bucknell University Press, 1982

Schuchard, Ronald, *Eliot's Dark Angel: Intersections of Life and Art*, New York: Oxford University Press, 1999

ed., T. S. Eliot, *The Varieties of Metaphysical Poetry*, New York: Harcourt, 1993

Schwartz, Sanford, *The Matrix of Modernism: Pound, Eliot, and Early Twentieth-Century Thought*, Princeton: Princeton University Press, 1985

Schwarz, Daniel, R., *Reading Joyce's Ulysses*, New York: St. Martin's Press, 1987

Senn, Fritz, "Nausicaa," in Clive Hart and David Hayman, eds., *James Joyce's Ulysses*, Berkeley: University of California Press, 1974, 277–311

Shelley, Percy Bysshe, "Preface" to *Frankenstein; or, The Modern Prometheus*, in Abrams, Gen. ed., *The Norton Anthology of English Literature*, II:907–908

Shelley's Poetry and Prose, eds. Donald H. Reiman and Sharon B. Powers, New York: Norton, 1977

Shusterman, Richard, *T. S. Eliot and the Philosophy of Criticism*, New York: Columbia University Press, 1988

Sigg, Eric, *The American T. S. Eliot: A Study of the Early Writings*, Cambridge: Cambridge University Press, 1989

Smith, Grover, *T. S. Eliot's Poetry and Plays: A Study in Sources and Meaning*, Chicago: University of Chicago Press, 1956

Sokal, Alan and Jean Bricmont, *Fashionable Nonsense: Postmodern Intellectuals' Abuse of Science*, New York: Picador, 1999

Spencer, Theodore, "Introduction," in James Joyce, *Stephen Hero*, eds. Theodore Spencer, John J. Slocum, and Herbert Cahoon, New York: New Directions, 1963

Spencer, Theodore, John J. Slocum, and Herbert Cahoon, eds., James Joyce, *Stephen Hero*, New York: New Directions, 1963

Spenser, Edmund, *The Faerie Queene*, ed. Thomas P. Roche, Jr., London: Penguin Books, 1987

Stead, C. K., *The New Poetic: Yeats to Eliot*, Philadelphia: University of Pennsylvania Press, 1987

Steinberg, Erwin R., "G. E. Moore's Table and Chair in *To the Lighthouse*," *Journal of Modern Literature* 15 (1988), 161–68

Stendhal, *The Life of Henry Brulard*, trans. Jean Stewart and B. C. J. C. Knight, Minerva Press, 1968

Sterne, Laurence, *The Life and Opinions of Tristram Shandy*, Oxford: Oxford University Press, 1983

Stevenson, Randall and Jane Goldman, "'But What Elegy?': Modernist Readings and the Death of Mrs. Ramsay," *The Yearbook of English Studies* 26 (1996), 173–86

Stocks, John Leofric, *Aristotelianism*, Bristol, England: Thoemmes Press, 1993

Strawson, Galen, "A fallacy of our age," *Times Literary Supplement* 5288 (Oct. 15, 2004), 13–15

Sullivan, Kevin, *Joyce among the Jesuits*, New York: Columbia University Press, 1958

Swanton, Christine, *Virtue Ethics: A Pluralistic View*, Oxford: Oxford University Press, 2003

Symons, Arthur, *The Symbolist Movement in Literature*, New York: E. P. Dutton, 1958

Tallis, Raymond, *Why the Mind Is Not a Computer: A Pocket Lexicon of Neuromythology*, Charlottesville, VA: Imprint Academic, 2004

Taylor, Charles, *The Ethics of Authenticity*, Cambridge: Harvard University Press, 1991

    Sources of the Self: The Making of Modern Identity, Cambridge: Harvard University Press, 1989

Torchiana, Donald T., *Backgrounds for Joyce's Dubliners*, Boston: Allen and Unwin, 1986

Trilling, Lionel, *Matthew Arnold*, New York: Harcourt, 1979

Tymoczko, Maria, *The Irish Ulysses*, Berkeley: University of California Press, 1994

Urmson, J. O., *Aristotle's Ethics*, Oxford: Blackwell, 1988

Van Doren, Charles, *A History of Knowledge: Past, Present, and Future*, New York: Ballantine Books, 1991

Veatch, Henry B., *For an Ontology of Morals: A Critique of Contemporary Ethical Theory*, Evanston, IL: Northwestern University Press, 1971

Virgil, *Virgil's Aeneid: Books I–VI*, eds. H. R. Fairclough and Seldon L. Brown, Chicago: Benj. H. Sanborn & Co., 1925

Watt, Donald J., "G. E. Moore and the Bloomsbury Group," *English Literature in Transition* 12 (1969), 119–34

Webb, Eugene, *Samuel Beckett: A Study of His Novels*, Seattle: University of Washington Press, 1970

Wellek, René, *A History of Modern Criticism*, 7 vols., New Haven: Yale University Press, 1955–86

Whitaker, Thomas, *Swan and Shadow: Yeats' Dialogue with History*, Chapel Hill: University of North Carolina Press, 1964

Whitehead, Alfred North, *Science and the Modern World*, New York: Simon and Schuster, 1967

Wicke, Jennifer, "'Who's She When She's at Home?': Molly Bloom and the Work of Consumption," in Richard Pearce, ed., *Molly Blooms: A Polylogue on "Penelope" and Cultural Studies*, Madison: University of Wisconsin Press, 1994, 174–95

Wilde, Oscar, *Complete Works of Oscar Wilde*, ed. J. B. Foreman, New York: HarperCollins, 2001

Williams, Carolyn, *Transfigured World: Walter Pater's Aesthetic Historicism*, Ithaca: Cornell University Press, 1989

Wood, James, *The Broken Estate: Essays on Literature and Belief*, New York: Random House, 1999

Wood, Rupert, "An Endgame of Aesthetics: Beckett as Essayist," in John Pilling, ed., *The Cambridge Companion to Beckett*, Cambridge: Cambridge University Press, 1994, 1–16

Woolf, Virginia, *Between the Acts*, San Diego: Harcourt, 1970

    Collected Essays, 4 vols., London: Hogarth Press, 1966

The Complete Shorter Fiction of Virginia Woolf, ed. Susan Dick, San Diego: Harcourt, 1985

The Diary of Virginia Woolf, ed. Anne Olivier Bell, 5 vols., New York: Harcourt, 1977–84

Freshwater: A Comedy, ed. Lucio Ruotolo, New York: Harcourt, 1976

Jacob's Room, San Diego: Harcourt, 1978

The Letters of Virginia Woolf, eds. Nigel Nicolson and Joanne Trautmann, 6 vols., New York: Harcourt, 1980

Moments of Being, ed. Jeanne Schulkind, 2nd edn., San Diego: Harcourt, 1985

Mrs. Dalloway, New York: Harcourt, 1925

Orlando, San Diego: Harcourt, 1928

A Room of One's Own, New York: Harcourt, 1929

Three Guineas, San Diego: Harcourt, 1938

To the Lighthouse, San Diego: Harcourt, 1989

The Voyage Out, San Diego: Harcourt, 1920

The Waves, New York: Harcourt, 1978

The Years, San Diego: Harcourt, 1939

Wordsworth, William, *Poetical Works,* eds. Thomas Hutchinson and Ernest de Selincourt, Oxford: Oxford University Press, 1936

Yeats, W. B., *Autobiographies: Reveries Over Childhood and Youth* and *The Trembling of the Veil,* New York: Macmillan, 1927

The Collected Poems of W. B. Yeats, ed. Richard J. Finneran, New York: Macmillan, 1989

The Collected Works of W. B. Yeats, eds. Richard J. Finneran and George Mills Harper, 14 vols., New York: Charles Scribner's Sons, 1989–

Dramatis Personae, New York: Macmillan, 1936

Essays and Introductions, New York: Macmillan, 1961

Ideas of Good and Evil, 2nd edn., A. H. Bullen: London, 1903

"Introduction," in W. B. Yeats, ed., *The Oxford Book of Modern Verse 1892–1935,* New York: Oxford University Press, 1935, v–xlii

The Letters of W. B. Yeats, ed. Allan Wade, New York: Macmillan, 1955

Mythologies, New York: Macmillan, 1969

A Vision, New York: Macmillan, 1966

W. B. Yeats and T. Sturge Moore: Their Correspondence, 1901–1937, ed. Ursula Bridge, New York: Oxford University Press, 1953

Yeats, W. B., ed., *The Oxford Book of Modern Verse 1892–1935,* New York: Oxford University Press, 1935

Young, G. M., *Victorian England: Portrait of an Age,* 2nd edn., London: Oxford University Press, 1960

Index

Printed in Great Britain
by Amazon.co.uk, Ltd.,
Marston Gate.